# POWER LINES

# POWER LINES

## Connecting with Teens in Urban Communities Through Media Literacy

JIMMEKA ANDERSON and KELLY CZARNECKI

ALA Editions

CHICAGO | 2022

Extensive effort has gone into ensuring the reliability of the information in this book; however, the publisher makes no warranty, express or implied, with respect to the material contained herein.

ISBN: 978-0-8389-3790-7 (paper)

**Library of Congress Cataloging-in-Publication Data**

Names: Anderson, Jimmeka, author. | Czarnecki, Kelly Nicole, 1974- author.
Title: Power lines : connecting with teens in urban communities through media literacy / Jimmeka Anderson and Kelly Czarnecki.
Description: Chicago : ALA Editions, 2022. | Includes bibliographical references and index. | Summary: "The book provides strategic and practical approaches toward building relationships and making a space for teens to engage and learn media literacy skills"—Provided by publisher.
Identifiers: LCCN 2022006894 | ISBN 9780838937907 (paperback)
Subjects: LCSH: Libraries and teenagers—United States. | Libraries and community—United States. | Libraries and minorities—United States. | Libraries and metropolitan areas—United States. | Libraries—Activity programs—United States. | Media literacy—United States.
Classification: LCC Z718.5 .A645 2022 | DDC 027.62/60973—dc23/eng/20220401
LC record available at https://lccn.loc.gov/2022006894

Book design by Alejandra Diaz in the Rooney and Sofia Pro typefaces.

♾ This paper meets the requirements of ANSI/NISO Z39.48-1992 (Permanence of Paper).

Printed in the United States of America

26  25  24  23  22      5  4  3  2  1

WITHOUT COMMUNITY,
THERE IS NO LIBERATION.
–AUDRE LORDE–

## JIMMEKA'S DEDICATION

First and foremost to Whitney, my daughter,
for being the reason I give life my all.

To the teens I've shared space and time with past and present, for helping me
to discover my passion and for giving me purpose
to make this world a better place for all of us.

To Belinha, for giving me the opportunity to believe in the power of my pen
and write my first contribution in your book.

To my mother, sisters, and friends who always fill my cup
with love so that it may spill into the lives I touch.

To my father in heaven, for teaching me to be fearless
and always find laughter in spite of.


## KELLY'S DEDICATION

To all the teens who came through the Loft at ImaginOn
to inspire these pages.

To Rebby, whose "Fully Integrated" workshop during the first summer
of the pandemic helped me to give voice to this project
to challenge systems of oppression.

To my love, Wes.

# CONTENTS

**Foreword**, by Belinha S. De Abreu   *xiii*

**Preface**, by Chance W. Lewis   *xvii*

**Acknowledgments**, by Jimmeka Anderson and Kelly Czarnecki   *xix*

**Introduction: Remembering the Why**, by Jimmeka Anderson   *xxi*

## PART I: HAVING AN "EMPIRE STATE OF MIND" WITH TEEN PROGRAMMING

**1**   **The Train Has Arrived: Understanding Their World**................ 3

JIMMEKA ANDERSON

Teen Reflection: Bereket Temesgen   **15**

Voices from the Field: Jeff Share   **16**

Voices from the Field: Jayne Cubbage   **17**

**2**   **It Never Sleeps: The Current State of Teens and Media** ..... 21

ABBY KIESA

Teen Reflection: Alasia Hicks   **28**

Voices from the Field: Merve Lapus   **29**

Voices from the Field: Brittany N. Anderson   **30**

**3**   **Flashing Lights: What Is Media Literacy?** ............................ 35

DONNELL PROBST and MICHELLE CIULLA LIPKIN

Teen Reflection: Kaella Racshenberg   **49**

Voices from the Field: Theresa Redmond   **50**

4 **Road Closed, Detour Ahead: Challenges and Opportunities with Serving Urban Teens in Libraries** ....... 53
KELLY CZARNECKI

Teen Reflection: Zakariyah Hanif **64**

Voices from the Field: Mary J. Wardell-Ghirarduzzi **65**

Voices from the Field: Jasmine McNeil **66**

5 **Under Construction: Creating Space and Relationships for Media Literacy with Urban Teens** ..................................... **69**
JIMMEKA ANDERSON and KELLY CZARNECKI

Teen Reflection: Matthew Rosa **82**

Voices from the Field: Natasha Casey **83**

6 **Power Lines: Empowering Teens Who Have Been Disempowered Through Partnerships** .................................... **87**
R. ALAN BERRY

Teen Reflection: Jeneva Claiborne **102**

Teen Reflection: Maia McElvane **103**

Voices from the Field: Nygel D. White **103**

Voices from the Field: Elis Estrada **104**

## PART II: STRAIGHT OUTTA THE LIBRARY

7 **Traffic JAMS! Music and Podcasting** ..................................... **109**
7.1: Media Literacy and Community Connection: A Profile of Virginia Tech's "Digging in the Crates" Hip Hop Studies Program **110**
LA' PORTIA J. PERKINS, JASMINE WEISS, JONATHAN KABONGO, FREDERICK PAIGE, and CRAIG ARTHUR

7.2: Let Your Voice Be Heard: Create Podcasting Programming for Your Library **114**
LAUREN KRATZ PRUSHKO

7.3: Podcasting the Possibilities **120**
MOLLY DETTMANN

**8** **City Blue PRINTS: Books and Print Literature**..................125

8.1: Alt RA: Looking Beyond Books in Readers' Advisory **127**
HEATHER LOVE BEVERLEY and CYNDI HAMANN

8.2: The Education of Blacks in Charlotte,
An Online Youth Exhibition **130**
PAMELA MCCARTER and JIMMEKA ANDERSON

Teen Reflection: Rachel Edmonds **135**

Teen Reflection: Ariah Cornelius **136**

8.3: The Zine Club **137**
LIZ ALLEN, NICOLE RAMBO, and KRISTINE TANZI

**9** **SCREEN Doors: TV, Film, and Broadcasting** .........................143

9.1: Girls Rock Film Camp: The Future of Film **144**
LONNA VINES

9.2: Keepin' It Reel: Black Girls Film Camp **149**
DENEEN S. DIXON-PAYNE and JIMMEKA ANDERSON

9.3: Girls on the Beat @ Charleston County Public Library **154**
DARCY COOVER

**10** **Bridges, Tunnels, and City CONNECTIONS:**
**Social Media, Information, and News Literacy**...................161

10.1: The Journalistic Learning Initiative **162**
ED MADISON, ROSS C. ANDERSON, and RACHEL GULDIN

10.2: An Introductory Lesson Plan in News Media Literacy
for YA Librarians **168**
MICHAEL A. SPIKES

10.3: Analyzing the News Through Infographics **174**
MARK J. DAVIS

**11** **City Zip CODES and Community PLAYgrounds:**
**Tech, Gaming, and Coding** .........................................................179

11.1: Dewey and Dragons (Dungeons and Dragons for Teens):
Connecting Teens with Technology at the Library **181**
LAURA VALLEJO, JAMEY RORIE, and CHRIS SPRADLIN

**11.2: Boston Public Library: Teen Technology Mentor Program    185**
BRIANNE SKYWALL and CHRISTOPHER JACOBS

**11.3: The Beauty of S.T.E.M.    191**
ANDREA MCNEIL and SHIMIRA WILLIAMS

**11.4: Blissful Coding Club    195**
ANUSHA BANSAL and MAISY CARD

**11.5: After-School Coding and Technology Clubs    201**
ALLY DOERMAN and PAMELA JAYNE

Conclusion: The Takeaways    *207*
Appendix: Collection of Resources for Continued Learning    *211*
About the Authors and Contributors    *215*
Index    *223*

# FOREWORD

One of the most subversive institutions in the United States is the public library.

—BELL HOOKS, *Rock My Soul: Black People and Self-Esteem*

**Libraries, community, and media literacy education are three central** themes covered in this book, *Power Lines: Connecting with Teens in Urban Communities Through Media Literacy*, coauthored by Jimmeka Anderson and Kelly Czarnecki. The first theme introduces us to a place embedded in many communities in the United States—the library. Libraries have always been the great equalizer in our society, though they have often gone unnoticed. They embody the community they exist in, through their programming and resources, by providing services where only limited ones exist, by offering media and mediated environments to people of all ages, and more. They reach out to various socially advantaged and disadvantaged groups in their localities—the visible and obvious, as well as citizens who are often overlooked.

As an institution, a library is about welcoming the public. Libraries provide shelter and respite, often servicing those experiencing homelessness and poverty. Simultaneously, they can also serve the struggling teen who needs a safe or quiet space, the person looking for jobs, or those learning new skills. In the library, there are no barriers to joining individuals or bringing them together within activities or programming. Libraries are in fact a blender for everything and everyone at all points in their lives: they are a welcoming place for a new mom while her child wanders through the stacks, a quiet place for someone who is shying away from the public, an access point for technology, an instructional place for someone who needs to research or who needs help with research, and so much more.

The programming offered by libraries bridges people and their community—the second theme of this book—and is particularly relevant when looking at the urban setting. In thinking about the ways in which we engage with information, specifically through the lens of media literacy education—the third theme of this book—the question of representation comes to the forefront. For example, the term *urban* comes with its own context. Consider the following text in stories written about urban communities when the term *urban* is searched online:

- "In many large *urban* school districts, three in four students or more are poor" (Weiss 2012).
- "Thirty-two percent of residents in *urban* areas are 50 or older" (The Associated Press 2017).
- "They fail to consider that the opportunities for involvement they are offering may not be what *urban* parents really need, at least initially" (Ackerman 2011).
- "This is not your average struggling *urban* high school" (Chiles 2015).

Media literacy instruction tries to take into account how representation matters, context matters, and voice matters—beyond what is characterized by the headlines. The value in analyzing and understanding various representations in the media, and imparting this type of learning to young people, is what brings the present book to life.

Libraries facilitate urban areas in both large and small ways. They become a central part of the community that they engage in and offer an extension to the schools, parents, and other regional services. Anderson and Czarnecki provide an opportunity for readers to consider how library programming connects with audiences, especially when it comes to teens, young adult programming, civics, and media literacy education. Further, the book considers the dichotomy of the term *urban* and looks at the influence of libraries as one of the greatest assets in many urban communities.

Media literacy education is an avenue to find the greater frame of reference, to explore ideas that are not represented, and to retell a story that is not limited by the images presented by the media. The value in offering this type of education is the principal subject of Anderson and Czarnecki's book. As a growing body of work in libraries, media literacy education has become the tool for bringing youth together and sharing in their connections as well as productions. Librarians have seen it all, and now they have taken up the work of helping youth engage in the issue of media literacy through discernment, action, and advocacy.

Finally, a preeminent feature of Anderson and Czarnecki's collection is that they share the ideas of a wide range of thinkers, from academics to practitioners to teens in their own voices, by means of their reflections on each of the individual chapters. The authors have ensured that the voices and ideas of young people, the generation that is most involved in the mediated world, are amplified in this book. In doing so, they offer to the reader a chance to glimpse indiscriminate possibilities, while also offering plausible ideas that can be utilized in a variety of settings. Each of the chapters in this book provides knowledge and inspiration for libraries, librarians, and media educators—who are ready to rise to the challenge of teaching media literacy education in their community.

**~Belinha S. De Abreu, Media Literacy Educator**

## REFERENCES

Ackerman, Patricia. 2011. "How and Why Urban Schools Fail to Engage Parents of Color." *Huffington Post*, August 27. www.huffpost.com/entry/how-and -why-urban-schools_b_885366.

The Associated Press. 2017. "Report: Minnesota's Urban Counties Growing, Rural Counties Shrinking." *CBS Minnesota*, January 27. https://minnesota.cbslocal .com/2017/01/27/demographic-trends/.

Chiles, Nick. 2015. "The Power of an Impassioned Principal." *The Atlantic*, November 17. www.theatlantic.com/education/archive/2015/11/principal -power-new-orleans-school/415911/.

Weiss, Elaine. 2012. "The Toxic Toll of Child Poverty." *Huffington Post*, October 1. www.huffpost.com/entry/child-poverty_b_1929225.

# PREFACE

**There are times in history when certain books must be written.** *Power Lines: Connecting with Teens in Urban Communities Through Media Literacy* is one of these books. The famous words of W. E. B. Du Bois (1903) are still relevant today when he asked, "How does it feel to be a problem?" Given the current state of our nation's political and educational climate, teens, particularly those who attend urban schools, have been relegated to a substandard system where they have garnered media attention and a national spotlight not for the positive attributes they bring to the educational setting, but for negative stories and headlines that are often manufactured to get likes and clicks.

I want to be crystal clear. Many teens in urban communities are facing an academic death in our nation's K–12 public, charter, and private schools. Unfortunately, educators, librarians, and many other stakeholders continue to make excuses about why it is not their fault that teens in urban communities are not achieving academically. However, these stakeholders never discuss what lies within their power to change when it comes to the question of educating teens in urban communities and school districts across the country. This book is a welcome addition to the education knowledge base, as it provides a new and fresh perspective on how to effectively serve teens in urban communities via media literacy and the role librarians can play to shape those teens' media literacy skills.

It is my hope that this book reaches educators, librarians, and media literacy advocates and makes a positive impact for teens in urban communities to achieve academically in the most affluent country in the world. We can no longer, in this age of educational accountability, continue to stand by and watch the achievement levels of this student population remain at or near the bottom of every major academic barometer and feel comfortable with our work as education professionals. Once the education profession chooses to fully embrace the educational potential of teens in urban communities, we will see transformations occur that will truly propel this population to want to achieve at a high level because their schools and libraries are taking a vested interest in developing their media literacy skills, which will allow them to reach their full potential.

*Power Lines* is also for Black parents who send their children to school expecting something great to happen, only to be met with disappointment at the door of the school building. The greatness they expect for their teens is why many work one, two, or even three jobs to make sure their children have food on the table and a roof over their head just so they can make it to school. Unfortunately, when their teens matriculate through our nation's schools, they are met with "educational rhetoric." This educational rhetoric tells the parents all that is perceived to be wrong with their children rather than how the schooling experience (media literacy skill attainment) will put them in the best position to have a positive impact on their lives.

Finally, this book embraces the voices, hopes, and dreams of so many who have died for teens in urban communities to have a right to a quality education in this country. We thank you for making the ultimate sacrifice so that one day the education profession can reach its full potential by serving the educational needs of this population. I have come to learn that we have to continue to push until this change happens. This is why I commend the authors, Jimmeka Anderson and Kelly Czarnecki, for this valuable contribution to the education profession. An intentional focus on the positive impacts of media literacy on teens in urban communities is exactly what we need at this moment. It is my hope that this book will spark a new movement of media literacy that is specifically focused on teens in urban communities.

~**Chance W. Lewis, Carol Grotnes Belk**
**Distinguished Professor of Urban Education**

REFERENCE
Du Bois, W. E. B. 1903. *The Souls of Black Folk.* New York: Random House.

# ACKNOWLEDGMENTS

**We would like to thank Marie Harris for her editing expertise and atten-**tion to detail as we crafted this book. Your feedback on this project was invaluable.

Thank you to the Teen Loft—both teens and colleagues—for influencing our work and this project in so many ways. A special shout-out to some of our teens who played an immense role in our lives and challenged us for the better: Scottie Stowe, D'Quayvion Cloud, Matt Rosa, and Shavontaye Rowzey. We are extremely grateful for the trust and vulnerability that you granted us.

Thank you to Angela Craig, Theresa Redmond, Belinha De Abreu, Michelle Ciulla Lipkin, Chance W. Lewis, and Tina Heafner for your professional mentorship throughout the years. All of you have been a catalyst and inspiration in our journey and careers. We only hope to pass on to others the immense amount of wisdom and opportunities you have granted us.

Thank you to Charlotte Mecklenburg Library and ImaginOn, where it all began.

# INTRODUCTION
## Remembering the Why

JIMMEKA ANDERSON

Media can be used to oppress or liberate. It is up to us to teach the next generation how to use this *powerful* tool for the good of humanity.

~JIMMEKA ANDERSON

**I am a Black woman, a single mother, born from poverty, and making** less than $30,000 a year with a college degree. The year is 2009. Every day I am surrounded entirely by White women and men who are my colleagues. Their clothes are pressed, creased pants and white linen tops that blow as freely when they walk by as they themselves appear to be. They appear to have it all together. I speak their language and mimic their gestures. I work uptown, two blocks from the bus transit and across from the construction site on 7th Street at the library. There is a homeless woman on the corner I walk by every day who clutches her Bible and screams at demons when they pass by. She looks like me. I work with teens every day who are raised in the same streets and neighborhoods where my family and I lived. These teens all look like my family, extended cousins perhaps. We share the same language. While at work, my mind drifts away in deep thought at times. Like . . . I worry if I will have enough money to pay my rent at the end of the month. One day, one of the teens told me she has no idea where her family is going to live at the end of the month. Our struggle is one and the same. We're both longing to do more than just struggle and barely survive. The teen's story I know very well, but mine is buried behind the smile I use to greet them and my colleagues. I wake up the next day and every day for them. I know they are depending on me to be there when they walk through those doors. For me to be a listening ear. For me to create a space for them to express and be their authentic selves as freely as the white linen shirt my colleague has on that blows as she walks by. As freely as I, myself, would like to be. They are depending on me to help them see a world and a life beyond our neighborhood every chance that we share time and space. So I wake up the next day and every day for them. Because through them, I found purpose.

It was 2008 when I started my job at the ImaginOn library in Charlotte, North Carolina, after graduating from college. I was making very little money but was extremely rich with ambition. I never would have imagined that I would be working at a public library, but the supervisor who hired me was looking for a strong community programmer. When I first walked through the doors of ImaginOn, the walls were painted in bright vibrant colors, yellows and oranges, with toys, origami figures, and festive trinkets hanging from the ceiling. If there was ever a place to just go and dream of tomorrows, this appeared to be it. In the building there were two large theaters, a decorative costume room, and a scenery shop for designing the sets for stage plays and box office performances. The place was absolutely magical.

By the end of my first week, I couldn't help but notice that I was the only Black woman in my department and only one of three in an entire building with at least fifty or more staff. I didn't realize at the time that this was largely due to the fact that more than 80 percent of librarians and those in the field of librarianship were White. Needless to say, code-switching naturally became embedded in my everyday routine at work, partly because I was afraid I wouldn't be accepted or deemed professional otherwise. Interestingly enough, the majority of the teens who entered the doors of our library were BIPOC. I observed how these teens were sometimes met with resistance and microaggressions from White staff and security guards in the building who didn't understand them or didn't know their stories—and were hyper-criminalized because of their presence.

When I started working at the library, I immediately immersed myself in doing what I did best: programming. During my first year at the library, I tested the waters with all types of nontraditional programs. Teens immediately began to gravitate toward some of my random programming ideas. For instance, I coordinated an actual step team that performed at library events, and I hosted Krumpin' (a style of dance) contests to support a documentary on that art form, jump rope challenges to discuss literature on health and wellness, and open mics for teens to share their own music and poetry with a speakeasy lounge ambiance.

Through the power of programming, I built strong bonds with teens and connected with my colleagues in meaningful ways from collaborations. The large number of participants and the active engagement I had with teens in the building caught the attention of managers and colleagues in other departments, and I eventually segued into creating system-wide initiatives and events. After two years spent finding what resonated the most with the teens I served in the community and what I felt most comfortable doing, I realized that my niche for programming was in media literacy.

Unfortunately, in 2010 our library experienced substantial budget cuts. Nearly 200 employees were laid off from work at the library, and I was merely one of the numbers. Now unemployed and with a child, I realized I had to come up with a plan for what to do next with my life. So I enrolled back in school and took classes in digital media and web design. Given the fact that I had developed a strong passion for media literacy education with teens, I decided in 2011 to create the nonprofit organization I AM not the MEdia. At the time, I focused on providing media literacy outreach programs to teens throughout the city of Charlotte. The organization immediately took off in its first year. Bookings came from schools, clubs, churches, and recreation centers in North Carolina and other states to request media literacy programs with youth, predominantly in urban communities.

I returned to my same position at the library in 2012. Now, I was working full-time at the library and doing media literacy outreach for I AM not the MEdia in the evenings and on my days off. Kelly Czarnecki and I had crossed paths when I began working at ImaginOn in 2008, but it wasn't until 2012 that we collaborated on our first program together, The Fashion Apprentice. From that collaboration I realized how dynamically our programming skills meshed. We began to create locally and nationally recognized programs for the teens of Charlotte and won an award from the Young Adult Library Services Association (YALSA). By 2015, I was teaching digital media courses at the Carolina School of Broadcasting in North Carolina and volunteering with organizations such as the National Association for Media Literacy Education, Media Literacy Now, and other groups to build relationships in the media literacy community. From these experiences I met some amazing folks who stretched my thinking of who I was as a Black woman in the field and who assured me that my voice was valued and necessary. I am forever grateful because those moments of mentorship helped empower me to become the devoted media literacy educator I am today and challenged me to be my most authentic self while doing this work.

After working at the library for ten years, I decided to pursue my PhD full-time in the field of urban education and focus my research efforts on media literacy education with historically marginalized youth. My research in the urban education PhD program at the University of North Carolina at Charlotte inspired the vision behind this book. Once I came up with the vision for it, I immediately reached out to Kelly to see if she would be interested in taking this writing and editing journey with me. Needless to say, I am extremely grateful she said yes.

## WHY THE TITLE *POWER LINES?*

It may have been my inner poet that led me to fall in love with the ambiguity of the phrase *Power Lines* and the different messages, hidden and unhidden, that it afforded, just like the media. Power lines are one of the most visible features found in inner-city urban communities, but the phrase could also represent certain connections with people and places such as libraries. In hip-hop culture, *lines* are words, lyrical verses, or text. So if someone were to tell you "those lines are tight" after reading something you wrote, know that it means your words and how you used them were exquisite. Thus, power lines could also metaphorically represent the influence of words and text found in media. Moreover, the word *power* alone is ambiguous in its use for the title and is coded to denote both hegemony and media. Understanding power and how it functions is a large part of the work of doing media literacy instruction with teens in urban communities. Thus, Kelly and I have sought to provide a compelling perspective toward understanding the influence of power structures on both ourselves and the communities we serve. Furthermore, we have collaborated with field experts and practitioners to develop a strategic guide for implementing media literacy programming with teens in urban communities.

## WHY FOCUS ON TEENS IN URBAN COMMUNITIES?

Now more than ever before, information and digital literacies are essential skills for survival and for staying informed in our media-saturated world. Unfortunately, historically marginalized and economically disadvantaged youth in urban communities score the lowest in information and communication technology proficiency, and they lack critical media literacy skills to successfully navigate and disseminate information online, according to national data (Nation's Report Card 2018). Although libraries have begun to invest in media literacy education initiatives with adults, immediate attention is needed to educate librarians on how to serve teens. Specifically, further insight on serving teens in urban communities is needed due to challenges with technology and internet accessibility, instructional inequities, and their high risk of media and informational illiteracy. Therefore, we believe this work is essential as it robustly acknowledges the challenges that come with teaching media literacy to teens in urban communities.

This book is divided into two parts. Part I provides strategic and practical approaches to building relationships and making a space for teens to engage and learn media literacy skills. Each chapter in part I concludes with reflections from teens, experts, and researchers in the field. Part II provides program profiles and case studies from librarians, practitioners, and scholars from all over the United States for implementing media literacy programs in libraries. The book concludes with next steps and resources for librarians.

In conclusion, as I reflect back on my "why" or purpose for doing this work and for writing this book, I am reminded of the reason why we as educators are extremely valuable. The world needs us and the youth we serve, especially in urban communities. They are depending on us every day to help them thrive—and not just survive—in a world that was not intended for them to succeed in. Moreover, I hope this book inspires you to reflect on your own "why," and I hope that you acquire knowledge you can apply and use to spark change in your community. I am extremely thankful to Kelly for agreeing to be my coauthor, and for the many colleagues in the media literacy field who invested in the vision of this book and believed in its potential to make a difference.

I am truly appreciative of everyone who contributed their time and poured out their stories to create these pages. Without this village of teens, practitioners, researchers, and librarians coming together, this book would not have been possible.

**REFERENCE**

Nation's Report Card. 2018. "National Achievement Level Results in Technology & Engineering Literacy." National Assessment of Educational Progress. www.nationsreportcard.gov/tel/results/achievement/.

# PART I

## Having an "Empire State of Mind" with Teen Programming

The title of Part I is named after the Jay-Z song released in 2009, featuring Alicia Keys, on *The Blueprint 3* album. Having an "Empire State of Mind" means to empower yourself to see the big picture and think strategically to overcome obstacles. This part of the book focuses on preparing librarians to build relationships and create spaces for teens in urban communities to learn, discuss, and create with media literacy education. Each chapter concludes with teen reflections and voices from the field.

# The Train Has Arrived
## Understanding Their World

JIMMEKA ANDERSON

We've seen the *power* of the collective. We've seen what happens when we join for the same cause. Please continue to be the voice for the voiceless. Never forget, we can disagree in a way that is productive to arrive at decisions that foster real change.

—**BEYONCÉ**, Commencement Speech to Class of 2020

**For many years, I felt the term *urban* had been contextualized as a form** of coded or adverse language to characterize marginalized people (primarily Black people) and neighborhoods negatively. I'm sure you have heard the term used rhetorically to mean "those people" or "those neighborhoods you should not indulge after dark." Figuratively speaking, the stigmatization of the term *urban* draws its dark connotations from the social inequities that plague the people and communities that comprise a good part of our nation's cities. Due to the increasing amount of social inequity reflected in schools with marginalized youth residing in large metropolitan areas, a focus on research was established in a field known as "urban education." Intrigued to further explore and understand the implications of urban life and its influences on youth academically, I pursued my PhD in urban education in the summer of 2018 in search of answers. What I have learned from research and literature is that *urban* is more than a coded word; it is a socially constructed reality that exists. Further, I learned that "urban" life for adolescents is rich in culture yet multilayered and conflictual.

The interconnectedness of race, poverty, gender, sexual orientation, family context, and other layers that go to form the identities and experiences of adolescents makes it impractical to focus on or seek to understand just one single issue. Most importantly, these multiple identities and the marginalization of adolescents in urban communities are interwoven like a web, in which there are individual differences but similar challenges. There is a famous quote by the astute intellectual Audre Lorde that states: "There is no such thing as a single-issue struggle because we do not live single-issue lives." This quote rings true for every teen who resides in an urban community and enters the library. In this chapter, I will first contextualize the word *urban* as characteristic. The word *characteristic* is defined by the *Oxford English Dictionary* as the features that belong to a person, place, or thing. In this case, I am speaking of the features that define the communities and experiences of the people who reside in them as being *urban*. Next, I will highlight the disparities that influence adolescents in urban communities and share an overview of how these disparities have been attributed to policies and practices that have plagued urban communities and marginalized groups. Lastly, this chapter enables librarians to understand the importance of providing media literacy with a "critical" lens and of working with marginalized communities.

## CONTEXTUALIZING "URBAN" AS CHARACTERISTIC

An article written by Richard Milner in 2012 titled "But What Is Urban Education?" has become a seminal work for contextualizing the meaning of the word *urban* in the field of education. Therefore, I felt that Milner's work would be quite applicable to apply in a library context for defining the communities and populations in which libraries are situated and provide service. According to Milner (2012), the field of urban education is characterized by three conceptual frames: (a) urban intensive, (b) urban emergent, and (c) urban characteristic. These frames are defined by various characteristics such as population density and by environmental factors such as housing, poverty, and transit. An urban-intensive library system, according to Milner's framework, would reside in the context of a large metropolitan city with a high population density and whose community may experience inadequacy and inequity from those environmental characteristics. For instance, cities such as New York, Chicago, Los Angeles, and Atlanta would be characterized as urban-intensive areas. By contrast, my hometown of Charlotte, North Carolina, would be characterized as an urban-emergent community due to its population size and the characteristics of inequity throughout the city. Then there are cities or towns that don't have a high population density, yet the characteristics of the area experienced by certain groups with housing and poverty may contextualize it as "urban characteristic." When most people think of urban communities, they think of New York or Chicago, but the factors that make up an urban community can come together in a wide range of places across the country, including smaller cities. For this book, we have sought to center the experiences of teens and libraries in all three defined frames that characterize the urban experience.

It is also important to note that Black and Hispanic youth consist of the majority population in inner-city urban communities (Wilson 1990). Therefore, it should come as no surprise to learn that Black and Hispanic youth consist of the majority population in urban public schools, specifically those situated in high-poverty communities. Currently in the United States, economically disadvantaged Black and Hispanic adolescents are provided with free education in the form of overcrowded public schools in isolated communities of highly concentrated poverty (Lipman 2004). Moreover, it is pertinent to acknowledge the immense role that the federal government has played in maintaining poverty in Black and Hispanic urban communities. Most poverty today is urban poverty and is caused by unaffordable housing, low minimum wages, and discriminatory laws against Black and Hispanic populations (Anyon 2005). In fact, the American economist Alan Greenspan, who served as chair of the Federal Reserve from 1987 to 2006, stated that poverty in America is good for business (Anyon 2005).

## CHALLENGES AND DISPARITIES EXPERIENCED BY TEENS IN URBAN COMMUNITIES

While the idea of "profitable" poverty may be a disheartening pill to swallow, as librarians and educators, we must understand why the cards are stacked against certain groups of people. We must acknowledge and reckon with the explicit and at times invisible barriers of systemic "isms" that perpetuate the injustices felt by many adolescents in urban communities and their families on a daily basis. For instance, social dislocation is an invisible barrier caused by government policies, events, or crises that alter the social lives of people and their opportunities to succeed. The impact of social dislocation can be felt immediately and may last for generations. What's more alarming is that the descendants of those who experienced the actual crisis may not realize that their physical realities are linked to the social dislocation of their ancestors. The majority of poverty today in the United States is also generational poverty that is historically linked to events and governmental policies from the past that interrupted the lives of majority BIPOC communities in this country. The challenges of poverty, social dislocation, inadequate education, and many other issues have caused several disparities that influence the daily lives of teens residing in urban communities. So whether you are in a library that is located in an urban intensive, emergent, or characteristic environment, it is important to understand the disparities that exist to better serve the teens who enter your doors.

## Poverty and Social Dislocation

According to Wilson (1990), the exodus of both White and Black middle and working classes from the inner city in the mid-twentieth century created what is known as a "concentration effect," thus centralizing poverty, causing social dislocation, and forming urban communities. Tarabini and Jacovkis (2012) define poverty through a series of dimensions that focus on access to opportunities, security, and empowerment. Youth who reside in environments with a high concentration of poverty do not receive access to the same opportunities and affordances as their peers from affluent backgrounds. Instead, youth from urban low-income communities substantially experience poor health, limited access to rich language experiences, and less participation in quality after-school and summer activities that enhance learning (Ladd 2012). For this reason, research has asserted that the concentration effect increases negative outcomes experienced by youth residing in communities with a majority high-poverty population in an enclosed area.

It is essential for librarians to understand how the concentration effect of poverty influences the experiences of people in the communities they serve. For instance, when looking at the contexts of urban schools with low academic performance, they are economically isolated in highly concentrated poverty communities. These high-poverty schools struggle with the challenges of having a student body whose members lack proper nutrition, come from unstable home environments, and experience violence in the form of crime and gangs (Orfield and Lee, 2005). It is no secret that there is a high correlation between poverty and crime. Although there are challenges associated with the concentration effect of poverty, socially dislocated urban youth who are exposed to opportunity and positive social norms through relationships and valuable learning experiences undergo positive and transformative outcomes (Anyon 2005). For this very reason, relationships with librarians and the availability of teen spaces within the library are vital for youth from low-income communities. The experiences provided by teen librarians have the potential to serve as social buffers that contribute to positive outcomes and influence the trajectory of teens' lives for the better.

## Segregated Communities

On December 3, 2019, in my hometown of Charlotte, North Carolina, the local public radio show *Charlotte Talks* aired a news story that examined how the Charlotte-Mecklenburg Schools (CMS) were just as segregated as they were before the 1954 *Brown v. Board of Education* ruling (Steinmetz 2019). The news story highlighted that although the CMS public school system had once served as a national pioneer for school integration, it was now considered the most racially segregated school district in North Carolina. Similar to what was experienced in my hometown, the desegregation of public schools in the United States only began some years after the 1954 *Brown v. Board of Education* ruling and was not put into effect nationwide by school districts until the 1960s. This racial integration model was implemented in the Charlotte-Mecklenburg district for three decades, until a 2001 ruling was upheld by the Fourth U.S. Circuit Court of Appeals that ended busing there. Though it once served as a national model for school desegregation in the 1970s, my hometown of Charlotte has now reverted to being highly segregated racially and socioeconomically.

A year prior to the *Charlotte Talks* news story, on September 5, 2018, our local newspaper, the *Charlotte Observer*, published an article which highlighted that graduation rates in eight Charlotte-Mecklenburg schools had declined substantially (Helms 2018). The article stated that the decline in graduation rates "hit the hardest among high poverty neighborhood schools and impacted predominantly Black, Hispanic, and economically disadvantaged students" (Helms 2018). My hometown of Charlotte may resemble several other urban communities across the nation in this respect. These communities are not just isolated by income, but also by race. It is not unusual for libraries in urban localities to primarily serve certain races or ethnicities due to the barriers of segregation that still exist and are attached to zip codes. For several years, I worked as a library outreach coordinator and just by knowing the zip code of a school or child care facility for which I was requested to provide services, nine times out of ten, I would know the income and ethnicity of the majority population there. According to Richard Rothstein's book *The Color of Law*, the federal government has historically been the chief force behind constructing racially segregated communities and creating the realities that exist in urban neighborhoods. Rothstein (2017) emphasizes that laws crafted by the federal government dating back to the 1930s enforced a practice known as "redlining." Through redlining, the government supported policies that only provided housing to white families in new suburban communities, while forcing Black families into inner-city housing projects.

Thus, it is essential to understand the historic intersections of race and poverty in urban communities and how many youth have identified their circumstances as normative due to the color of their skin. W. E. B. Du Bois's seminal work *The Souls of Black Folk* coined the term *double consciousness* to characterize the ongoing mental plight of Black people, as well as other marginalized races in America. As described by Du Bois in 1903, being white in America constitutes a struggle of self-consciousness in which one only has to understand the world through one's own experiences. Yet belonging to a marginalized race in America causes individuals to see the world not only through their own experiential lens but also through the lens of how white people view them. By looking at others as the standard, marginalized people on the daily contemplate how their otherness influences their own experiences and opportunities. By the stage of adolescence, marginalized teens from urban communities have developed a sense of double consciousness. They are aware of segregation, racism, and how their race is influenced by the opportunities and encounters they have with members of other races. As stated earlier, the challenges experienced by urban youth are multilayered yet contribute to the realities and double consciousness effect that each of them experiences when you greet or interact with them at any moment in time. What is most important for librarians who serve teens from historically marginalized communities to understand is the need to be aware of and critically explore how every encounter and experience they have with teens is shaped by teens' perceptions, realities, and the double consciousness that exist.

## Social Capital and Upward Mobility

The phrase *social capital* denotes the amount of positive interactions and relationships that adolescents encounter in their environment. These positive interactions may take the form of adult and peer relationships which provide exposure and access to experiences that the adolescents may not otherwise have at home or in their community. Research has shown that an absence of strong positive peer influences is correlated with youth who attend high-concentrated poverty schools and can have a negative impact on academic achievement (Orfield and Lee 2005). Additionally, the Coleman Report from the federal government in 1996, which was the first national study of segregated and desegregated schools, revealed that peer and non-family adult influence was a stronger factor than family background in student success. Although social capital has not been proven as a measurable indicator, some research studies have concluded that it is associated with higher SAT scores and higher education enrollment among adolescents (Moore and Lewis 2012).

To understand the role of social capital and upward mobility in urban communities, I want to use my hometown as an example again. Charlotte's historical landscape has been built on decades of racial and economic segregation that have divided its inhabitants along the lines of prosperity and poverty. In 2014, Harvard University and UC Berkeley published a study that ranked Charlotte-Mecklenburg 50th out of 50 large cities to experience upward mobility in adulthood for children born into poverty (Chetty et al. 2014). As a child born into poverty in Charlotte, I would be remiss if I didn't acknowledge the positive role that mentors, camp counselors, and library professionals played in creating social capital in my life. For instance, the after-school program I attended as a child was inside the same building as the neighborhood library. At an early age, my experiences outside of school were embedded in free community programming that centered the library and literacy. I eagerly anticipated the scary stories that were told during Halloween and the Black History Quiz Bowls that were hosted by librarians in my community in February. The programs that were provided to us young people at that time were about more than just exposure to literacy and Black history facts; they were also about the meaningful relationships that were built with our community librarian, which allowed us to see thriving professionals who were passionate about their work.

## Literacy

Only 15 percent of Black children in the eighth grade are at grade-level proficiency in reading in the United States (Nation's Report Card 2019). Black children have consistently scored the lowest in reading proficiency of any race on national assessments. Hispanic children are not too far behind on national assessments, with only 22 percent of eighth-grade students reading at proficiency level. The National Assessment of Educational Progress (NAEP) data highlights a 27-point reading gap between White and Black students in the eighth grade. Consequently, the reading gap between White and Black students is not the only large disparity gap assessed in the NAEP's Nation's Report Card (2019). A reading gap of 26 points was also found between students from affluent backgrounds compared to those from low-income households, with only 20 percent of students reading at proficiency level. What the Nation's Report Card (2019) reveals to us is that large inequities in reading exist among Black and Hispanic students compared to White students, and among students who live in poverty.

While disparities in reading proficiency among marginalized students were captured in the 2019 national data, a national questionnaire conducted by the NAEP in 2015 provided insight on how students' views of reading differed based on their socioeconomic status. One of the key questions in the study asked the children whether reading was one of their favorite activities. About 29 percent of eighth-grade students from affluent backgrounds had positive views about reading, compared to 24 percent of students from low-income households. These percentages show a small difference between students from different economic backgrounds and their interest in reading. Thus, it is clear that motivation is not a factor in reading proficiency inequity with marginalized youth in urban communities. Librarians can use this knowledge to creatively ignite the interest of urban youth with literacy and seek ways to enhance their proficiency and skills through culturally responsive approaches. (Chapter 8 of this book provides examples of media literacy programs and services that you can implement with teens in your library to gauge their interest in finding books that they would enjoy and thus increase their engagement with reading print literature.)

## Technological Inequity

The spread of the COVID-19 virus in 2020 was declared a global pandemic and pushed schools across the United States to implement forced shutdowns. Educational institutions turned to classroom instruction delivered online and began desperately seeking technological alternatives for students to confront the challenges with accessibility that disadvantageously impact high-poverty urban and rural communities (King and Gaudiano 2020). Considering the critical issues that plague our national educational system during the COVID-19 pandemic, the need to explore radical possibilities to relieve technology instruction inequity is more urgent than ever before. And the need to address the inequities in information communication technology (ICT) proficiency that exist among students in high-poverty communities is vital, given the fact that only 30 percent of U.S. students from low-income families are proficient in ICT (Nation's Report Card 2018). Teens today must possess the technology skills to participate with digital media collaboratively. Technology proficiency has been proven a necessity for academic success in higher education. Much coursework is now delivered and submitted online through learning management systems, and students engage with their classmates through virtual discussion boards. It is safe to say that technology proficiency is now considered a college readiness skill, yet only 23 percent of Black students and 31 percent of Hispanic students in the eighth grade in the United States are equipped with those technology skills (Nation's Report Card 2018). Therefore, implementing solutions in libraries to address the homework gap and the digital divide are essential for alleviating the inequitable barriers and achievement gaps experienced by economically disadvantaged students as compared to economically advantaged students.

Technology proficiency today now aligns with media creation and is contingent upon knowing how to use and decipher various media formats and tools (Jocson 2018). Understanding how to participate in online communities and how to access and analyze credible information are literacy skills that are necessary for thriving in a new post-truth era (Mirra et al. 2018). And while schools push digital devices into the hands of students during the day and academic year, when these students return home, economically disadvantaged families are still less likely to have access to a computer and a broadband internet connection. This divide between the digital haves and have-nots has resulted in a "homework gap" (Meyer 2016) and the fact that economically disadvantaged eighth-grade students have the lowest scores in ICT proficiency in the United States (Nation's Report Card 2018). In many cases, the public library is the only source of access to computers and high-speed internet that teens from low-income urban communities have outside of school. Programming in libraries that teaches teens digital and media literacy can help close the homework gap and bridge the digital divide. Many libraries have begun creating programs that offer Wi-Fi hotspots and laptops for checkout. If your library is located in an urban community, partnerships with local tech companies, college tech programs, and businesses may also be beneficial to establish and help support the technological needs of its patrons. (Chapters 10 and 11 explore programs by scholars and practitioners that address tech inequity and teach online digital and information literacy skills to teens.)

## Media and Misrepresentation of Teens in Urban Communities

Mass media have been considered a powerful tool that communicates hidden messaging to children daily regarding power and privilege through stereotypes, misrepresentation, and underrepresentation of oppressed cultures. According to Price Jr. (2005), tools such as media that reinforce the existing power structures in society must be countered by education that raises consciousness and inspires hope and vision. Teens engage with the media on average 7.5 hours each day and so it's important to understand the influence of messaging on their identity and beliefs (Kirsh 2011). While 7.5 hours a day may not seem alarming at first, this means that youth engage with the media on average 2,737 hours a year, as compared to being in school the minimum of 1,025 hours a year required by most states. Therefore, it is evident that youth spend more time engaging with the media than they spend in school, and with family or friends. Specifically, Black youth report spending more than the average amount of hours engaging with media than white youth do and thus have a heightened daily media usage and consumption.

Additionally, the mass media that Black youth consume continues to reinforce negative and limiting stereotypes of Black people as violent, immoral, and uneducated. As was highlighted by #OscarsSoWhite in 2015, positive media depictions of BIPOC are rare, and the latter often do not receive recognition equal to that of white performers. These representations shape or support group norms and are detrimental to BIPOCs' self-concept, behavior, and achievement. Media representations can contribute to negative evaluations of marginalized groups and to institutional practices that limit access to opportunities and resources for youth. While institutions are slow to change, youth can be empowered to push against negative portrayals and create their own media. Teaching critical media literacy has shown promise in changing perceptions about marginalized groups, social norms, and violence, and in increasing young people's self-esteem and self-efficacy.

## APPLYING A "CRITICAL" LENS WITH TEENS IN URBAN COMMUNITIES

The term *critical* in the phrase "critical media literacy" was derived from the foundations of critical theory. Critical theory examines relationships of power that exist within the institutions of society. It has been explored in education research and practice to deconstruct systems of economic oppression (DeMarrais and LeCompte 1998). Many critical theorists of education assert that the commodification of education has enforced an ideological apparatus that oppresses the minds of the poor for the benefit of sustaining power among the wealthy (Bowles and Gintis 2011). Gaining notoriety in the 1970s, critical theory was applied in education to conceptualize the challenges in schooling as a result of hegemony and was led by the Brazilian philosopher Paulo Freire. Freire developed "critical pedagogy" in the belief that education which is liberating should encourage inquiry and critical consciousness instead of the forced learning of information. Critical pedagogy is designed to embrace diversity and utilizes cultural knowledge for learning with students. Freire (2000) asserted that oppressed people must be involved in the struggle for their own liberation in education, activism, and social justice, and this has become a core component of critical pedagogy with students (Morrell et al. 2013).

According to Freire (2000), children "read the world" before they read the word. For this reason, critical literacy has been implemented in education with historically marginalized students to analyze power structures in society. Research has also shown how critical literacy enhances oppressed young people's critical consciousness of their social conditions and provides them with access to transformative outcomes. Critical literacy has been used as a tool to deconstruct systems of power and privilege with marginalized students through sociocultural practices such as poetry and hip-hop. Over time, critical literacy has evolved and extended additional literacy frameworks that are grounded in the work of Freire, such as critical media literacy. As stated previously, the media are one of the most powerful and influential tools that are used to disseminate hegemonic ideology. The hegemonic power of the media has also proven to form oppressive paradigms among marginalized youth through its Eurocentric ideology and imagery as they interpret the world.

In response, critical media literacy is a counter-hegemonic approach toward the influence of power systems in education and media. It is defined as the ability to acquire the literary tools to access, analyze, evaluate, and create media through critical practices (Kellner and Share 2019). Librarians should always apply a critical lens to media literacy when serving historically marginalized teens in urban communities because this has shown promise in changing perceptions about social norms and in increasing self-efficacy. In this book you will learn about media literacy and how to implement it in library programming. (Chapter 3 provides insight and more depth on the purpose of media literacy, as well as a conceptual framework for practice.) But before we dive deeper into understanding the media literacy framework, it is important to understand how teens are using and engaging with media today. Thus, chapter 2 will provide insight on the current state of teens and media.

●  ●  ●

## TEEN REFLECTION

**What challenges do you experience in your community that you think librarians should take into consideration when serving teens?**

Something I've realized through the pandemic is how many of my deep-seated interests stemmed from experiences. For example, the console demos in the video game sections at Best Buy and Target were where I first experienced what video games could be and where my love for video games really took off. But, as someone who is of a low socioeconomic background and a teen, experiences that might spark a lifelong passion often seem unavailable, often through price or timing.

While video games are a relatively inexpensive passion, other things in STEM are not. Music, for one, can get very expensive, even if it's just to try it out. I know that I would not be at the same level now musically if I didn't have friends who were willing to share their copies of Ableton Live with me. Even more expensive are things like robotics and lab time, both of which give immensely valuable skills and can spark passions but are less available to teens, especially those who are lower socioeconomically.

I enjoyed my work at the Teen Center because the price was always free, and the timing was something we gave great thought to. We strived to give other teens and tweens experiences in STEM that were fun for the hour and might spark a passion, like our PowerPoint escape room, which had concepts from computer science and music theory. I myself was able to further my passions as a result of the program, as I got my first MIDI keyboard through my job and the program provided me with connections and mentorship in music. ⏻

—BEREKET TEMESGEN, 16, Boston, MA

● ● ●

## VOICES FROM THE FIELD: Jeff Share

Jeff Share teaches in the Teacher Education Program at the University of California, Los Angeles.

**Why is it important to implement a critical approach to media literacy when educating historically marginalized youth?**

It is important to recognize the differences between dominant approaches to schooling that incorporate neoliberal education and transformative models of learning that support critical approaches to media literacy. Educators have come under attack for daring to question the dominant narratives instead of just repeating inaccurate whitewashed ideologies. Debates over what to teach and how to teach clearly demonstrate that schooling is neither neutral nor objective. Education has always been political because it is a powerful tool that can promote obedience, rationalize injustice, and limit inquiry; or alternatively, it can encourage critical thinking, develop empathy, and empower people to act for social and environmental justice.

For historically marginalized youth, schooling is often an exclusionary space that reinforces deficit frames and funnels them into vocational tracks that rarely capitalize on their assets. At the same time, commercial media often underrepresent and misrepresent people of color and other marginalized groups, appropriating their cultures, denigrating their experiences, and reinforcing harmful stereotypes.

Critical media literacy can provide pedagogy to critique the social structures, systems, and representations that organize society and reproduce these hierarchies of power. Students should be guided to read both the word and the world (Freire and Macedo 2005) as they question injustice and challenge oppression through critical media analysis and production.

A critical approach to media literacy empowers students to think critically about the media sphere in which they swim and use those tools to express their voices and create alternative media that are more compassionate, environmentally sustainable, and socially just. ⏻

● ● ●

## VOICES FROM THE FIELD: Jayne Cubbage

Jayne Cubbage is an associate professor of communications at Bowie State University and editor of the upcoming volume *Critical Race Media Literacy: Themes and Strategies for Media Education*.

**Why should librarians in urban communities implement critical media literacy skills in their programming and services?**

Imparting critical media skills to youth in urban communities is a collective responsibility. When trained on critical media literacy, librarians are able to provide this skill set to their students. Urban youth are known to "over-index," or spend more hours each day engaging with multiple media platforms than youth from varying socioeconomic backgrounds. Educators in an urban setting play a special role in this process because they are able to work with their students in multiple ways using existing media texts. The use of favored media texts in educational settings has been shown to foster increased student engagement and enhanced student performance.

Educators have a unique opportunity, over sustained periods of time, to learn the specific motivations and usage patterns among this group, while at the same time working with their students to help them to reimagine their interactions with media. In structured educational environments equipped with caring and compassionate librarians, young media consumers can be imparted with critical media literacy skills, which in turn opens up a variety of possibilities for their media engagement to become a liberating force in their lives rather than a predatory and exploitative entity. This process can move young media consumers to the stage of being producers and creators who actually benefit financially from their online presence. Once fully acculturated on the benefits and the challenges with digital media today, these newly enlightened youth can serve as cultural and digital ambassadors to their peers as they shape the next generation of mindful media users. ⏻

## REFERENCES

Anyon, Jean. 2005. *Radical Possibilities: Public Policy, Urban Education, and a New Social Movement*. New York: Routledge.

Bowles, Samuel, and Herbert Gintis. 2011. *Schooling in Capitalist America: Educational Reform and the Contradictions of Economic Life*. Chicago: Haymarket Books.

Chetty, Raj, Nathaniel Hendren, Patrick Kline, and Emmanuel Saez. 2014. "Where Is the Land of Opportunity? The Geography of Intergenerational Mobility in the United States." *Quarterly Journal of Economics* 129, no. 4: 1553–1623.

DeMarrais, Kathleen Bennett, and Margaret LeCompte. 1998. *The Way Schools Work: A Sociological Analysis of Education*. 3rd edition. New York: Longman.

Du Bois, W. E. B. 1994. *The Souls of Black Folk*. New York: Dover.

Freire, Paulo. 2000. *Pedagogy of the Oppressed*. Continuum International.

Freire, Paulo, and Donaldo Macedo. 2005. *Literacy: Reading the Word and the World*. Routledge.

Helms, Ann Doss. September 5, 2018. "Grad Rates Plummet at Several CMS High Schools. Here's What It Means." *The Charlotte Observer*. www.charlotte observer.com/news/local/education/article217798175.html.

Jocson, Korina M. 2018. *Youth Media Matters: Participatory Cultures and Literacies in Education*. Minneapolis: University of Minnesota Press.

Kellner, Douglas, and Jeff Share. 2019. *The Critical Media Literacy Guide: Engaging Media and Transforming Education*. Boston: Brill.

King, Maya, and Nicole Gaudiano. September 23, 2020. "The Pandemic Could Widen the Achievement Gap. A Generation of Students Is at Risk." *Politico*. www.politico.com/news/2020/09/23/how-the-coronavirus-is-making -school-segregation-worse-420839.

Kirsh, Steven J. 2011. *Children, Adolescents, and Media Violence: A Critical Look at the Research*. Los Angeles: Sage.

Ladd, Helen F. 2012. "Education and Poverty: Confronting the Evidence." *Journal of Policy Analysis and Management* 31, no. 2: 203–27.

Lipman, Pauline. 2004. *High Stakes Education: Inequality, Globalization, and Urban School Reform*. New York: Routledge.

Meyer, Leila. 2016. "Home Connectivity and the Homework Gap." *Technological Horizons in Education* 43, no. 4: 16.

Milner IV, H. Richard. 2012. "But What Is Urban Education?" *Urban Education* 47, no. 3: 556–61. https://doi.org/10.1177/0042085912447516.

Mirra, Nicole, Ernest Morrell, and Danielle Filipiak. 2018. "From Digital Consumption to Digital Invention: Toward a New Critical Theory and Practice of Multiliteracies." *Theory into Practice* 57, no. 1: 12–19. https://doi.org/10.1080/00405841.2017.1390336.

Moore III, James L., and Chance W. Lewis. 2012. *African American Students in Urban Schools: Critical Issues and Solutions for Achievement*. New York: Peter Lang.

Morrell, Ernest, Rudy Dueñas, Veronica Garcia, and Jorge López. 2013. *Critical Media Pedagogy: Teaching for Achievement in City Schools*. New York: Teachers College Press.

Nation's Report Card. 2018. "National Achievement Level Results in Technology & Engineering Literacy." National Assessment of Educational Progress. www .nationsreportcard.gov/tel/results/achievement/.

———. 2019. "National Achievement Level Results in Reading Grade 8." National Assessment of Educational Progress. www.nationsreportcard.gov/reading/nation/achievement/?grade=8/.

Orfield, Gary, and Chungmei Lee. 2005. *Why Segregation Matters: Poverty and Educational Inequality*. Harvard University Civil Rights Project.

Price Jr., Robert J. 2005. "Hegemony, Hope, and the Harlem Renaissance: Taking Hip Hop Culture Seriously." *Convergence* 38, no. 2: 55.

Rothstein, Richard. 2017. *The Color of Law: A Forgotten History of How Our Government Segregated America*. New York: Liveright.

Steinmetz, Jesse. December 3, 2019. "Charlotte Talks: Segregation in Charlotte Education." Charlotte Talks. Podcast, website, 49:04. www.wfae.org/show/charlotte-talks-with-mike-collins/2019-12-03/charlotte-talks-segregation -in-charlotte-education.

Tarabini, Aina, and Judith Jacovkis. 2012. "The Poverty Reduction Strategy Papers: An Analysis of a Hegemonic Link between Education and Poverty." *International Journal of Educational Development* 32, no. 4: 507–16.

Wilson, William J. 1990. *The Truly Disadvantaged: The Inner City, the Underclass, and Public Policy*. Chicago: University of Chicago Press.

# It Never Sleeps
## The Current State of Teens and Media

ABBY KIESA

The media's the most powerful entity on earth. They have the *power* to make the innocent guilty. They have the *power* to make the innocent guilty and to make the guilty innocent.

—MALCOLM X

**Before we delve too deeply into approaches to media literacy education,** let's take a step back and put into some perspective what the current relationships between teens and different types of media look like. While a high-profile media report may cover dramatic events like young people using TikTok to influence a rally of former President Trump, or it may note teens' increased use of screen time during the global pandemic, the reality can be very different by community. Conversations about the state of youth and media often revolve around screen time and social media, and while these are certainly relevant topics, they are not the only considerations. This chapter will try to go beyond screen time and who uses what digital platform to consider other factors that influence young people's relationships to media. In fact, what this chapter will lay out is an argument for a deeper understanding of the teens that media literacy programs serve, as young people's relationship to media can differ considerably based on their access to digital technology, the interests they bring to online spaces, and the networks that influence their relationship to media.

## MEDIA ACCESS AND USE DIFFER AMONG YOUTH

It almost goes without saying that, speaking generally compared to other generations, the current generation of teens are "digital natives." While that's undoubtedly true on a generational level, it should not be the basis for assuming much before working with a group of young people in your community. Like many things about young people in the United States, huge differences can exist *among* young people.

This begins with the time spent viewing screens for entertainment. According to Common Sense Media (Rideout and Robb 2019), screen time varies among teens, but the majority spend anywhere from 4 to 8 hours a day viewing screens for entertainment, while 29 percent spend more than 8 hours a day doing so. One of the reasons why these figures differ among young people is differences in access. In fact, while 77 percent of adults in U.S. urban areas have home broadband, only 70 percent of those aged 18–29 do (Pew Research Center 2021). At the same time, young people are much more likely than other age groups to have a smartphone but not high-speed internet at home (Perrin 2021). Pew also found that in 2018, 95 percent of teens from ages 13 to 17 reported having a smartphone, but that figure ranged from 75 to 96 percent according to income, and this aligns with research from Common Sense Media (Parker and Igielnik 2020; and Rideout and Robb 2019). These differences manifest in young people's lives regularly. Common Sense Media (Chandra et al. 2020) estimates that 21 percent of K–12 students in urban areas across the country are without adequate internet connectivity and points out that these divides can differ dramatically by state. This warrants a concerted effort among educators and those who work with youth to seek to understand the experiences of the young people they are specifically working with in their community. Their experiences have implications for the approach, program design, technology needed, and activities used in educating teens.

Like screen time, the topic of youth and media often draws concerns over the potential negative influence on young people. However, this is another way in which the relationships between young people and media are diverse. Exposure to media can have disparate impacts on diverse youth. The detriments of online participation have often been discussed (Patton et al. 2014; Nesi et al. 2021; Twenge 2017), but there are also benefits. As Genner and Süss write, "[youth] actively construct an understanding of the world through interactions with their social and cultural environment, of which media is a part" (2017, 4–5). For example, young people from minoritized and marginalized communities can find online spaces to be a support. McInroy and Craig (2017) find that LGBT youth are finding support to develop their identity through online spaces. Stevens et al. (2017) find that online spaces contribute to sexual risk reduction among youth of color. Additionally, Rice and Barman-Adhikari (2014) find that access to digital spaces allows homeless youth to sustain and develop social capital. And research finds other benefits among youth, including benefits to positive youth development (Lee and Horsley 2017), and nonprofits can use social media to counter "white racial resentment" (Maxwell and Schulte 2018). In fact, teens themselves report both positive and negative benefits from social media:

> Teens have mixed views on whether social media has had a positive or negative effect on their generation. About three-in-ten (31%) say the effect on people their own age has been mostly positive, 24% say it's been mostly negative, and 45% say it's been neither positive nor negative. (Parker and Igielnik 2020)

Analysis done by students working with our research institute found that 18–19-year-old teens were more likely than their near-peers to see or hear information about the 2020 presidential election via digital spaces more known for media creation, like Snapchat, TikTok, and Instagram (Belle Booth 2021). Figure 2.1 shows that young people who are 18–19 years old were more likely than their 20–29-year-old peers to hear about or see information about the 2020 election on Instagram (49 versus 38 percent), TikTok (47 versus 23 percent), and Snapchat (44 versus 20 percent). These platforms have some aspects of media production embedded in their user experience in ways that other platforms do not.

The varied benefits and drawbacks that the media's influence can have on youth point to a need for educators to remember the possible negatives while also recognizing the potential positive benefits of online spaces. This is especially true among youth from minoritized and marginalized communities, for whom we should not write off digital media as being always dangerous and negative. The media can be used as a tool to improve young people's power and potential.

FIGURE 2.1

**Young people reported seeing information about the 2020 election on different platforms more or less frequently based on their age**

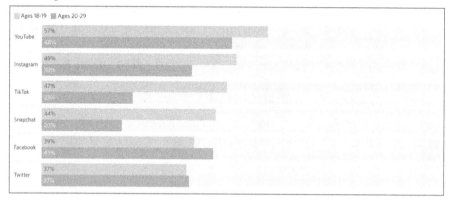

Source: CIRCLE (Center for Information and Research on Civic Learning and Engagement), "Young People Created Media to Uplift Their Voices in 2020," https://circle.tufts.edu/latest -research/young-people-created-media-uplift-their-voices-2020.

An asset-based perspective is important and can be facilitated through the known positive impacts of a media creation approach. The experiences that young people have with online spaces should be seen as an asset to media literacy education. There are many approaches to teaching media literacy, as Kellner and Share (2007) documented over a decade ago. These approaches range from "protectionist" ones to a more critical approach, and it's important to think about these choices in the context of young people's everyday lives. An asset-oriented approach to thinking and inquiring about youth and media, as recommended by Alper, Katz, and Clark (2016), is of particular importance to working with youth who don't fit the dominant U.S. cultural experience—for example, youth of color, youth from low-income families, and LGBTQIA youth. An asset-based approach leverages and leans on the knowledge, experiences, and power of young people themselves, and in the case of young people from marginalized communities, the power they may not always see in themselves or have reiterated for them.

A particularly valuable approach to teaching media literacy using an asset-based approach is working with young people to *create* media content. Creation and action are an essential part of an asset-based approach. The National Association for Media Literacy Education (NAMLE), the central body for media literacy educators in the United States, specifically includes this in its vision:

> NAMLE envisions a day when everyone, in our nation and around the world, possesses the ability to access, analyze, evaluate, create, and act using all forms of communication. Media literacy education refers to the practices necessary to foster these skills. (NAMLE 2021)

Media creation benefits youth development in many ways (Buckingham 2008; Goldfarb 2002; Jenson, Dahya, and Fisher 2014; Ranieri and Bruni 2013 as cited in Dahya 2017; Chan and Holosko 2020; and Chan 2019) within a politically polarized environment. The media creation process, as Dahya (2017) summarizes, benefits young people from "non-dominant communities" in using their voices. As a form of narrative development to counter minoritization and marginalization processes, "young people write themselves into existence" (Stornaiuolo and Thomas 2018) in a process of "restorying."

It's likely that the tumultuous year 2020, which saw a global pandemic hitting youth and communities of color hard, as well as a continued racial reckoning and political mobilization mostly led by Black youth, played into how young people in the United States used digital spaces. Online spaces are ripe for building collective efficacy, sharing impactful stories, and reaching out to those you're in relationship with to engage them. These are reasons why it's not surprising that in 2020 Black and Latinx youth were more likely to create media and share their own experiences in online spaces (Belle Booth 2021). For example, Black and Latinx youth were 10 percent more likely than white and Asian youth in the United States to share their experiences via media (see figure 2.2). Additionally, a 2020 pre-election youth survey carried out by CIRCLE (Center for Information and Research on Civic Learning and Engagement) found that a majority of young people who reported engaging in these sorts of digital creation processes reported feeling more informed about politics and civic life as a result. They felt that their voice was more powerful, and they felt more represented as a result of creating media content (Belle Booth et al. 2020).

FIGURE 2.2

## Black and Latino youth created online content more than their white and Asian peers did

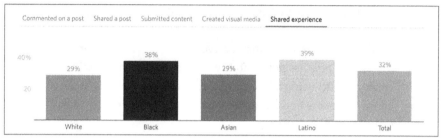

Source: CIRCLE, "Young People Created Media to Uplift Their Voices in 2020," https://circle .tufts.edu/latest-research/young-people-created-media-uplift-their-voices-2020.

It's imperative that educators consider the approaches to media literacy education that will build young people's agency for themselves, their families, and their communities (Kiesa and Vito 2018). "Media literacies that focus on participation in local issues can frame the critique and creation of messages as connected to one's sense of place, belonging and community" (Mihailidis and Viotty 2017, 451). Research on civic education has found that more interactive instructional practices, when implemented well, can stimulate young people to build their capacities and continue to be engaged in their communities (Kawashima-Ginsberg 2013; Gingold 2013; Ballard, Cohen, and Littenberg-Tobias, 2016), including in urban contexts (Cohen et al. 2018).

## MEDIA LITERACY EDUCATION REQUIRES A CRITICAL LENS

An asset-based approach also means helping young people make sense of challenging information and leveraging the opportunity to enable young people's power and self-confidence. The plethora of forms of media, the political polarization that has led to associations between political party and identity (Huddy and Bankert 2017), and the increase in ideologically motivated media mean that it's not unlikely for young people, especially those from marginalized communities, to encounter ideas or images that disrespect them, their family, or their community. While we may see small but important changes in this sort of representation, the changes don't always mean that there are no negative implications for youth development (McInroy and Craig 2017; Gillig and Murphy 2016; Adams-Bass et al. 2014).

In their early descriptions of the type of media literacy education that existed, Kellner and Share (2007) worried about "water[ing] down the transformative potential" of youth media creation without a critical lens (as cited in Johnston-Goodstar et al. 2014). As Garcia et al. (2015) write, "It is urgent that spaces be created that build critical literacy practices with youth, as these can provide a critical counternarrative that challenges dehumanizing policies and practices that disenfranchise the youths' communities." This focus on uplifting young people's assets, value, and tools is echoed in Kwon and de los Ríos's writing about urban classroom contexts: "Teachers simply incorporating students' social media practices, photography and digital apps in the classroom will not automatically lead to social transformation. Without an acute lens of systemic racial inequity and the honing of students' critical digital literacies, these classroom projects can easily reproduce harm and 'damage-centered' narratives" (Tuck 2009 as cited in Kwon and de los Ríos 2019).

Therefore, in urban spaces and spaces where young people of color are program participants, an approach that supports young people telling their own stories, talking about their experiences, and understanding how power works is important to consider. Kersch and Lesley (2019) lay out a theoretical framework for understanding how the perspectives of non-dominant groups fit into a broader critical media literacy framework, one which includes "student-centered inquiry" and which inherently values young people's questions, as well as having a "testimony" aspect and a focus on "production for social action" (45). And longitudinal research by Barron et al. (2014) illuminates the positive outcomes associated with this general approach in an urban context, as well as interrogating assumptions about digital divides and "digital natives," while Evans (2020) reminds us of the role that musical creation as a form of media creation can play in improving critical media literacy and other positive outcomes. The case study of *Latinitas*, a youth-created digital magazine, also reinforces the many benefits of this approach with young Latina women, including the work against harmful stereotypes in media (Sousa and Ramasubramanian 2017). And the harm that can come from online spaces is part of Volpe et al.'s (2020) research to understand the relationship between "liberatory media literacy" ("the ability to critically read, evaluate, support, and create media and technology that represents people of color in their full humanity") and traumatic events witnessed online. These authors find that another positive outcome from this approach is helping young people of color to play a "protective" role.

As educators think about building media literacy supports for youth in urban spaces, the research laid out in this chapter is a reminder of the truly transformative potential of an approach that considers context. Young people's relationships to media can differ dramatically, and educators should be taking those factors into consideration to design programs that help young people make sense of what they see and center their own power and value. In addition to learning how to distinguish between fact and opinion, this instruction holds the potential to expand both positive youth outcomes and young people's sense of what they can do.

● ● ●

## TEEN REFLECTION

**How do you feel you and your peers engage with the media today?**

I do not believe social media is "social" anymore. It has been completely turned away from that in my eyes. That's why my peers and I tend to engage less. Social media is no longer about staying in touch with others but more about keeping up with others' online identities. There's constant pressure to post only the best and most flattering pictures of yourself on social media, especially if it's going on your main profile. There is not much casual posting going on within my generation. We don't share what we ate for breakfast or how we worked out for thirty extra minutes that day. We leave that to the millennials!

A lot of people who I'm friends with don't post that much. They only have a few posts, sometimes none. I personally have only twenty-two posts total on my Instagram page, spanning back from 2018 to now. I had a lot more up in the past but have since deleted them. I felt like they didn't fit my image anymore.

I hope one day social media can become social again, less about keeping up and more about staying present. ⏻

—**ALASIA HICKS,** 16, Brunswick, MD

● ● ●

## VOICES FROM THE FIELD: Merve Lapus

Merve Lapus is the vice president of education outreach and engagement for Common Sense Media.

**Why is it important for educators to understand the ways in which teens are using media to better teach media literacy skills?**

It is important now more than ever for educators to understand the ways teens are using media to better teach media literacy skills. Not only are media and technology continuing to evolve at a rapidly changing pace, but so are the function and impact they have on teens and younger children. Approximately 95 percent of teens in America will have their own mobile device and will, on average, spend almost nine hours a day texting, playing games, posting to social media, watching videos, and more (Rideout and Robb 2018). These apps and tools are much more than just utilities and platforms for them; in many ways, the media are their "space." These platforms are where they interact with friends, explore information, and express creativity. As educators, we typically focus on the skills students need to learn and less often on fostering the disposition needed to act on those skills. Educators need to better understand the complex decisions and experiences of teens with media so as to better align and validate their approach to addressing ongoing media literacy skills.

Dispositions guide students' thoughts and behaviors as they go about their lives. We support the development of dispositions when we attend to students' (1) sensitivity to situations where careful, critical thinking and action are warranted, (2) and their inclinations and motivations to follow through with putting to use the skills they have learned (Perkins, Jay, and Tishman 1993). In a diverse classroom setting of cultures, access, and shifting media, students increasingly face dilemmas and sticky situations that lack clear-cut right or wrong answers. In order to help young people be reflective, responsible, and ethical decision-makers in their connected lives, we need to take their experiences and perspectives into account. Better aligning their dispositions and experiences with digital literacy skills will make these instructional efforts more valid and meaningful to their needs. ⏻

•  •  •

## VOICES FROM THE FIELD: Brittany N. Anderson ⎯⎯⎯⎯⎯⎯

Brittany N. Anderson is an assistant professor of urban education in middle, secondary, and K–12 schools at the University of North Carolina at Charlotte.

**Why is it important for educators who serve teens in urban communities to understand the ways in which historically marginalized teens are using media?**

As educators, we play a critical role in demystifying contemporary uses of new media and in teaching media literacy skills, particularly for historically marginalized teens. Therefore, I present the question: how can we, as a broader learning community, identify, engage, and empower our youth to employ media literacy as learners and doers in their informal and formal academic development? With media literacy skills, students learn to deconstruct dominant media narratives and to create their own counter-narratives to the media's depiction of marginalized youth. Due to the continuous cycles of the media, now, more than ever, we have to understand problem-sensing and problem-posing from a critical and emancipatory perspective.

Educators have to privilege marginalized perspectives, knowledge, and frameworks through the use of media literacy and try to understand societal systems, both systemic and structural. Our students are in great need of understanding how different images, concepts, and communities are shown in the media and how they can use historical and current events to unpack what this means for them. With these tools, educators have the opportunity to not only nuance hegemonic mainstream norms but also interrogate their own experiences with media. As we negotiate the development of antiracist and culturally responsive teaching, we must situate and foster learning that is empowering, active, authentic, and emancipatory (Morrell et al. 2013) for historically marginalized youth. To do this requires us to remain present, informed, and open to change because the media never sleeps. ⏻

## REFERENCES

Adams-Bass, Valerie N., Howard C. Stevenson, and Diana Slaughter Kotzin. 2014. "Measuring the Meaning of Black Media Stereotypes and Their Relationship to the Racial Identity, Black History Knowledge, and Racial Socialization of African American Youth." *Journal of Black Studies* 45 (5): 367–95.

Alper, Meryl, Vikki S. Katz, and Lynn Schofield Clark. 2016. "Researching Children, Intersectionality, and Diversity in the Digital Age." *Journal of Children and Media* 10 (1): 107–14. doi: 10.1080/17482798.2015.1121886.

Ballard, Parissa J., Alison K. Cohen, and Joshua Littenberg-Tobias. 2016. "Action Civics for Promoting Civic Development: Main Effects of Program Participation and Differences by Project Characteristics." *American Journal of Community Psychology* 58 (3–4): 377–90.

Barron, Brigid, Kimberley Gomez, Nichole Pinkard, and Caitlin K. Martin. 2014. *The Digital Youth Network: Cultivating Digital Media Citizenship in Urban Communities.* Cambridge, MA: MIT Press.

Belle Booth, Ruby. 2021. "Young People Created Media to Uplift Their Voices in 2020." Center for Information and Research on Civic Learning and Engagement. https://circle.tufts.edu/latest-research/young-people-created-media-uplift-their-voices-2020.

Belle Booth, Ruby, Emma Tombaugh, Abby Kiesa, Kristian Lundberg, and Alison Cohen. 2020. "Young People Turn to Online Political Engagement during COVID-19." Center for Information and Research on Civic Learning and Engagement. https://circle.tufts.edu/latest-research/young-people-turn-online-political-engagement-during-covid-19.

Buckingham, David. 2008. "Beyond Technology: Rethinking Learning in the Age of Digital Culture." In *Youth Media Democracy: Perceptions of New Literacies*, edited by Jan Pettersen. Youth Media Democracy Conference, 37–43.

Chan, Chitat. 2019. "Using Digital Storytelling to Facilitate Critical Thinking Disposition in Youth Civic Engagement: A Randomized Control Trial." *Children and Youth Services Review* 107 (104522).

Chan, Chitat, and Michael J. Holosko. 2020. "Utilizing Youth Media Practice to Influence Change: A Pretest–Posttest Study." *Research on Social Work Practice* 30 (1): 110–21.

Chandra, Sumit, Amy Chang, Lauren Day, Amina Fazlullah, Jack Liu, Lane McBride, Thisal Mudalige, and Danny Weiss. 2020. "Closing the K–12 Digital Divide in the Age of Distance Learning." Common Sense Media. www.commonsensemedia.org/sites/default/files/uploads/pdfs/common_sense_media_report_final_7_1_3pm_web.pdf.

Cohen, Alison K., Joshua Littenberg-Tobias, Abby Ridley-Kerr, Alexander Pope, Laurel C. Stolte, and Kenneth K. Wong. 2018. "Action Civics Education and Civic Outcomes for Urban Youth: An Evaluation of the Impact of Generation Citizen." *Citizenship Teaching & Learning* 13 (3): 351–68.

Dahya, Negin. 2017. "Critical Perspectives on Youth Digital Media Production: 'Voice' and Representation in Educational Contexts." *Learning, Media and Technology* 42 (1): 100–111.

Evans, Jabari. 2020. "Connecting Black Youth to Critical Media Literacy through Hip Hop Making in the Music Classroom." *Journal of Popular Music Education* 4 (3): 277–93.

Garcia, Antero, Nicole Mirra, Ernest Morrell, Antonio Martinez, and D'Artagnan Scorza. 2015. "The Council of Youth Research: Critical Literacy and Civic Agency in the Digital Age." *Reading & Writing Quarterly* 31 (2): 151–67.

Genner, Sarah, and Daniel Süss. 2017. "Socialization as Media Effect." In *The International Encyclopedia of Media Effects*, edited by P. Rössler, C.A. Hoffner and L. Zoonen. https://doi.org/10.1002/9781118783764.wbieme0138.

Gillig, Traci, and Sheila Murphy. 2016. "Fostering Support for LGBTQ Youth? The Effects of a Gay Adolescent Media Portrayal on Young Viewers." *International Journal of Communication* 10 (23).

Gingold, Jessica. 2013. "Building an Evidence-Based Practice of Action Civics: The Current State of Assessments and Recommendations for the Future." Center for Information and Research on Civic Learning and Engagement. https://circle.tufts.edu/latest-research/building-case-action-civics.

Goldfarb, Brian. 2002. *Visual Pedagogy: Media Cultures in and beyond the Classroom.* Durham, NC: Duke University Press.

Huddy, Leonie, and Alexa Bankert. 2017. "Political Partisanship as a Social Identity." Oxford Research Encyclopedia of Politics. https://oxfordre.com/politics.

Jenson, Jennifer, Negin Dahya, and Stephanie Fisher. 2014. "Valuing Production Values: A 'Do It Yourself' Media Production Club." *Learning, Media and Technology* 39 (2): 215–28.

Johnston-Goodstar, Katie, Katie Richards-Schuster, and Jenna K. Sethi. 2014. "Exploring Critical Youth Media Practice: Connections and Contributions for Social Work." *Social Work* 59 (4): 339–46.

Kawashima-Ginsberg, Kei. 2013. "Do Discussion, Debate, and Simulations Boost NAEP Civics Performance?" CIRCLE Fact Sheet. Center for Information and Research on Civic Learning and Engagement. https://circle.tufts.edu/sites/default/files/202-01/discussion_debate_naep_2013.pdf.

Kellner, Douglas, and Jeff Share. 2007. "Critical Media Literacy: Crucial Policy Choices for a Twenty-First-Century Democracy." *Policy Futures in Education* 5 (1): 59–69.

Kersch, Dorotea Frank, and Mellinee Lesley. 2019. "Hosting and Healing: A Framework for Critical Media Literacy Pedagogy." *Journal of Media Literacy Education* 11 (3): 37–48.

Kiesa, Abby, and DC Vito. 2018. "A Civic Imperative for Media Literacy." Philanthropy for Active Civic Engagement. https-medium-com-infogagement-civic-imperative-for-media-literacy-youth-action-b9906f66bed1.

Kwon, L., and C. V. de los Ríos. 2019. "'See, Click, Fix': Civic Interrogation and Digital Tools in a Ninth-Grade Ethnic Studies Course." *Equity & Excellence in Education* 52 (2–3): 154–66.

Lee, Ah Ram, and Suzanne Horsley. 2017. "The Role of Social Media on Positive Youth Development: An Analysis of 4-H Facebook Page and 4-H'ers' Positive Development." *Children and Youth Services Review* 77: 127–38.

Levine, Peter, and Kei Kawashima-Ginsberg. 2017. The Republic Is (Still) at Risk—and Civics Is Part of the Solution." Jonathan M. Tisch College of Civic Life, Tufts University.

Maxwell, Angie, and Stephanie R. Schulte. 2018. "Racial Resentment Attitudes among White Millennial Youth: The Influence of Parents and Media." *Social Science Quarterly* 99 (3): 1183–99.

McInroy, Lauren B., and Shelley L. Craig. 2017. "Perspectives of LGBTQ Emerging Adults on the Depiction and Impact of LGBTQ Media Representation." *Journal of Youth Studies* 20 (1): 32–46.

Mihailidis, Paul, and Samantha Viotty. 2017. "Spreadable Spectacle in Digital Culture: Civic Expression, Fake News, and the Role of Media Literacies in 'Post-Fact' Society." *American Behavioral Scientist* 61 (4): 441–54.

Morrell, Ernest, Rudy Dueñas, Veronica Garcia, and Jorge López. 2013. *Critical Media Pedagogy: Teaching for Achievement in City Schools*. New York: Teachers College Press.

NAMLE. 2021. "Our Mission." https://namle.net/about.

Nesi, Jacqueline, Taylor A. Burke, Alexandra H. Bettis, Anastacia Y. Kudinova, Elizabeth C. Thompson, Heather A. MacPherson, Kara A. Fox, et al. 2021. "Social Media Use and Self-Injurious Thoughts and Behaviors: A Systematic Review and Meta-Analysis." *Clinical Psychology Review* 87 (102038).

Parker, Kim, and Ruth Igielnik. May 14, 2020. "On the Cusp of Adulthood and Facing an Uncertain Future: What We Know about Gen Z So Far." Pew Research Center. www.pewresearch.org/social-trends/2020/05/14/on-the-cusp-of-adulthood-and-facing-an-uncertain-future-what-we-know-about-gen-z-so-far-2/.

Patton, Desmond Upton, Jun Sung Hong, Megan Ranney, Sadiq Patel, Caitlin Kelley, Rob Eschmann, and Tyreasa Washington. 2014. "Social Media as a Vector for Youth Violence: A Review of the Literature." *Computers in Human Behavior* 35 (June): 548–53.

Perkins, D. N., Eileen Jay, and Shari Tishman. 1993. "Beyond Abilities: A Dispositional Theory of Thinking." *Merrill-Palmer Quarterly: Journal of Developmental Psychology* 39 (1): 1–21.

Perrin, Andrew. June 3, 2021. "Mobile Technology and Home Broadband 2021." Pew Research Center. www.pewresearch.org/internet/2021/06/03/mobile-technology-and-home-broadband-2021/.

Pew Research Center. 2021. "Internet/Broadband Fact Sheet." www.pewresearch.org/internet/fact-sheet/internet-broadband/?menuItem=89fe9877-d6d0-42c5-bca0-8e6034e300aa.

Rice, Eric, and Anamika Barman-Adhikari. 2014. "Internet and Social Media Use as a Resource among Homeless Youth." *Journal of Computer-Mediated Communication* 19 (2): 232–47.

Rideout, Victoria, and Michael B. Robb. 2018. "Social Media, Social Life: Teens Reveal Their Experiences." Common Sense Media. www.commonsensemedia .org/research/social-media-social-life-2018.

———. 2019. "The Common Sense Census: Media Use by Tweens and Teens." Common Sense Media. www.commonsensemedia.org/sites/default/files/ uploads/research/2019-census-8-to-18-full-report-updated.pdf.

Sousa, Alexandra, and Srividya Ramasubramanian. 2017. "Challenging Gender and Racial Stereotypes in Online Spaces: Alternative Storytelling among Latino/a Youth in the U.S." In *Beyond the Stereotypes? Images of Boys and Girls, and Their Consequences*, edited by Dafna Lemish and Maya Gotz, 75–83. Goteborg: Nordicom.

Stevens, Robin, Stacia Gilliard-Matthews, Jamie Dunaev, Abigail Todhunter-Reid, Bridgette Brawner, and Jennifer Stewart. 2017. "Social Media Use and Sexual Risk Reduction Behavior among Minority Youth: Seeking Safe Sex Information." *Nursing Research* 66 (5): 368.

Stornaiuolo, Amy, and Ebony Elizabeth Thomas. 2018. "Restorying as Political Action: Authoring Resistance through Youth Media Arts." *Learning, Media and Technology* 43 (4): 345–58.

Twenge, Jean M. September 2017. "Have Smartphones Destroyed a Generation?" *The Atlantic*, September. www.theatlantic.com/magazine/archive/2017/09/ has-the-smartphone-destroyed-a-generation/534198/.

Volpe, Vanessa V., Henry A. Willis, Patrece Joseph, and Brendesha M. Tynes. 2020. "Liberatory Media Literacy as Protective against Posttraumatic Stress for Emerging Adults of Color." *Journal of Traumatic Stress* 34 (5): 1045–55. https://doi.org/10.1002/jts.22640.

# Flashing Lights
## What Is Media Literacy?

DONNELL PROBST and MICHELLE CIULLA LIPKIN

Keep exploring. Keep dreaming. Keep asking why. Don't settle for what you already know. Never stop believing in the *power* of your ideas, your imagination, your hard work to change the world.

**—BARACK OBAMA**, Remarks at 2015 White House Science Fair

**What *is* media literacy? According to the National Association for Media** Literacy Education (NAMLE), media literacy is "the ability to access, analyze, evaluate, create, and act using all forms of communication" (2022). Media literacy expands on the concepts of traditional literacy to incorporate all media texts. In today's complex digital world, students must be prepared with the skills to consume and author all texts, not only print text. Media literacy skills activate critical thinking and production communication and empower power to participate actively as engaged citizens in society.

Media literacy education encourages a comprehensive understanding of the information landscape, such as representation, authorship, power dynamics, economics, storytelling, bias, and credibility. While media literacy education has been closely associated with fact-checking and combatting disinformation over the last several years, media literacy skills are much broader than merely assessing the accuracy of information. While accuracy and reliability should be identified, media literacy supports a deeper understanding of media messages, including purpose, agenda, and an exploration of media construction.

Media literacy is interdisciplinary. While media literacy is offered as a stand-alone course in some schools and institutions, media literacy skills can be incorporated into any classroom to support subject area learning. Giving students the opportunities to develop expertise with media analysis and creation throughout subject areas reinforces these relevant and practical skills.

Filmmaker George Lucas, the founder of Edutopia and the George Lucas Educational Foundation, asked a question in 2004 that still reverberates in education conversations today: "If students aren't taught the language of sound and images, shouldn't they be considered as illiterate as if they left college without being able to read or write?" (Daly 2004). Today's complicated media and information landscape require us to think differently about what it means to be a literate person in the world. We require a broader set of skills to successfully comprehend the messages we receive and productively author our own media messages. Media literacy is a necessary response to the ever-changing information ecosystem and must be an educational priority. Libraries are one of the many environments in which media literacy is practiced, and librarians are some of the field's most stalwart advocates.

## A DEEP DIVE INTO THE DEFINITION OF MEDIA LITERACY

Over the years, many definitions and visions of media literacy have been created. Still the purpose has remained consistent: to ensure every person is equipped with the skills they need to navigate the complicated media landscape as a literate, active participant in today's world. As a result, many scholars and educators turn to NAMLE's *Core Principles of Media Literacy Education* for their foundational understanding of media literacy. Drafted in 2007, these principles were created to solidify media literacy concepts, expand practice, and encompass the opportunities and possibilities of media literacy education to transform both learning and teaching—from kindergarten to college (NAMLE 2007).

The *Core Principles of Media Literacy Education* were written by media literacy scholars and experts and build on scholarship across multiple disciplines, including communication, education, media and film studies, public health, and psychology. The Core Principles reflect a very different media landscape than what exists today. While they require revision to reflect these changes and are not a substitute for defined teaching and learning standards, they present a unique opportunity for educators and practitioners to expand their current practices and identify opportunities for applying media literacy principles, regardless of the technology being used.

The Core Principles shift "the focus of the discussion from what we believe to be true about media to what we believe to be true about how people learn to think critically" (NAMLE 2007). With the principles, we consider not only *what* content we teach but also *how* we teach that content.

## Core Principles of Media Literacy Education

- Media literacy education requires active inquiry and critical thinking about the messages we receive and create.
- Media literacy education expands the concept of literacy to include all forms of media (i.e., reading and writing).
- Media literacy education builds and reinforces skills for learners of all ages. Like print literacy, those skills necessitate integrated, interactive, and repeated practice.
- Media literacy education develops informed, reflective, and engaged participants who are essential for a democratic society.
- Media literacy education recognizes that the media are a part of culture and function as agents of socialization.
- Media literacy education affirms that people use their individual skills, beliefs, and experiences to construct their own meanings from media messages. (NAMLE 2007)

## BREAKING DOWN THE DEFINITION

Each part of NAMLE's definition of media literacy (access, analyze, evaluate, create, and act) requires understanding and skill-building. While each part can stand independently, a fully media-literate person demonstrates skills in all five areas.

### Access

> *Access* is defined as how, when, where, and how often people have access to the tools, technology, and skills needed to thrive. This includes (but is not limited to) understanding how media, technology, and the internet work and how to locate content and use media (i.e., knowing what resources are available online). (NAMLE 2021a)

It is impossible to become media literate without *access* to the media, technology, and skill-building to navigate current communication systems. Access is the starting point. To access information, people must understand how to identify, locate, and use media and technology. Media-literate individuals understand how these tools work, know how to identify different types of content, and are aware of what resources are available both online and offline.

The way information is accessed, and the types of information that are accessible, have a profound impact on our ability to be media literate. Limited or no access to information hinders our ability to participate in society. For example, without access to news and relevant information about current events, people lack the knowledge to engage civically. In addition, lack of access to information disproportionately impacts those communities that are already marginalized, increasing inequity and decreasing educational and employment opportunities. Whether it be for education, for work, or to engage in their community, access to information is necessary.

Access also directly impacts inclusion and representation. With access to consume and create content, voices and experiences are heard. Without access to consume and create content, voices and experiences are silenced. This is another way access affects those already disadvantaged by dictating whose stories are told.

Despite the push for access, access to media and technology alone does not guarantee media literacy skills are being acquired. When considering access, it's important to consider access to media literacy education. Media literacy education is needed to move beyond access in order to be able to analyze, evaluate, create, and act using all forms of media. Media literacy education and skill-building ensure society has access to information from sources that are credible, diverse, and from varied points of view.

## Analyze

> *Analyzing* media content is the process of asking questions about a piece of media in order to identify its authorship, credibility, purpose, technique, context, and economics. A media-literate person understands who created a piece of media/information (the author) and is able to identify whether the author is credible and what the intent behind the media may be. (NAMLE 2021c)

Being prepared and ready to ask questions about all media messages is at the core of media literacy. Building habits of inquiry allows individuals to arm themselves with a range of questions to ask when encountering media content. Media-literate individuals inquire about the author's purpose, biases, and tactics designed to persuade people to feel, think, or act in a certain way. *Analyzing* media is active reflection that digs deep into the agenda and meaning behind media messages.

Analysis skills help media consumers break down the various components of media messages to better identify authorship, authority, accuracy, and techniques used to influence. For example, media-literate media consumers might identify different production choices, such as the types of sound, lighting, editing styles, and camera angles. Media-literate consumers will also ask who authored a piece of media and whether or not the information presented is accurate, factual, and complete. Analysis also includes thinking about the influence of economics on media content, including how financial relationships influence what points of view are represented or omitted.

## Evaluate

> *Evaluating* media content involves drawing one's own meaning, judgment, and conclusions about media messages based on the information gathered during media access, thoughtful analysis, and self-reflective interpretation. (NAMLE 2021e)

*Evaluating* media moves consumers beyond simply deconstructing media messages' techniques, authorship, and economics. Instead, evaluation allows individuals to consider their interpretations, beliefs, and bias to help them draw their meaning and conclusions about media messages. Media-literate consumers will use the information they gathered when analyzing a media message to evaluate the message's credibility; effectiveness; subtexts; how that media might influence themselves, others, or society at large; and the role of that message in power and privilege (NAMLE 2021e).

Media messages are nuanced and should move beyond binary determinations of true and false. Skilled individuals will learn to distinguish fact from fiction, opinion from analysis, and propaganda from creative texts. Additionally, we should investigate messages through a self-reflective lens. For example, how does who we are, our values, life experiences, culture, and identity impact the way we interpret media messages? Does the omission or inclusion of different stories and voices in the media—and the way they are told—contribute to the privilege or harm of diverse populations and cultures? Critically evaluating all media messages develops strong, lifelong media literacy skills.

## Create

> Media *creation* is a form of expression. It encompasses learning how to express ideas through media and communication tools and using that power to create media narratives beyond those that exist in the mainstream media. (NAMLE 2021d)

Given today's participatory culture, it is hard to believe that *create* was not included in the original definition of media literacy. Media creation is an integral part of our relationship with media in the current media landscape. With the development and growth of social media platforms, we are all content creators. Every time we post, share, comment, or react, we participate in the media ecosystem and create new messages to be analyzed and evaluated.

Creation at the core is a tool for expression and empowerment and allows people to share their thoughts, creativity, and voice. Creation is to media literacy as writing is to traditional literacy. Without being able to write, one is not considered literate. Likewise, if you cannot create and express using media, you cannot be considered media literate. The ability of all individuals to author content also allows for different and often suppressed media narratives to rise to the surface and gain attention.

To be media literate, content creators must also consider their intent and their responsibilities as participants in the media ecosystem. Issues of ethics, copyright, fair use, and digital citizenship all need to be considered when creating and sharing content.

## Act

*Act*, or action, is engaging civically as the result of our thoughtful access, analysis, and evaluation of the media messages we receive. We act as a way to do something that challenges the status quo (often in opposition to mainstream media). We act in response to breaking down thoughts, feelings, and ideas related to the media. (NAMLE 2021b)

As previously noted, how we think about and create media content is core to media literacy. Beyond that, though, what do we *do* after accessing, analyzing, and evaluating media messages? What are the *actions* we can and should take? Media literacy, at its core, is about empowering individuals to be active and engaged citizens.

Media literacy supports *productive* participation and action. Whether using social media accounts to support issues or causes one cares about, reporting harassment one sees online, or sharing your voice to counter narratives in the media, there are many ways to *act*. Actions don't have to be confined to the media ecosystem. One might also vote, demonstrate, donate, attend a community meeting, or volunteer as a result of their experience with media messages. Empowering others to be media literate by asking questions and modeling media literacy skills is also productive action.

## IMPLICATIONS FOR PRACTICE

NAMLE's Core Principles were written with classroom teachers in the United States in mind. They state that media literacy requires "integrated, interactive, and repeated practice" (2007). While the principles frame core concepts in media literacy, we also must think about how these principles are applied in educational practice. With this in mind, the original authors created "Implications for Practice" to expand the principles into a practical framework for teachers. Below are some examples of how educators can support media literacy skill-building in the classroom as outlined in the Core Principle's "Implications for Practice" (NAMLE 2007).

### The *Core Principles of Media Literacy Education*'s "Implications for Practice"

- Support students to ask the specific types of questions that will allow them to gain a deeper or more sophisticated understanding of media messages.
- Emphasize strong-sense critical thinking, that is, asking questions about *all* media messages, not just those with which we may disagree.
- Train students to use document-based evidence and well-reasoned arguments to support their conclusions.
- Explain that all media messages are biased, and it is important to understand *what* the substance, source, and significance of a bias might be.
- Provide students with numerous and diverse opportunities to practice and develop skills of analysis and expression.
- Invite and respect diverse points of view.
- Explore representations, misrepresentations, and the lack of representation of cultures and countries in the global community.

- Train students to examine how media structures (e.g., ownership, distribution, etc.) influence the ways that people make meaning of media messages.
- Recognize that *how* we teach matters as much as *what* we teach. Classrooms should be places where student input is respected, valued, and acted upon.
- Help students become aware of and reflect on the meaning that they make of media messages, including how the meaning they make relates to their own values.
- Recognize that students' interpretations of media texts may differ from the teacher's interpretation without being wrong.
- Use group discussion and analysis of media messages to help students understand and appreciate different perspectives and points of view. (NAMLE 2007)

## MEDIA AND INFORMATION LITERACY:
## A Shared Process

While the rise of mis- and disinformation in news and political media has led to media literacy's well-deserved and long-awaited moment in the spotlight, you might be asking, "What does media literacy have to do with libraries and with the information literacy that they support?" The short answer is that media literacy and information literacy are both literacies. The more complex answer is that they both address a need to access, evaluate, and use information effectively. Let's take a look at the definition of each:

*Information literacy:* ". . . the ability to locate, evaluate, and use effectively the needed information" (ALA's Presidential Committee 2006).
*Media literacy*: "The ability to access, analyze, evaluate, create, and act using all forms of communication" (NAMLE 2022).

At the core of both information and media literacy is the ability to access (locate), analyze (and evaluate), and use (create or act) information by utilizing a variety of sources and communication forms. Like traditional literacies, information and media literacy are types of learning that require progressive, repeated instruction across multiple contexts. In traditional literacy practice we start with pictures, letters, words, and sentences, and we eventually progress to more complex topics like context, author intent, and so on. Information literacy begins with the ability to identify an information need, then learn basic search skills and technology, and eventually graduate to more complex information-seeking and evaluation strategies using advanced search engines and databases.

As media consumers, we move beyond simply labeling images with words or intentionally seeking information to fill a defined need. We begin to unconsciously assign meaning and values to the content we encounter across all forms of media. We make meaning of the world around us through the ideas, values, and interpretations represented in the media we read, see, and hear. But without understanding the process for deconstructing these messages, we may even begin to replicate these messages in our own media creations. Media literacy begins unraveling those embedded points of view and provides a road map for analyzing media messages to help media consumers of all ages become more constructive participants in society. Like traditional and information literacies, those who are new to media literacy might begin with basic skills, such as asking questions about the author ("Who created this?" "Who paid for this?"), and eventually begin breaking down how a given piece of media content represents a particular perspective, culture, or point of view and how those embedded values contribute to the sustainment of inequitable power structures and who benefits or is harmed by the maintenance of those structures.

Whether media consumers are seeking information with intention, as described by Kuhlthau's "information search process" (ISP) (1989), or they follow a more fluid, reactive consumption and production process, similar to Bates's "Berrypicking" (1989), media literacy is a process through which media consumers learn to critically and responsibly interact with all forms of media to understand better the values embedded in them, regardless of how they encounter a piece of content.

Beyond their shared processes, information and media literacy hold many other values in common. Both types of literacy are aligned with intellectual freedom and anti-censorship advocacy, and media literacy practitioners believe that best practices require uninhibited access to all information. Media literacy intentionally guides consumers by identifying embedded information, points of view, and values so that consumers will have the necessary information to draw conclusions about the source and authority of content based on their personal beliefs and values. Additionally, media literacy seeks to spotlight how inequitable access to information as a consumer or creator impedes the civic engagement of citizens by limiting the voices of those who are often already marginalized. Both librarians and media literacy practitioners seek to ensure that diverse perspectives and voices are present in both the information and the media landscapes. This commitment to equitable access and information creation is the cornerstone of a civically engaged society.

## INTERSECTIONS: The *Core Principles of Media Literacy Education* and YALSA's *Teen Services Competencies for Library Staff*

One of the most pressing gaps in the field of media literacy is the absence of a defined set of teaching and learning standards. Many media literacy educators, practitioners, and professionals have done their best to independently create curricular standards and outcomes based on the competencies defined in the aforementioned *Core Principles of Media Literacy Education*. In this section we will explore how media literacy intersects with the content area competencies defined by YALSA's *Teen Services Competencies for Library Staff* (2017), a document hereafter referred to as the "Competencies."

One of the more esoteric intersections of information and media literacy—but possibly one of the most critical—is how we include and represent voices from diverse communities in our content acquisition and creation, programming, and decision-making in libraries. YALSA Competencies' "Content Area 2: Interaction with Teens" requires consideration of one of the core competencies of a media-literate person: seeking out, including, and amplifying diverse texts, voices, perspectives, and communities (which maps to Core Principles 4.4, 4.5, and 5.1). Media literacy practice compels us to evaluate and address which voices are included *and* which ones are excluded from various forms of media and texts, conversations, and decision-making processes.

When considering how and how often diverse voices are represented in collections, programming, or the leadership of community-directed programming, librarians must understand that the exclusion of voices that are frequently misrepresented or underrepresented serves only to perpetuate the marginalization of already underserved communities and to reinforce existing power structures. Building relationships with teens that prioritize and value the inclusion of diverse voices and perspectives promotes the development of programs and projects that will better reflect the diversity of the communities that libraries serve. When teens are given the opportunity to be the voice of their community and represent their culture accurately and authentically, they will view their voices as valued and important in society, breaking down centuries of marginalization and building foundations for shared progress and understanding among community members.

Another often undervalued aspect of media literacy among those outside of the media literacy community is the incorporation of media literacy education into learning environments. For example, the Competencies' "Content Area 3: Learning Environments" explicitly calls for both digital and physical resources and materials to help teens develop "creative skills and multiple literacies" (YALSA 2017, 8). When educators, in both formal and informal environments, embrace the principles of media literacy education, they begin to expand the concept of traditional literacies to include all forms of media (Core Principle 2) in a variety of settings, including the library (Core Principle 2.3), thus addressing the call for multiple literacies among learners.

To fully realize the idea of multiple literacies and develop imagination and creativity among teens, library learning environments must be designed to be accessible for all populations served by the library and include the tools and instruction necessary to both analyze and create media individually and collaboratively (Core Principles 2.7, 2.3). In other words, libraries cannot simply purchase equipment and automatically expect collaboration and creative content creation by teens. Libraries can begin addressing issues of equitable access by examining what populations are underserved or unserved; creating online, low-tech, and no-tech programming; and designing innovative, collaborative opportunities that satisfy this call for creativity and engagement.

In addition to ensuring access to the necessary tools, instruction, and programming regardless of teens' connectivity or prior participation, libraries must actively engage in skill-building using all forms of media to ensure that teens can demonstrate media-literate behaviors across all aspects of media literacy, including analyzing, evaluating, creating, and acting. It is not enough to simply provide the tools and programs that cultivate imagination, creativity, and collaboration. Teens are some of the most operationally savvy users when it comes to various types of media tools. Ensuring that teens have the opportunity to use media to responsibly access, engage, and act on media in ways that amplify their voices can help position them as valuable and authoritative voices in their community and promote respectful and inclusive discourse. The representation of diverse communities is central to creating media-literate individuals and environments.

Once we've ensured that we are building spaces and programs to gather all voices served by the library, we can look to the intersections between the Competencies' "Content Area 4: Learning Experiences" and the Core Principles to understand how we can most effectively help teens develop and demonstrate their media literacy skills. One of the most appealing qualities of media literacy is its inherent ability to be incorporated across different content areas. Librarians don't need to drastically modify their programming, topics, and content to address media literacy; instead they can work to incorporate media literacy learning opportunities into their existing curriculums.

Librarians are adept at creating year-round programming linked to specific holidays, celebrations, and other promotional activities. By engaging teens in programmatic topic exploration and selection, we can empower them to examine their personal preferences and tastes, identify possible connections within the social circles of the library or other related communities, and identify opportunities for growth, appreciation, and understanding through library programs and projects (Core Principle 6.7). By engaging a connected learning model as described in Content Area 4, teens can learn and develop through intellectual openness, active inquiry, and critical thinking about various topics, messages, and choices, a key value of media literacy.

As we continue to explore the Competencies' content areas, we begin to see the same recurring threads of media literacy throughout them. Representation, diversity of culture and thought, active inquiry, and critical analysis are themes that are strongly represented across other content areas. For example, in "Content Area 5: Youth Engagement and Leadership," we again see reference to critical thinking, problem-solving, and decision-making—skills explicitly required in media-literate practices (Core Principles 1, 1.7) in both formal and informal learning environments. Developing teens' self-reflection, empathy, and appreciation of diverse opinions and cultures aligns directly, again, to Core Principles 4.4, 4.5, and 5.1, which call for the inclusion of diverse points of view, media, and texts, as well as the exploration of representations, misrepresentations, and the lack of representation of cultures.

"Content Area 7: Cultural Competency and Responsiveness" continues the thread of cultural inclusiveness and awareness by requiring library staff to actively support and respect individual expression, and recognize barriers to participation such as "racism, ethnocentrism, classism, heterosexism, genderism, ableism, and other systems of discrimination and exclusion in the community and its institutions, including the library" (YALSA 2017, 12). Library staff are the gatekeepers to ensure that teens can not only access library programming and content but also have the ability to consume and create content that reflects their culture, thoughts, and opinions accurately and authentically—a cornerstone of being a media-literate person. When teens don't feel free to express their views and experiences authentically or don't see themselves reflected in the media, texts, and programs in the library, systems of marginalization and power over underrepresented communities are reinforced and *will* continue unabated.

Revisiting the idea of access as a media literacy concept, the Competencies' "Content Area 8: Equity of Access" aligns with the media literacy community's belief that intellectual freedom is essential to exercising and building media literacy skills (Core Principle 4.11). Media-literate behavior includes developing a deep interest in news and current events and being an informed, reflective, and active participant in society (Core Principles 4, 4.1). When teens develop digital citizenship skills, they understand the implications of their media consumption and creation and take responsibility for the effects of their media use in a civic context. This participation requires uninhibited access to content that reflects the civic interests of teens so they can begin to reflect on various types of media and critically analyze its impact on themselves and others. Developing this understanding of how various types of media are created and their effects can directly impact how teens understand the impact of the media they create and share. Developing critical and informed media habits is essential to empowering teens to break down preexisting barriers to participation in a democratic society and ensuring their productive engagement as citizens.

## CONCLUSION

To become a successful student, responsible citizen, productive worker, or a competent and conscientious consumer, individuals need to develop expertise with the increasingly sophisticated, multisensory media world. To equip youth to navigate that world successfully, we need to create opportunities and learning environments that allow for media literacy skill-building. To be literate in today's world, one needs to be *media* literate.

Media literacy involves a complex set of skills that require repeated practice and integration across disciplines. While the entire school is part of the media literacy endeavor, libraries and the librarians who teach in them are key to improving and spreading media literacy practices around the United States. It is their work and expertise that give us the greatest chance of ensuring that the next generation is media literate.

●  ●  ●

**TEEN REFLECTION** ─────────────────────

**Do you feel that media literacy is important? If so, why?**

During a time when billions of humans across the globe actively use media in their daily lives, the application and knowledge of media literacy are extremely important because people of all ages encounter some form of misinformation regularly. Trusting fake or misleading news can leave negative impacts upon individuals who are at a higher risk of believing the altered truth. It is undeniable that a majority of students, like me, mainly consume information through social media such as Twitter and Instagram, and these have become the new hub spot for "hot" and trending information. Misinformation and inaccurate facts have the ability to be harmful and can affect our opinions, as well as our grades and health. Learning to identify these fabricated details can benefit us and help us to clearly see the truth as it is. Implementing programs that teach students the skills needed to fight the lies that lurk online can lead to a more factual and positive experience. A reality that focuses on the actuality and certainty of daily information is a safer and more productive environment that I definitely feel is important to pursue. ⏻

—**KAELLA RACSHENBERG**, 18, Normal North High School, OK

● ● ●

## VOICES FROM THE FIELD: Theresa Redmond ⎯⎯⎯⎯⎯⎯

Theresa Redmond is an associate professor of media studies and teacher education at Appalachian State University in Boone, North Carolina.

### Why should educators implement media literacy skills in their instruction?

I came to media literacy early in my professional educator training, and for me, it was readily apparent that my expertise and preparation were of little worth to the lives of my students if my curriculum didn't speak to their interests, experiences, and futures. Outside of our classrooms and schools, young people come of age in complex, mediated spaces comprised of endlessly novel blends of information and communication technologies that combine text, audio, images, video, and more. Their experiences of media are simultaneously empowering and ensnaring— both completely their own and entirely contrived, as online engagement is monetized and new ways of participating are repeatedly commodified. Gradually, our collective awe at the information age has turned to angst. Befuddled by an increasing loss of consensual reality, media literacy can no longer be a luxury incorporated into curricula as an aside or add-on. Today's youth deserve an urgently relevant education that is rich with the perennial skills inherent in media literacy. They need to build, practice, and refine their abilities to access, analyze, evaluate, create, communicate, and act using media in all forms. But even these words are not ambitious enough, not substantial enough to reflect media literacy as an educational imperative. For, at its heart, media literacy education is about cultivating in young people the knowledge of their most inalienable and valuable gifts—their attention, their imagination, and their free will. ⏻

## REFERENCES

ALA's Presidential Committee. *Presidential Committee on Information Literacy: Final Report.* Washington, D.C.: American Library Association, July 24, 2006. www.ala.org/acrl/publications/whitepapers/presidential.

Bates, M. J. 1989. "The Design of Browsing and Berrypicking Techniques for the Online Search Interface." *Online Review* 13 (5): 407–24. https://doi.org/10.1108/eb024320.

Daly, James. 2004. "Life on the Screen: Visual Literacy in Education." *Edutopia.* George Lucas Educational Foundation, September 14. www.edutopia.org/life-screen.

Kuhlthau, Carol C. 1989. "Information Search Process: A Summary of Research and Implications for School Library Media Programs." *School Library Media Quarterly* 18 (1). www.ala.org/aasl/sites/ala.org.aasl/files/content/aaslpubs andjournals/slr/edchoice/SLMQ_InformationSearchProcess_InfoPower.pdf.

NAMLE (National Association for Media Literacy Education). 2007. *Core Principles of Media Literacy Education in the United States.* New York: NAMLE. https://namle.net/wp-content/uploads/2020/09/Namle-Core-Principles-of-MLE-in-the-United-States.pdf.

———. 2021a. "Access." Media Literacy Week, October 25. https://medialiteracy week.us/about/theme/access/.

———. 2021b. "Act." Media Literacy Week, October 29. https://medialiteracyweek .us/about/theme/act/.

———. 2021c. "Analyze." Media Literacy Week, October 26. https://medialiteracy week.us/about/theme/analyze/.

———. 2021d. "Create." Media Literacy Week, October 28. https://medialiteracy week.us/about/theme/create/.

———. 2021e. "Evaluate." Media Literacy Week, October 27. https://medialiteracy week.us/about/theme/evaluate/.

———. 2022. "Media Literacy Defined." https://namle.net/resources/media-literacy-defined/.

YALSA (Young Adult Library Services Association). 2017. *Teen Services Competencies for Library Staff.* Chicago: YALSA. www.ala.org/yalsa/guidelines/yacompetencies.

# Road Closed, Detour Ahead

## Challenges and Opportunities with Serving Urban Teens in Libraries

KELLY CZARNECKI

> Never underestimate the *power* of dreams and the influence of the human spirit. We are all the same in this notion: The potential for greatness lives within each of us.
>
> —WILMA RUDOLPH

**"Do white librarians know how much their BIPOC patrons don't trust them? I know the answer is no, but I don't think they even understand how deep the mistrust goes"** (Nins 2020). This was a tweet from a children's librarian, Tasha Nins, in Saint Paul, Minnesota, in October 2020. How do we (if we identify as white) respond when we read a statement like this? Is there any truth to it? Do we like to think of ourselves as the exception? Are we ourselves a barrier to teens coming to the library, and if so, how do we change that? Let's take a look at our libraries for some answers.

According to a recent article in *Places Journal*, 87 percent of American librarians are white (Mattern 2019). While that's a very high number, it's also likely not surprising, especially if we've frequented libraries and have experienced this statistic while visiting or working in them. Unfortunately, hiring more people of color isn't a magic bullet to eradicate the white values that often get translated—knowingly or otherwise— into bodies of culture. The anti-oppression consultant McKensie Mack tweeted: "Hiring more people of color doesn't dismantle structural racism within an organization. A white dominant organization could hire 100 people of color, but if the policies and the practices stay the same, that's 100 more people that can be harmed by them" (Mack 2020). She adds, "We're here for transformation, not tokenism." This is not to completely dismiss having more representation of BIPOC in the library, particularly in leadership and senior management roles. This can in fact be helpful in some areas, especially when reflecting back to urban teens that they can see themselves as community connectors as a volunteer, mentor, librarian, library worker, social worker, teacher, or change-maker if they decide to pursue their passion or a related career path. If you're in a position to influence hiring or have ideas on how to market job postings to cast a wider net, let your voice be heard.

You may be thinking right now about what areas in your library could possibly be perpetuating inequalities. You may even have heard that one of the most common areas is through library classification systems, which are still in place today and which have been criticized for organizing information through a white lens. For example, "non-Western" languages are labeled together instead of being more specifically differentiated. This chapter takes a deeper dive into examining how the cultural context and white supremacist values get translated and can often directly impact how teens experience the library. Unfortunately, "stories of patrons and librarians facing discrimination or hostility for their race, class, sexual identity, or disability are common." But before we think to ourselves, "I would never do that" or "That's not me!" or "Not here!" let's allow ourselves some space to pause and reflect. Even if something is done unintentionally or unknowingly, the impact of our behaviors and practices is what leaves an impression on the lives of teens.

## CHECK YOUR PRIVILEGE

You can find a lot more information online about what is sometimes referred to as *social location* or an *identity wheel*. This is an activity that encourages students (and others) to think about the various ways they identify socially and then reflect on the ways those identities manifest themselves in social interactions with others. If you've been through a diversity training or any kind of race and bias workshop, you will probably have been asked to examine these identity characteristics about yourself. If not, we do encourage you to spend time to dialogue in the community and reflect further on how who you are and who you believe yourself to be can influence your interactions with others. For example, the University of Michigan engages students in a social identity timeline activity where they choose an aspect of their identity (gender, for example) and visually map it out, following its course over their lifetime and noting any lessons learned (University of Michigan 2021). Because identities can be fluid, the exercise will likely give insight into how socially constructed—as opposed to unchanging—certain parts of our identity can be.

The closer to power you are means your identities are thought to have more value and worth than those that are different than that standard. This can play out particularly if you're bringing in your own subjectivity and bias with regard to the behaviors of teens that are in the library. For instance, two of my identities are white and female. When I see a group—say, five male teens who are persons of color—come into the library, I can ask myself some questions. Are my biases showing up when I think they may be disruptive because a similar-looking group of teens recently was? Do I find myself surveilling them more often than I would another group of teens or customers in general? When I bring awareness to these possible undercurrents, I can often create change for the better. This is especially important because as a library staff member who already carries some amount of power or authority, I can set the standard for transmitting my library's policies. If you're not familiar with what implicit bias is, here is a reminder: "They are the beliefs that sit in the back of your brain and inform your actions without your explicit knowledge. In times of stress, these unexamined beliefs can prove deadly" (Oluo 2018). Anyone can have implicit bias—it's not something particular to white folks. However, if you are white and hold power by being a staff member *and* you hold implicit bias, you can cause damage to developing minds if you're not aware of your bias.

How many times have we been tired at the end of a shift and responded differently than if we were fresh into the day? Just like with our own kids, our patience probably wears thin when it's being tested—for example, when the library is going to close for the day, or we've just gotten out of a stressful meeting, or had an unpleasant interaction with a customer.

At these moments it's important to ground ourselves, check in with our breathing, and take a pause before responding by picking up the phone and calling security or even the police, when we may not need to escalate the situation to that point. You have options and choices—just like the teen(s) that you are reacting to does. Try and create space to allow those choices to present themselves rather than responding out of anger and force. We also can't assume that if a teen is acting out, they're just being difficult. Their behavior might point to a situation at home that they want to avoid and put off as long as possible. They might not be familiar with other tools they can use to express their fear or avoidance. Developing a relationship with them may help shed some more light on their circumstances.

Having an awareness of the identities you carry with you is really key to understanding how to make changes both in your library and in your relationships with teens. These characteristics can be thought of as visible or even invisible lines and boundaries that play out in our interactions regardless of whether we acknowledge them or they remain verbally unspoken.

Related to identities is the unearned privilege that they come with, and this too affects how we interact with teens in the library. Privilege isn't just limited to white folks either, but given the fact that most of the staff and decision-makers in the library are white, it is important to acknowledge how this can play out. As an example, our libraries are likely ADA accessible. If they were not, it would be against the law and we'd need to make the necessary changes. Not having an elevator or pathways wide enough to accommodate a wheelchair comfortably would be obvious violations of ADA regulations. One identity I carry with me at the present moment is that I am able-bodied. I fit comfortably in most of the seating that is easily available. Given this worldview, I may not consider the height of tables that I've placed programming supplies on if someone is in a wheelchair. I also may not consider larger-bodied folks who might prefer a booth seat if it is available rather than a small folding chair. While it's not necessary to bring out every possible option that your library has, you might consider asking as part of registration if there are any special accommodations that are requested. You will also want to have some choices available that can be implemented quickly—even if that means having a staff person on standby to help if needed, or some other seating in a nearby room that can be brought out. While sometimes we may feel that we barely have enough time to buy all the supplies we need and balance three other things we're doing, much less consider alternative seating, it's important to keep an open mind. We don't want to be so rigid and flustered that it shows in our presentation and interferes with the teens being able to feel safe and comfortable in the library, nor do we want to make them feel that they're somehow being a burden to us. We don't have to be perfect, but we can try our best to meet the needs that are out there. Connecting with the community by reaching out to local organizations that would be willing to give suggestions on how to be a more inclusive and welcoming environment, based on an analysis of your space, might also be an option. If there are no local organizations to contact, consider a virtual appointment to gather ideas and resources, a practice that is not uncommon.

## POLITICS IN THE SPACE

Though we may have been taught in library school and believe even now that libraries are neutral places, they're not. They are political, just like any other public space is. Some ways this shows up is in the decision to have gendered bathrooms, to have armed security guards, or to enforce a dress code policy for staff and customers. This doesn't mean these decisions are inherently bad or good, or right or wrong. It does mean, though, that there are some lines drawn that we may not see—especially if we're part of the dominant culture. For example, if my sex aligns with my gender and I've never thought too much about which bathroom to use, it may not occur to me that it's different for folks who may not identify the same way. So we can create a welcoming space for all by having non-gendered bathrooms, or we can create an unwelcoming space due to the disciplinary measures we enact to uphold the policies that are in place.

## SCENARIOS, IDENTITIES, AND BARRIERS

In addition to the identities I've already mentioned that I carry with me into the library space—those of an able-bodied white female—there are also the facts that I am middle class and middle-aged. Because of my position as a librarian, you probably assumed that I have at least one higher education degree. Let's take a look at the following scenarios to see how these identities can be a barrier, particularly to urban teens in the library. We will also consider ways we can mitigate those factors to restore balance to the power dynamics in the library.

### Relationship-Building Before Rule Enforcement

Here is a scenario. I see a group of three Black male teens coming into the teen space after school one day. One of them is carrying a basketball that I hear bouncing before I even see them in the space. They all have book bags, which indicates they have just gotten out of school. I don't recognize them as having visited the library before, but they seem to know where to go. They get comfortable by sitting at a table, some propping their feet up on the furniture and grabbing snacks from their bags. They don't know me, but they can tell that I am a middle-aged white female and an authority figure because I work at the library. What message do I want to convey? They probably have a majority of teachers at school who are white—either male or female. They may have had good or bad experiences with them. I can shift some of those power dynamics that are already at play by acknowledging them with a smile and a welcome. Full stop. If I start focusing right away on a library rule they may be violating (even though it's not egregious), I'm sending the message that the rules of my organization are more important than their needs. Perhaps we can both get our needs met at the same time if I welcome them into the library, introduce myself, and start building a relationship with them by noticing something about them—their music, the graphics on their clothes, a book they're reading, their name from the previous time they were here, and so on. The teens deserve respect because this is their space and they are here, which is exactly what it is intended for. I also have to earn their approval—it's not just automatically given. This probably means things as simple as repeated engagement with a smile on my part and remembering their names when they return.

## What Is the Story You Are Telling Yourself?

Here is another scenario. I notice a teen who comes in to read a magazine in the teen space at the library during school hours, when the public school system is in session. I give him a minute to get situated before approaching him, but then the phone rings and I have to handle a customer need. Next time I look over at the teen who was reading, I notice he has dozed off and is asleep in the corner. My coworker sees me about to approach the teen and pulls me aside instead and asks, "Have you met Amari yet?" "He came this weekend and I talked to his mom. They just moved to the area not too long ago and he is enrolled in A+ Charter School. I meant to write their days off on our calendar because it's a bit different than XYZ school system. He mentioned that he hasn't gotten much sleep lately because there's a lot going on at home." This probably differs from the story you told yourself as you were about to go over and wake Amari up for "violating" the library policy of being there while school was in session and also sleeping, which isn't allowed either. But after you found out his story, hopefully this changed your framework and this story helped you make sense of the situation. Not having all the pieces can lead to a lot of conjecture— and to understandable aggravation on the part of the teen who is tired to begin with. This is not to say that we should simply not approach a teen who is violating a library rule. It does mean that we can show some empathy in our tone of voice and body language for starters, and realize that we might not know the whole story.

In looking at another scenario, one year, my library branch had an incident where the glass on the door leading to the parking lot was damaged. Camera footage showed teens present and a partial view of the actual perpetrator doing the damage. A group of teens comes into the library who somewhat resemble the teens in the footage, but no one can be for certain. I notice security heavily surveilling the teens while trying to keep a noticeable distance from them. The teens don't appear to be doing anything wrong that day at the library. Next thing I know, our armed security officer approaches me and tells me they are certain these are the teens seen recently on camera damaging the door. In essence, the teens have been profiled, and I am being asked to verify this assumption. I don't know the teens, but I can choose to welcome them to the library and get to know them better. I can remind myself that each day is a new day and even if they are responsible for the damage, they start a clean slate each day. Rather than accuse them off the bat, because the identification remains murky to me, I can instead decide to build a relationship with them. Perhaps one of my coworkers who is not here today might know the teens better than I do. Hopefully, the teens will continue to return to the library, which is the goal—though this time, with any luck, they will feel more responsible for the space because I've helped make them feel a part of it. If they really were the group that damaged the door, it will probably be found out through conversation or their own admission, and then we can determine together what the appropriate consequences should be.

## LEAD WITH CURIOSITY

The last scenario we're going to review that may be creating an unnecessary hurdle for a teen wanting access to a safe and welcoming place involves a coworker from another department who happens to be in the teen space after school shelving materials. The employee notices a teen taking a handful of snacks out of the basket that's got granola bars and chips—and stuffing their pockets with the food. The shelver quickly gets a disgusted look and stops the teen before they try to leave the area by putting them on blast in front of their peers. The teen is understandably embarrassed and will do whatever they can to defend themselves (and keep the food!), which is to run out of the building. Not only are we conveying a message to the teen that we don't care about exploring their needs a bit deeper, but we're also communicating to those in the area that they are being policed, and we will respond punitively. I can now either choose to approach my coworker directly about this or pretend that I didn't even witness the situation (and thus tacitly convey that the shelver acted appropriately). I decide to invite the coworker into the office and have a conversation. When I ask questions such as what happened from their viewpoint, I can better understand where they're coming from, instead of making accusations right away. None of us is given a guidebook on working with teens, no matter how many years we've been a part of teen services—and not even if we're raising a teen on our own!

## PART OF A SYSTEM

It's important to remember the cultural context of our responses. While we've discussed in the above examples how the stories we tell can lead to certain assumptions or behaviors on our part as staff, it's also not just about us as individuals. I may be the "friendly teen librarian" who is not like those other "mean" staff who don't particularly like teens, but if I'm not actively trying to disrupt the systems in place that have the effect of creating barriers for all teens—especially those who are furthest removed from the sources of power—then I am also enabling the system as it is intended to work. We might be asking ourselves right about now: "But how can that be? Almost all of the staff are friendly and kind. We're welcoming to all. A wide range of materials sits on our shelves, available for anyone to check out, and they have multiple viewpoints." Most of these sentiments are well intentioned and are not done with malice. However, as stated earlier, it's the impact (rather than the intention) that matters most.

Now we'll take a look at some more potential major barriers for urban teens in the library, which include library security and the stressors at home that teens may bring with them to the library.

## SECURITY IN LIBRARIES

It's not unusual to have security at the library—just like in schools—and there may even be metal detectors and a security guard who is armed. While these may be able to intervene in situations in the library so that you felt temporarily safer, they may also be creating the illusion of safety and "law and order."

I am based at a children's library, and we contract with a company that has armed security in the building during all of the hours that we're open. In the time that I have been here, incidents involving the officers' guns have been unnecessary and have even caused situations that put patrons at more risk of harm. Sometimes the security guard may have escalated a situation to the point that no matter what the teen decided to do, the teen would not be viewed favorably. At what point does the institutionalization of guns in libraries became "part of normal business" is a story in itself. Of course, this phenomenon is not unique to libraries but is common in other businesses as well.

This isn't a complete rebuke against having security at the library, but their role does need further examination and continuous updating with regard to training and reflection, if an incident does happen that is not in alignment with the policy of creating a safe space for all at the library. When it comes to teens, especially those who are Black and Brown, because of the "school-to-prison pipeline" and the history of police brutality, it's not surprising to see similar patterns play out with the disciplinary actions undertaken in libraries. "The school-to-prison pipeline starts with the high level of suspensions and expulsions made against black and brown students" in school (Oluo 2018). The equivalent in libraries would be the "banning" or "suspension" of youth from the building.

While the relationship between disciplinary systems and Black and Brown youth is a complex issue, the following are recommendations to heighten your awareness of how you and the policies of your library may be punitively punishing and thus further contributing to alienating such youth from the community.

Do not allow language to go unchecked. Do you, your coworkers, administrators, or security use racist terms (or even include them in reports) such as "thug," "hoodlum," or "gangbanger" to describe a teen who is in the library? According to the antiracist educator Ibram X. Kendi, "When you view me as dangerous, you view my existence as dangerous" (Kendi 2020). When we talk about teens (or any customers, for that matter) as less than a human being, we are dehumanizing them based on our own beliefs.

Perform an audit on the number of Black and Brown youth involved in incident reports and what the consequences are, compared to the percentage of them in the population served as a whole. If you aren't able to collect the data because you're not tracking demographic information, suggest the changes to make this happen. This can give you a baseline for being able to see any disparities in incidents. If we can't see what may be racist policies, then we won't be able to change them.

Take a look at your library's disciplinary policy. If there is not a separate one for youth, put a team together to start revamping and creating one. Do your research on restorative justice as a model that can serve to empower youth to take responsibility for their behaviors instead of enacting punitive punishments against them. The International Institute for Restorative Practices has abundant resources including books, workshops, and even pocket reminder cards to respond to challenging behavior. Instead of thinking, "What is wrong with this person?" ask, "What happened?" or "Who has been affected by what you have done?" YALSA dedicated its November 2020 issue of *YALS* to trauma-informed responses when working with youth at the library. Because this is a lifelong learning practice, keep the training constant and embedded in the culture of the library. Invite security to be part of the training and expect the same level of service from any staff member, whether they're in the teen department or not.

Review the role of security in the building. Has it become evident that there is some training they may need and aren't being given? The Madison Public Library in Wisconsin, for example, has officers who sit at the staff desk in the teen area and build relationships with teens. While they don't need to be best friends, creating opportunities for security guards to interact with customers outside of their role of telling them to stop doing something can create a relationship that can be mutually beneficial if a problem does arise with a teen patron in the future. It also gives the security guards a chance to view the teens and the library in another light—to see the opportunities a library offers and to know that they themselves can play a role in that.

## AT-HOME STRESSORS

The last barrier we will examine with regard to making all urban teens feel safe and welcome at the library is the stressors they may bring from their home life. As we mentioned earlier in this chapter using the examples of teens who may be "acting out" by sleeping or taking extra snacks, we don't want to make up stories as to why they're behaving this way, just because we may have privilege in this area and might never have ourselves experienced the need or automatically feel we have to "punish" them right away. We also want to be careful about assigning some deep reason as to why certain teens take more food than others do. It may have nothing to do with starving at home—they may just be having a growth spurt. We need to understand that people with different experiences than ours may behave or express their feelings somewhat differently; this doesn't automatically mean that it's wrong or bad. If we're measuring everyone against our own worldview, that's not realistic and often invalidating. We need to consistently challenge the ways in which we tell ourselves stories to justify a course of action (disciplinary or otherwise) that we think is appropriate.

The teen years can be challenging in and of themselves. We don't need to add additional barriers to teens' safety and freedom at the library because we're upholding harmful practices. Don't be afraid to step back and dig in when policies are challenged. This might be just what we need to change some things that never really worked in the first place.

● ● ●

## TEEN REFLECTION

**How can the library better support real-world success through the use of media literacy?**

The Middle Country Public Library (MCPL) has a diverse selection of programs that aim to grow media literacy. Traditional book clubs are intimidating to many people, and there's no real-world application for what is discussed in these clubs. MCPL has put a modern twist on the traditional book club, where meetings are more relaxed and members get to choose what they read. This opens the discussion to more topics than a traditional book club would cover. As much as a book club helps foster media literacy education, one of the best ways to understand media is to create it firsthand. MCPL's writing cafe allows teens to get together and write whatever they wish, and the Zine Club brings teens together to create all types of zines. Creativity is promoted in these clubs, an invaluable quality that is often ignored in schools and traditional book clubs. These special clubs offered at MCPL make media literacy education engaging and enjoyable for youth at my age. More modern clubs like these will allow libraries to teach skills that will ensure that our generation flourishes in the real world. ⏻

—**ZAKARIYAH HANIF**, 16, Centereach, NY

● ● ●

## VOICES FROM THE FIELD: Mary J. Wardell-Ghirarduzzi ——

Mary J. Wardell-Ghirarduzzi is the president of the San Francisco Public Library Commission, board chair of the Urban Libraries Council in Washington, DC, and the vice president for diversity, equity, and inclusion at the University of the Pacific.

### How can libraries better support historically marginalized teens in their facilities and through their services?

When was the last time you observed a group of teens in your neighborhood public library? Did you notice them? In the northern California cities where I'm located (San Francisco, Sacramento, and Stockton), the public library is a central hub for a diverse array of communities of color, particularly historically marginalized teens.

The teens I observe seem to find solace in the library. They may meet up with friends, or sometimes they are alone. They are makers and creators: musicians, writers, dancers, and so on. I would definitely say these young people are both today's and tomorrow's leaders.

As a library trustee, what I know for certain is that libraries are lifelines of liberation in the movement for racial and social equity, especially for teens. I also know how certain adolescents, through no fault of their own or their families, experience life at the margins: BIPOC teens, queer teens, undocumented teens, unhoused teens, working teens, religiously targeted teens, parenting and care-giving teens, and teens with psychological, neurological, or other disabilities.

As one of our most enduring institutions, what should public libraries do now to help our historically marginalized teens dream big and prosper in a society that doesn't equitably invest in their futures? As I see it, our essential duties to support these teens are to:

- First, lead the way for digital democracy. We must ensure that every child in a digital desert in our community has access to Wi-Fi in public spaces.
- Second, conduct outreach to teens from disenfranchised families and communities. To help our teens express their voices, they need our help in making sense of information.
- Third, commit to the work of racial equity. All inequities are linked to racial injustice.
- Fourth, convene, facilitate, and collaborate with K–12 partners. To solve serious problems like learning loss, we must be a part of their educational team.
- Lastly, approach teens as individuals in transition. Our role is to help them safely transition into their next developmental phase of life.

All library workers are essential workers, even library trustees. The spaces and opportunities we support are necessary for the advancement and betterment of all historically marginalized teens in every community we serve. ⏻

● ● ●

## VOICES FROM THE FIELD: Jasmine McNeil

Jasmine McNeil works as an outreach specialist at Charlotte Mecklenburg Library.

**How can library outreach programming address the barriers of access and transit to programming with historically marginalized youth?**

Leveraging resources and community partnerships through outreach programming is a key way to bridge the digital and resource gap experienced by marginalized youth. Resources are distributed to neighborhood schools and their students based on the taxes received from those communities. As a result, many schools that are in low-income neighborhoods and serve predominantly BIPOC students receive significantly less resources and have lower-quality teachers in comparison to predominantly affluent white schools.

Providing innovative and creative programs that increase media literacy skills can be the difference between a reluctant reader and an avid reader, and can break down the racial barriers caused by intentional and unintentional hierarchies. As Emily Style, with the National SEED Project, stated regarding the concept of mirrors and windows, "mirrors reflect one's own culture and help them with identity," while a window offers us a view into someone else's experiences. These mirrors and windows help to dismantle the hierarchies by allowing youth to see themselves and others in the stories they read and the media they engage with.

When library outreach programming is heavily invested in marginalized communities, it allows youth to be exposed to resources and quality education that they otherwise would never have experienced. Outreach programming creates the opportunity to introduce concepts that complement the curriculum and allows a deeper dive into topics, a dive that sometimes deviates from the restrictions created by school systems. For some youth in urban communities, field trips and outreach programs are their only way to see a world outside of their neighborhood.  ⏻

## REFERENCES

Kendi, Ibram X. 2020. "The Difference between Being 'Not Racist' and Antiracist." YouTube video, 51:14. www.youtube.com/watch?v=KCxbl5QgFZw.h?v =KCxbl5QgFZw.

Mack, McKensie (@mckensiemack). 2020. "Hiring more people of color doesn't dismantle structural racism within an organization. A white dominant organization could hire 100 people of color, but if the policies and the practices stay the same, that's 100 more people that can be harmed by them." Twitter, October 10. https://twitter.com/mckensiemack/status/ 1314982559944769541.

Mattern, Shannon. 2019. "Fugitive Libraries." *Places Journal*, October. https://doi .org/10.22269/0000.

Nins, Tasha (@TashaCMN). 2020. "#LibraryTwitter." Twitter, October 9. https://twitter.com/TashaCMN/status/1314760993789149184.

Oluo, Ijeoma. 2018. *So You Want to Talk about Race*. New York: Seal.

University of Michigan. 2021. "LSA-Inclusive Teaching: Mapping Social Identity Timeline." https://sites.lsa.umich.edu/inclusive-teaching/wp-content/ uploads/sites/853/2021/02/Mapping-Social-Identity-Timeline-Draft-2.pdf.

# Under Construction
## Creating Space and Relationships for Media Literacy with Urban Teens

JIMMEKA ANDERSON and KELLY CZARNECKI

The relationship of morality and *power* is a very subtle one. Because ultimately power without morality is no longer power.

—**JAMES BALDWIN,** Interview with Nikki Giovanni, *A Dialogue* (1973)

*This chapter is cowritten by Jimmeka Anderson and Kelly Czarnecki. Kelly Czarnecki wrote the first section, "Creating Space," and Jimmeka Anderson wrote the second section, "Building Relationships."*

## CREATING SPACE

Many readers may already be familiar with sociologist Ray Oldenburg's concept of the "third place." He explains it as "the public places on natural ground where people can gather and interact" (Oldenburg 1999). In the context of youth and media literacy, that "third place" is our libraries, digital media centers, and after-school meet-ups such as cafes, malls, and community centers. It can also be spaces within digital platforms such as chat rooms, virtual worlds, or social media. The third place is not home or school/work, which are typically defined as the first and second "places" in this framework. However, just because you work at a third place such as a library, this doesn't automatically mean that your library is a place for relaxation and socialization, which are important characteristics of a "third place" according to Oldenburg. You are responsible not only for fostering these conditions in the library space, but more importantly, for maintaining them there as well. Most of us have probably also realized that spaces can shift—particularly those third spaces. What worked a few years ago with the teens who frequented your space might change completely this year. A new school may have been built nearby, technology may have advanced, or a tragedy might even have occurred that would influence the users of the space. It's important that the space be flexible as the needs of teens shift and change as a result of forces within the community and even larger, the geography of the world. For example, when the YALSA and IMLS report *The Future of Library Services for and with Teens: A Call to Action* was first written in 2014, the challenges that teens faced then as compared to today living in the pandemic or after are magnified compared to what was identified almost a decade ago (Braun et al. 2014). But while the report seems a bit dated now, it still provides a foundation with which to look at rethinking services for and with teens—which is something we need to do consistently for this constantly changing population if we're to remain relevant and meet their needs to grow as productive adults.

Aligned with the concept of the "third place" is that of the library as a "counterspace." "Counterspaces . . . are often considered 'safe spaces' at the margins for groups outside the mainstream," according to an article published in the *Journal of Research in Science Teaching* (Ong et al. 2017). When we're looking at serving urban teens in the library, these patrons are often considered to be the opposite of the standard library patron. While this particular article focuses mainly on women of color in STEM educational spaces, much of what it says is also applicable to libraries. For example, we know that representation is important and that the library profession is made up of a very high percentage of white females, as discussed in chapter 4. Creating a safe space within the library, and thus sending a message to teens that they are represented, would involve taking a look at the makeup of the staff and the hiring practices of the library. Are there networks or job boards that employment opportunities could be posted to, such as the American Library Association Spectrum Scholars, on alumni discussion lists, or with other special-interest groups that might garner a more diverse set of applicants than are currently applying? While you yourself may not work in the library's human resources department, you could still ask yourself: what is my role in the hiring process, and what could I be doing to create a more welcoming space for all in terms of who work at the library?

Ong et al.'s article also tackles the topic of microaggressions, which often play a role in the need for safer spaces. These are defined as "brief and commonplace daily verbal, behavioral, or environmental indignities that communicate hostile, derogatory, or negative racial slights and insults toward people of color." Institutional microaggressions can also occur beyond the individual level and within structures. The library space is an area to pay particular attention to in this regard; are materials by Black authors or about the Black experience highlighted only during Black History Month in February? Are posters that promote reading or other library initiatives truly representative of a diverse array of folks, instead of merely token attempts to include the marginalized or underrepresented among them? The teen space in my library branch, for example, has a wall of quotations that we created in our makerspace using a vinyl cutter. When we were deciding what to put on the wall, I made the decision to include music quotes along with print materials. It was important to me that we include texts from a format that did not consist of printed material. Secondly, we needed to involve the teens who were at the library and get their feedback on what they wanted. We ended up with quotes ranging from the rapper Drake to the author J. K. Rowling. In creating these "safer" or even "brave" spaces (ScottBey Jones 2020), "it is far more urgent to create spaces that celebrate marginalized experiences" (Cardoza 2021). In other words, creating counterspaces is not about making members of the dominant culture feel better about themselves but about truly uplifting and positively focusing on those whose identities may have some negative aspects or connotations attributed to them.

As we saw in chapter 4, actively calling out microaggressions when they occur, whether it's from a staffer to a customer, a teen to another teen, or a security guard to a customer, also supports the counterspace beyond what images are on the wall or what books are on display. A safe or brave space requires vigilance and maintenance to address instances that transgress how we ideally want to treat each other. This can involve updating our policies and practices, and being in tune when the policies are not being used for their intention.

## Affinity Space

More and more public libraries are providing dedicated spaces for teens, and as part of this approach, one common theme is to have teens involved in the whole process, from the planning of the actual space to the policies adopted for it. This is recommended by YALSA in its *National Teen Space Guidelines* (2012). While this publication is a decade old, the foundation of involving teens in the planning process is still applicable.

A more recent publication, *Library Staff as Public Servants: A Field Guide for Preparing to Support Communities in Crisis*, was put together by researchers in the field after hosting virtual sessions in the summer of 2020 with more than 100 library staff (Subramaniam et al. 2021). While the impetus for this field guide was the COVID-19 pandemic and more widespread participation in the Black Lives Matter movement, understanding how to serve communities in crisis is, of course, not limited to these two phenomena. The guide can be a helpful resource in the context of this chapter in understanding how to work with the community rather than making decisions for them.

The book *Real-World Teen Services* has a chapter dedicated to teen library spaces in which the author, Jennifer Velásquez, examines various models, including the Carnegie style, which is a traditional concept of the library as a warehouse of materials (Velásquez 2015). She also explores the framework for an "affinity space," which is about "producing social experiences and incorporating user meanings." Velásquez goes on to say that "libraries that cultivate an affinity space for teens create a venue focusing on the relationships teens have with information and one another, and the creation of content, artifacts, and knowledge." In this setting, teens are allowed to be the experts and innovators while staff are more the guides and facilitators. My library—the ImaginOn branch of the Charlotte Mecklenburg Library—is mentioned as an example of an affinity space in the book, and in the subsections below I will point out several features that make up this framework and give teens the opportunity to participate in the space at varying levels. If this is the outcome you are trying to achieve with your teen space, you may consider adopting these ideas in your own library.

## Flexible Furniture

At the ImaginOn library branch, we acknowledged that teens have a need to create their own spaces depending on how they are interacting with information. A more open space, for example, would allow for a small performance and tables and chairs, which could easily be set up if some teens are working on a hands-on group project. This doesn't mean we don't set limits on how the chairs and tables are used (prolonged sitting on tables can cause damage over time), but we do allow them to be moved quite frequently.

The teen area was always designed with a digital/makerspace in mind, for personal creation. This is different than the central space, which is mostly used by teens for studying and by staff and teens for programming. In this creation space, teens can do anything: record their voices, act in front of a blue screen, or print their favorite vinyl saying on their T-shirt. Teens unfamiliar with the space are encouraged to explore and try their hand at whatever might interest them. We do ask that if they're in this creation space, they engage with the equipment on some level rather than just hanging out, so we can keep our focus on assisting those who need it. The space is used for programming as well, so there is "hang-out" time per se as well. The space is not super rigid either; if teens want to take some time and observe because it's their first time there, or if they want to try something different, they're welcome to do so. It is also an iterative space, in that the ways youth interact with one another are inspired by being together in the space.

## Staff Desk

We've had a variety of staff desks and configurations in the area throughout the years. When the teen space was first opened, the desk was small and was placed among the teens—where the booth seating and computer stations were. As compared to a few years later when there was a large fortress-style desk (over ten feet long) that met the teens as they came up the ramp. Some of the thinking behind this was to have a customer service point readily available to meet and greet the youth when they approached the space. But this desk proved to be more of a barrier and a gate than a welcoming entrance. Moreover, our backs were to the youth who had already walked past the desk because all of the programming space, computers, and booth seating were behind us. This didn't allow for a lot of natural interaction with the teens.

To sum up, it's helpful to have flexible furniture if a setup causes some unanticipated issues. As the teens themselves change, you may want to use different seating arrangements and move the furniture accordingly to allow for the appropriate service. Once we were able to see the problematic "social experience" that the fortress-like desk created, and were in a position to remove it (having obtained management's approval), we began to reconfigure the space. We ended up repurposing some standing table desks with wheels that supported the staff's computers; these repurposed tables were more physically open and less of an impediment to being able to engage with the teens.

## Display Work

Showcasing teens' work—whether it's something written such as quotes or poems, or artwork such as hand drawings, paintings, digital artwork, or even images of teens themselves in the library or library users on social media (as appropriate and with consent)—can be a great way to integrate teen participation into the library. Displaying the teens' content creation can help give them some agency and a feeling of ownership of the library. As Velásquez points out, a policy of allowing teens to constantly change or create what is on the wall "will always reflect the users' tastes, interests, and desires." It also adds spontaneity to the space, rather than something static and thus predictable over time. As teens age out into a different area of the library, their artwork will too, and this will make way for up-and-coming teens. Displaying the work can be done in a variety of ways. It can range from a bulletin board maintained by both the teens and the library staff, to a digital board on a flat screen or a giant video wall. It all depends on your budget, the interest of the teens, and what materials are available for display. If you don't have the budget, starting out small can be a way to test the waters and see if the displays are something to pursue and grow over time.

Both counterspaces and affinity spaces can be lenses through which we can look at reorganizing the way we build library spaces for teens. While there's more work to be done in these areas as they relate to marginalized teens, this is part of an exploration of tenets that can be considered to build bridges for all teens and support them to become well-rounded adults, which is a goal we can all rally around.

## BUILDING RELATIONSHIPS

There is a quote in the classic 1989 film *Field of Dreams* where the main character, played by Kevin Costner, hears the words whispered to him "If you build it . . . they will come." Although libraries are not cornfields that need to be transformed into magical baseball stadiums for spirits of the past to reappear, they are spaces that need to be transformed for urban teens to gather and feel safe, validated, and celebrated. The word *build* here involves more than just creating a physical space. It's about establishing something greater than what the eye can see. Teens don't become consistent patrons because of how the library looks; they come back because of how being there made them feel. I like to use the *Field of Dreams* quote when thinking about building relationships because it implies that there is work to be done and effort to be made in our quest to truly serve others. So as we ponder the work that is needed to build relationships and safe spaces with teens, we must first ask ourselves "What exactly does it take to make urban teens feel safe in the library?"

While having police officers and security guards standing around in your library facility may create a sense of safety among adults, urban teens who are constantly profiled and targeted, and who experience microaggressions daily from authority may beg to differ. Creating a safe space is merely the foundation toward transforming your library into your own "Field of Dreams," metaphorically speaking. So think of building relationships as the maintenance work needed for sustainability with urban teens. For instance, I remember in 2012 when our public library began supporting the Safe Space initiative in our city, which was spearheaded by the county and a local agency that worked with homeless teens. We received large bright yellow signs with bold black letters that read "Safe Space" to hang outside the doors and throughout the building. Libraries, along with churches, schools, and even gas stations, received these signs to signal them as a designated place for urban youth to go when they were in danger and to receive assistance from a trained staff member at the site. While these signs declared safety for teens who may have needed urgent help or assistance, they were only intended to be temporary in function. Once the emergency was addressed and a teen received the help that was needed, the sign and the space had met their obligation. You see, the sign and the building it designated, although extremely meaningful, served only a temporary purpose for teens. It takes more than a big yellow sign, an officer in a suit standing at an entrance, and just saying the words "this is a safe space" to actually create a consistently safe space for urban teens to belong. Consistent safety for teens is not a declaration, it is a feeling that is created through authentic relationships with adults.

For the past ten years, I have used media literacy programming to create safe dialogic spaces and build relationships with teens. The relationships that I have formed over the years with urban teens through our library's media literacy programming were based on three major components, (1) taking interest, (2) being an active listener, and (3) not applying pressure. In the next subsection, I will share how I have used media literacy programming to build relationships with teens whom I've worked with throughout the years. Many of the teens that I have worked with and mentored in the past are now adults. At the end of this chapter, I have asked one of my former teens to share a reflection on the influence that relationships and programming had on his life as an urban teen who frequented the library.

## Take Interest

It was in my second year working at the public library in uptown Charlotte when I learned that some adults in the facility were afraid of urban teens. I remember having a conversation one day with a coworker in another department after our library had been in the local news due to a recent fight that had broken out in the facility. While answering the many questions about the incident, my coworker, who was a middle-aged white woman, proceeded to inform me that she had never felt safe walking to the bathroom or anywhere near the teen space of our library. After having this conversation with her, I began to notice several other colleagues avoided coming to the bathroom in the teen space of our library (which was the closest to their office), and those who did make their way to the teen area avoided any form of eye contact with the teens there. One day while playing a video game with a few of my teens, I noticed that my coworker had decided to venture out and use the bathroom in the teen space. As I watched the stiffness in her shoulders and her avoidant body language, with her eyes staring down at the floor, one of my teens yelled out to her, "Hey ma'am, I like your shoes! Are those Coach?" My coworker stopped in her tracks, continued to look down, positioned her eyes to look at her own shoes, and then looked at the teenage girl who had grabbed her attention. "Yes . . . yes, they are Coach," she replied nervously. "Oh, I have some that look similar to those at home," the teen responded. I then watched as my coworker smiled and continued to proceed to the restroom. She had made a simple connection with a teen just through her interest with shoes, and I saw firsthand a sense of contentment.

While that one experience could not possibly alleviate the fear that my coworker confessed she felt toward the teens in the space, it was a first step of many more that she could have taken to try and get to know the teens who entered our doors, understand them, and peel away layers of the implicit biases that she possessed. The "shoe experience" I just recounted always pops into my mind when I think about how misunderstood teens, and specifically urban teens, can be by adults and the world. Although teens today engage in music and pop-culture trends that I certainly find questionable at times, I understand that there is still great value in meeting them where they are. When I say "meeting them where they are," that means exploring their interests. Too many times, as adults we try to force our interests onto teens rather than learning about their passions and their own special interests. One of the programs I created at the library with teens that allowed me to build relationships based on their music interests was titled "The Top 10 Teen Video Countdown." Each week, teens in the library could vote for a song from Saturday to Wednesday to be entered in our Video Countdown, which was held every Friday. Music videos that received the most votes during the week would be shown on the big screen in our teen space on YouTube, with popcorn for teens to eat as they watched. After each video, I would have the teens discuss the lyrics and imagery of the songs in order to articulate the overall message. I must say that it is important to review the videos for language and content before making your YouTube playlist, if you are thinking about replicating this program. In many cases, I had to find the clean version of certain songs. If I was unable to locate a clean version, I would still highlight the ranking of the video for the Countdown but inform the teens that we could not view it due to content. As a result of doing this program, I began to receive regular visits on Fridays from teens who looked forward to watching the videos that made the cut and wanted to have authentic conversations with me about the music. I began to build authentic relationships with teens as we discussed the videos and songs that reflected their interests.

## Active Listening

While working in the library with teens, there will be times when you may hear and encounter inappropriate language. You will hear words that make your heart ache, skin crawl, and ears bleed. I would hear this kind of language most often in the music studio that was made just for teens at our library. While on duty in the studio, I would occasionally listen in to some of the recording sessions of teens expressing their art, and it eventually dawned on me that a lot of the content that they sang and wrote about was extremely violent. Of course, I did my job by warning them about their inappropriate language and informing them that if that language continued, they would lose access to the recording studio for the day. But for me, there was a bigger issue that I wanted to tackle after consistently hearing the language used by the teens who frequented the studio booth. I wanted to know the root of that language and the purpose behind its use. Was it to impress their peers, or were they just aspiring to be like the other rock stars and rappers they see in the media? Therefore, I built some community partnerships with local organizations and built a program at the library called Music Over Violent Entertainment (MOVE).

As part of the MOVE program, we hosted a series of dialogue sessions that talked about violence in music, film, and videos. Specific teens were selected to participate in the weekly sessions and were told at the end of the project that they could work collaboratively to create a song that promoted positivity over violence in the community. In the course of this project, I listened to a lot of the challenges that the majority of Black teens who participated shared with being profiled, judged, and treated negatively by adults. I learned about the conflicting struggles they felt between trying to please their parents on the one hand and winning the respect of their peers on the other—which held the most value for them at the time. The youth who participated in the program were so eager to learn and have discussions in which others just listened to them as they released their thoughts, fears, and hopes for the future. Our group continued to grow each week as participants invited other youth to join our MOVE workshops held on Wednesday afternoons. The most important lesson that I learned from this program I did many years ago was the power of listening to youth for understanding. It is important to practice active and patient listening with urban teens to understand their experiences and the challenges that they face. But most importantly, to better serve them. This involves controlling your voice and allowing youth to share their thoughts freely without interruption or judgment. To do this, we as adults have to develop humility as we take on the role of learners and demonstrate genuine interest in discovering teens' lives and passions. When working with a group of teens in a program, policing your voice is still essential to engage in active listening and to avoid dominating the space. Allow the teens to lead the conversation at times, while you just serve as a guide or curator of content to probe the discussion.

If you have worked with teens before, you are well aware that getting them to talk is sometimes a challenge in itself. In many cases, you have to warm up teens into conversation. Prompt them to discuss their interests, but you should also understand that deep down they do want to discuss and make sense of the nonsense in the world. Help them! In the book *Not Light, but Fire: How to Lead Meaningful Race Conversations in the Classroom*, Matthew Kay does a great job of describing how to adopt the role of an active listener and hold probing, critical conversations about race with teens in the classroom (2018). These sessions often incorporate an element of critical media literacy. For example, when teaching a lesson on cultural beauty standards, Kay uses the Chris Rock film *Good Hair* and a scene from *Malcolm X* to stimulate a discussion among teens. In the scene from the film, Malcolm X is getting a perm and enduring burns from the experience. As Kay provides a transcript of the scene, he sets up a media analysis for the teens to evaluate the connections with culture and society under the context of race and assimilation. The teens then share their thoughts and lead a discussion from the prompts provided. Beyond film and literature,

Kay also uses critical media literacy through a music analysis activity with Kendrick Lamar's "Alright" lyrics. Kay connects Lamar's song with current Black Lives Matter activism, and with news coverage of college students chanting the lyrics as modern-day hymns to signify hope over injustice. The teens were then able to ground themselves in a conversation through the resources provided by Kay, and discuss their thoughts and feelings about race relations and events that had been bothering them—thoughts and feelings which no prior outlet had allowed them to discuss. Librarians can use some of the same strategies with teens that Kay used and incorporate media to engage students in timely conversations and discourse around critical issues that impact their daily lives.

## No Pressure—Don't Force It

As a former library outreach coordinator and a current media literacy educator, I have learned how important relationships and building rapport with those you serve and educate can be. At times it can feel like pressure to make a connection with certain teens who—like the title of one of my favorite chick flicks—"are just not that into you!" I warn you, don't force it. Allow relationships with teens to form organically by taking a consistent interest in them, checking in on their social well-being, and inviting them to participate in programs. But don't become frustrated when teens repeatedly say no, they are not interested in participating in your workshop. Instead, remain reassuring, grateful to them for their considering the matter, and appreciative of the fact that you are slowly establishing trustworthiness with young, vulnerable teenagers. Continue to acknowledge these teens by name, ask how their day has been, and find out what artists they listen to or what YouTubers they watch. Perhaps, once you've gauged their interests, you can ask them if they would be interested in assisting with creating a program that aligns. Consistency, not force, is key in fostering a relationship with urban teens.

In her book, *Juárez Girls Rising: Transformative Education in Times of Dystopia,* Claudia Cervantes-Soon shares her experiences in getting to know ten unique Hispanic teenage girls from vulnerable backgrounds at Preparatoria Altavista, an urban high school (2017). I chose to highlight this text because Cervantes-Soon does a great job of being her authentic self and allowing many of her relationships with urban teen girls from violent backgrounds and communities to form organically through what she refers to as "hanging out." She shares how through her relationship-building, teen girls eventually asked her to join them in their conversations, activities, and classes. She further shared how this in turn allowed her to meet some of their friends, who were then invited to participate in her workshops. When I worked in the library, I spent a lot of time "hanging out" with teens. This encompassed just being available in the teen area with playing cards or checkers to ask a random teen if they cared to join me for a quick game. Setting up puzzles in your library space where teens can jump in and join you in completing them while conversing is another great way to form organic relationships.

At times it is extremely challenging to get teens to participate or stay committed to an experience. Understand and accept that this may be the case some days. You don't want to push any teen to do anything they feel is uncomfortable or that they just don't want to participate in. It is also okay to choose not to pursue certain teens where you may feel resistance. Sometimes the library is just an escape for urban teens. It may just be a place where they need to clear their head that day, and they want to be left alone with their thoughts and just relax. As adults we can certainly understand this, and we should have the same grace with teens as many of these teens are balancing life stressors that we know nothing about. Just remember, there will be times where the best service you can provide a teen is the reassurance that you are there for them if needed and by giving them space. In some instances, a safe space is just that . . . space.

●  ●  ●

**TEEN REFLECTION** ───────────────────────────────

**What types of media-centered programs were brought to you from the library, and how have these positively impacted your life?**

I always thought I was creative, but I never believed that my creativity would mean something to anyone else. Where I grew up, that was the expectation. You have dreams and then you forget about them. You listen to all the people telling you that you can't, and you accept that they might be right. Then I went to ImaginOn. At first, I didn't even know the people there were librarians. To this day, it's still hard to believe. Very much like Superman, they just seemed to be concerned citizens living in my city. I never thought they would teach me about my own creativity and how to make a difference. It started with programs like Rock the Mic and ended with my acceptance at a university thousands of miles away. The journey, however, was fueled by the people who smiled at me every day, asked me how I was doing, helped me study, and pointed me in the right direction. After all was said and done, I realized that the time I spent at ImaginOn with librarians such as Ms. Jimmeka was special. They understood that my circumstances were special and created a safe space for people like myself to dream.

The first time I went to the Rock the Mic event that Ms. Jimmeka would host at the library, I didn't think anyone was listening. I remember it like it was yesterday. I did a cover of Eminem's song "Stan" and was completely embarrassed because I forgot what I wrote. It was so bad that I stopped in mid-performance to ask my friend to pass me the sheet of paper that contained the words I had written down prior. The truth is that the words didn't actually matter much because I still stuttered and fumbled my way through the rest of the performance, and at that moment, I felt like the world was crashing down. Then someone in the audience came to talk to me. He told me that my words made him feel something deep inside of him and that he wanted to connect with me outside of the program. His kind words changed my life. They made me realize that my voice had an audience and that my work was valuable. I spent the next several years working to improve my public speaking and confidence. As a result of that work, I've had opportunities that I could have never imagined. I often look back to that moment at Rock the Mic with gratitude, and I just hope that other kids from where I'm from are given that same opportunity to let their voices be heard. Now that

I'm older I wish there were more ImaginOns because I've met kids around the country who deserved that same opportunity, and I truly hope more kids like us get it one day. ⏻

—**MATTHEW ROSA,** former teen patron, San Jose, CA

● ● ●

## VOICES FROM THE FIELD: Natasha Casey

Natasha Casey is a communication professor at Lincoln Lab Community College, an affiliated faculty member at the Media Education Lab, University of Rhode Island, and serves on the *Journal of Media Literacy Education* editorial advisory board and the Youth Be Heard board.

**How can relationship-building be intentional and purposeful with implementing critical media literacy with historically marginalized teens in urban communities?**

> Critical media literacy not only teaches students to learn from media, to resist media manipulation, and to use media materials in constructive ways, but is also concerned with developing skills that will help create responsible citizens who are motivated and competent participants in social-political life. (Kellner and Share 2019)

Ingredients for the successful implementation of critical media literacy are peppered throughout Anderson and Czarnecki's thoughtful chapter and include flexibility, humility, authentic interest, decentering the librarian educator, creating affinity spaces, and active and patient listening. In some ways these are the same ingredients for any successful learning experience irrespective of the venue or audience. The authors' ideas echo the work of many critical pedagogy theorists such as Paulo Freire, whose writing has heavily influenced critical media literacy. Co-learning (because the one who teaches is also always taught), as famously described by Freire, is a natural outcome of authentic interest and reciprocity. Critical media literacy shouldn't be top-down or transactional (if it is, it isn't critical media literacy).

I have written elsewhere that critical media and information literacy should seek to disrupt traditional "banking" models of education and eschew individualistic, competitive approaches to learning by replacing them with collaborative, creative, and problem-posing strategies (Brayton and Casey

2019). In this framework, the students' agency is key. Anderson and Czarnecki note the sometimes uncomfortable reality (not for teens, but for librarians and other educators) when this is practiced. The assumptions, stereotypes, and microaggressions (ironically often influenced by mediated images) about who that urban teen audience is and what interests they have are commonplace in white-dominated spaces, including many classrooms and libraries. But allowing teens from "historically excluded" communities to choose their own media texts to create and analyze is key (Zvobgo 2021). At the same time, white educators need to be wary of self-serving savior complexes and performative allyship and ensure they "police their voice" in order to create the space required to listen. Anderson and Czarnecki remind readers that intentionality, purposeful relationship-building, and working alongside (rather than above) communities are key components, and as such should always be baked into the critical media literacy pie. ⏻

## REFERENCES

Braun, Linda W., Maureen L. Hartman, Sandra Hughes-Hassell, and Kafi Kumasi. 2014. *The Future of Library Services for and with Teens: A Call to Action.* Chicago: Young Adult Library Services Association. www.ala.org/yaforum/ sites/ala.org.yaforum/files/content/YALSA_nationalforum_final.pdf.

Brayton, Spencer, and Natasha Casey. 2019. "Reflections on Adopting a Critical and Media Information Literacy Pedagogy." In *Critical Approaches to Credit-Bearing Information Literacy Courses,* edited by Angela Pashia and Jessica Critten, 117–38. Chicago: Association of College and Research Libraries.

Cardoza, Nicole. 2021. "Stop White Centering." Anti-Racism Daily, February 5. www.antiracismdaily.com/archives/stop-white-centering-anti-racism -daily?utm_source=Anti-Racism%2BDaily&utm_campaign=5930107fe4 -EMAIL_CAMPAIGN_7_14_2020_4_16_COPY_01&utm_medium=email &utm_term=0_c1e01f2335-5930107fe4-211379700.

Cervantes-Soon, Claudia G. 2017. *Juárez Girls Rising: Transformative Education in Times of Dystopia.* Minneapolis: University of Minnesota Press.

Kay, Matthew R. 2018. *Not Light, but Fire: How to Lead Meaningful Race Conversations in the Classroom.* Portsmouth, NH: Stenhouse.

Kellner, Douglas MacKay, and Jeff Share. 2019. *The Critical Media Literacy Guide: Engaging Media and Transforming Education.* Leiden: Brill.

Oldenburg, Ray. 1999. *The Great Good Place: Cafes, Coffee Shops, Bookstores, Bars, Hair Salons, and Other Hangouts at the Heart of a Community.* 3rd edition. Marlowe.

Ong, Maria, Janet M. Smith, and Lily T. Ko. 2017. "Counterspaces for Women of Color in STEM Higher Education: Marginal and Central Spaces for Persistence and Success." *Journal of Research in Science Teaching* 55 (2): 206–45. https://doi.org/10.1002/tea.21417.

ScottBey Jones, M. 2020. "Jennifer Bailey and Lennon Flowers – An Invitation to Brave Space: The On Being Project." On Being. https://onbeing.org/programs/jennifer-bailey-and-lennon-flowers-an-invitation-to-brave-space/.

Subramaniam, Mega, Linda W. Braun, S. Nisa Asgarali-Hoffman, Keanu Jordan-Stovall, and Christie Kodama. 2021. *Library Staff as Public Servants: A Field Guide for Preparing to Support Communities in Crisis.* College Park, MD: University of Maryland. https://yxlab.ischool.umd.edu/wp-content/uploads/2021/02/Field-Guide-2021-Final.pdf.

Velásquez, Jennifer. 2015. *Real-World Teen Services.* Chicago: American Library Association.

YALSA (Young Adult Library Services Association). 2012. *National Teen Space Guidelines.* Chicago: YALSA. www.ala.org/yalsa/guidelines/teenspaces.

Zvogbo, Kelebogile (@kelly_zvobgo). 2021. "Motion to replace 'underrepresented' with 'historically excluded.' Precision matters; the former is a consequence of the latter. Let's not forget." Twitter, June 25. https://twitter.com/kelly_zvobgo/status/1408419297945395202.

# Power Lines
## Empowering Teens Who Have Been Disempowered Through Partnerships

R. ALAN BERRY

As you enter positions of trust and *power*, dream a little before you think.
—TONI MORRISON

**My very first experience with media literacy was through a library** partnership. I had been facilitating film production courses at community centers in Queens and Brooklyn for the previous year, but I found that I was moving further away from a traditional film production curriculum (write, shoot, edit) toward a more multimedia and critical approach. I was asking the students to experiment with different forms, such as advertisements and news, and they were more than happy to make music videos and podcasts. We also began deconstructing different media texts together and making our own media in response, as parody or critique. When we would return to making short narratives, the students brought fresh ideas and approaches to their projects, often with a more critical and personal point of view. As a novice educator, I lacked the language to articulate what exactly we were doing together, the students and me, through these informal, experimental learning experiences.

Fortunately, I was introduced to The LAMP (Learning About Multimedia Project), an organization that was delivering programming on media literacy education across New York City. The LAMP worked with schools, workforce centers, community organizations, and libraries, bringing media technology and innovative, hands-on programs to every neighborhood and to all ages. What immediately hooked me about The LAMP's philosophy toward media education was that empowering learners to be more literate producers and consumers of all forms of media wasn't enough—media literacy should empower people to be more critical and more engaged citizens as well. I went from volunteering at its programs, to facilitating programs, to managing programs, to serving as director of education at The LAMP, where I honed my skills as a media literacy educator and advocate, as well as a facilitator of partnerships, as all of our programming was based in, and thrived on, collaborations with schools, community-based organizations, and libraries.

Back to that first experience. I was volunteering with The LAMP at the Stone Avenue Branch of the Brooklyn Public Library in the Brownsville neighborhood. I was excited about this program because it was in the same neighborhood where I had been facilitating film production courses, at the nearby Brownsville Recreation Center, and this was an opportunity to engage with the community in a different space and a different way. The Brooklyn Public Library had partnered with The LAMP to deliver a variety of programs at several of its branches. At Stone Avenue we were collaborating with the staff to do a five-session news literacy program for young teens. The goal was for the teens to make short news stories about and for the Brownsville community that countered the typical news media coverage of that community, which was often negative. Teens in the community were developing critical thinking skills along with communication and media production skills, while also exploring their community through counter-narrative storytelling and digital media technologies.

Production teams were formed, and as a volunteer, I had the privilege of supporting one of the teams that chose to construct a video news story about the Stone Avenue library. I observed as the teens interviewed library staff and members of the community about the role the library plays in their lives and the life of the community. The team improved with each interview—they remembered to ask follow-up questions, they moved their microphone closer to the person speaking, and they started to develop a narrative. As their story started to take shape, they wanted to interview more people to make sure they included everyone and everything. They were actually excited about a news story! Then one of the Stone Avenue library staff mentioned that the library had a museum, which the teens had been unaware of. The librarian led us up to the third floor and unlocked the door to a large room decorated with murals and collages, and a number of displays of photographs and objects telling the story of Brooklyn and the Brownsville neighborhood.

The team's story then became about this hidden museum at the top of the Stone Avenue Library; a museum tracing the long and proud history of their neighborhood, and the community library that had been at the center of that story for the last century. The teens were learning about their community with agency, curiosity, and a sense of civic pride, while also challenging traditional media narratives through creative and participatory methods. The librarians, in turn, were proud to see the kids exploring the library and using digital media technologies in purposeful and constructive ways. As for me, I was able to learn so much more about a neighborhood I only thought I knew, and to see how media literacy learning and community partnerships are empowering. My media literacy practice began in earnest through that experience. Community partnerships have been and continue to be essential to my development as an educator and learner, as I believe that partnerships are essential to a place-based media literacy centered on critical thinking, civic engagement, and citizen empowerment.

This chapter will detail several partnerships and programs that I have been involved with through my work as the education director and program facilitator at The LAMP in New York, and as an educator and researcher in Kosovo on a Fulbright grant, where I spent nine months mapping the media literacy landscape and conducting applied research and facilitating programs and workshops across the country. This chapter will also try to articulate a vision of media literacy education that moves beyond transactional learning and prioritizes learner empowerment and healthy media relationships through a civically intentional framework. Partnerships are at the center of this vision, as I believe that media literacy partnerships provide powerful connections between educators and learners and between communities and organizations. These connections are the conduits for the media literacy skills, processes, and outcomes that are essential to fostering engaged and empowered citizens and communities.

## CONDUITS FOR SKILL DEVELOPMENT AND HEALTHY DIGITAL RELATIONSHIPS

In the late 1990s, as personal computers became more ubiquitous and the number of people using the internet grew exponentially, a conversation arose around the *digital divide*. That conversation centered primarily on ensuring that all communities, especially those traditionally left behind, would have meaningful access to new media technologies as the digital revolution rolled on (Van Dijk 2006). A few of the flawed assumptions of these early conversations about the digital divide's "haves" and "have-nots" were that access to a computer and the internet was enough and that learning and skills would be generated simply through the use of those new technologies (Warschauer 2003). As access became more commonplace and traditional inequalities persisted, the conversation shifted to a second-level divide that focused on disparities in internet usage and digital skill development, and then to a third-level divide that occurs when internet access, skills, and usage lead to healthy or beneficial outcomes for some and to unhealthy or less beneficial outcomes for others (Scheerder et al. 2017). We now know that internet access alone is not enough, though quality access continues to be a problem in many communities across the country and globally. We also know that deep inequities exist in the different ways we engage with new media technologies and for what purposes, and that these technologies have become unhealthy and unproductive for many communities. The COVID-19 pandemic has further exposed and exacerbated those digital divides, as students across the country have been forced to learn and work remotely, with varying levels of success determined largely by existing structural inequalities (Katz et al. 2021).

Libraries have been an important source of computer and internet access for many of the communities on the wrong side of these digital divides for the last three decades. During the pandemic libraries have maintained this vital connection to their communities, particularly as many families have been studying and working remotely without adequate or consistent online access at home. While libraries across the country have played an important role in providing access for all, media literacy education is one of the most important tools we have for bridging the second-level and third-level divides. Fundamental to media literacy is the development of healthy, participatory, and purposeful relationships with media technologies and media content, as well as the navigational skills, critical thinking skills, and creative skills needed to facilitate those relationships. These are essential skills for everyone, especially teens who will continue to spend more and more of their time playing, socializing, and learning with and through digital media. Community and media literacy partnerships should prioritize healthy digital relationships and digital skill-building as a way to eliminate digital divides, challenge social inequality, and empower teens. In the two subsections below, I will discuss two program models and three partnerships that were aimed at bridging digital divides in very different contexts.

## Digital Storytelling with Twine
**(Partners: Vuk St. Karadžić City Library and its American Corner, North Mitrovica, Kosovo)**

Kosovo is a young nation of great potential but also one of lingering divisions, the most salient being Albanian- and Serbian-ethnic tensions, which fueled the Kosovo War in the late 1990s and persist more than a decade after Kosovo declared independence. The country contains within its borders several Serbian-ethnic communities that do not recognize Kosovo's independence or the Kosovo government. This division affects many aspects of social and civic life, from language to politics to education. Nowhere in Kosovo is this division as stark as in the city of Mitrovica, which is split by the Ibar River into an Albanian-majority municipality in the south and a Serb-majority municipality in the north. Crossing the pedestrian bridge from South Mitrovica to North Mitrovica is like crossing a border into another country, where even a different currency is used (see Pinos 2015 for more on the unique identity of Mitrovica).

Within this context, I partnered with a small library in North Mitrovica, the Vuk St. Karadžić City Library, which serves the Serb-majority community, with a focus on summer and after-school youth engagement. The library was already partnering with the U.S. embassy to host one of their American Corners, a partnership that provides cross-cultural programming, grant funding, and donations, in the library's facility. In a Serb-majority community that doesn't recognize the authority of the Kosovo government, the youth of North Mitrovica are shut out of a lot of opportunities available to youth in Pristina and other cities around the country. Internet access and usage in Kosovo are very high (STIKK Kosovo ICT Association 2019), but significantly less so in the Serbian enclaves, though official data from these communities is sparse. Media production, computer coding, and digital skills training opportunities for youth are also rare in North Mitrovica, and the Vuk St. Karadžić City Library wanted to do more of that type of programming to fill the void and to make better use of the new technology provided by the American Corner. English-language learning was also a priority—Albanian youth throughout Kosovo, especially in urban centers, are being instructed in English from the early primary grades on, while students in Serbian-run schools are largely not receiving any English-language instruction.

I partnered with the Vuk St. Karadžić City Library to develop a media literacy program that would help local teens develop digital literacy skills and English-language skills and would utilize some of the new technology that was largely underutilized in the library's American Corner. What came out of that collaboration was a digital storytelling program using the free online software Twine, which allows users to create interactive, nonlinear stories or games through basic coding languages. Twine has been utilized effectively in media literacy learning (Thevenin 2017), and I had used the tool in previous partnerships as a means of integrating digital literacy, coding, and counter-storytelling. The teens participating in this new program at the Vuk St. Karadžić City Library were supported in and challenged to create interactive stories that could be played as games, or choose-your-own-adventure stories, about their daily lives in North Mitrovica, with specific details about the language, culture, food, and so on, in both Serbian and English. In order to create engaging stories, the teens did a lot of planning and a lot of troubleshooting with their colleagues, they learned some basic coding skills, and they gained more confidence communicating in English. Most importantly, they were afforded the opportunity to share their stories as teens living in North Mitrovica, stories that are not often heard either inside or outside of Kosovo, and Twine provides the ability to publish your story/game and share it as a URL so anyone can play it from any device around the world. This was a powerful partnership because it connected an access point—the library and its American Corner—with sustainable and engaging learning that focused on digital skills, literacy, communication, and the fostering of healthy and participatory digital relationships. Through a media literacy framework that focused on critically examining and challenging traditional media narratives and representations, the teens were empowered to use Twine and the skills they had developed as tools for purposeful media creation and sharing their experiences and stories with others.

## Digital Career Path Programs
**(Partners: Hudson Guild, New York City, and New Settlement Community Center, Bronx, NY)**

Some of the most rewarding partnerships I experienced as education director and as a facilitator at The LAMP was through our Digital Career Path programs, which were aimed at older teens and young adults who were already participating in workforce training interventions and which had the goal of combining digital literacy skill development with civic engagement. We were able to forge several multiyear partnerships through this programming model, including ones with workforce training centers in Queens and the Bronx and with community organizations in the Bronx and Manhattan. What I found so rewarding about these programs was not only the relationships with the partners we collaborated with but also the connections participants were able to make in their communities and with local businesses. Whenever possible, these programs not only afforded participants the opportunity to develop digital media skills, like graphic design and video production skills, but also the opportunity to apply those skills for local businesses or toward a local campaign and to build a portfolio of work in the process. This model introduced participants to different digital career paths, showed them that there is a demand for those skills in their own communities and beyond, and provided them with an outlet to practice those skills in purposeful and creative ways that complemented the traditional workforce training skills they were already developing.

Hudson Guild is a multi-service community organization serving residents of the Chelsea neighborhood in Manhattan. When they opened up a new college and career training center, The LAMP was brought in as a partner organization and, in collaboration with Hudson Guild, we adapted our Digital Career Path model to focus on graphic design skills. Hudson Guild thought that focusing on graphic design (and Adobe Photoshop and InDesign) would be a fun and creative way to engage more young people at the center, teach them valuable skills, and keep them engaged in the center's other training opportunities. We believed that a focus on graphic design would provide an opportunity to engage participants in digital literacy and visual literacy learning, understand and analyze the construction and impact of media messages, and challenge traditional graphic design practices and norms. It also presented a great opportunity for participants to collaborate with local businesses and organizations in the course of applying their skills and producing graphic design projects. To facilitate this, we recruited several community partners with specific graphic design needs that they pitched to the program's participants. Design teams were formed for each project based on interest, and participants communicated with their "clients" over several rounds of edits before presenting their final projects, which included logos, menus, and event fliers.

The LAMP was invited to facilitate its Digital Career Path program with young adults at the New Settlement Community Center, which serves students and their families in Mount Eden and surrounding neighborhoods of the southwest Bronx. New Settlement was trying to bring fresh and productive training opportunities to young adults in the neighborhood who were either unemployed or underemployed. In collaboration with New Settlement staff, we reframed our Digital Career Path model as a Digital Entrepreneurship program, with the same goal of connecting media literacy and digital skills development with civic engagement, but with the focus on crafting a community-oriented business plan or advocacy campaign using multimedia production, social media, and crowdsourcing sites, like Kickstarter, as a model. Participants formed teams based on shared interests and identified challenges in their community that they wanted to solve through a small business venture or advocacy campaign, including starting a community arts organization and raising money for a local food pantry. Each team conducted research, crafted a plan of action, produced videos and graphics, and presented their final campaign to other members of the community. Participants forged collaborative relationships with other young adults in their community, developed valuable skills, and produced projects that they could implement or that could inspire them toward further community engagement.

## CONDUITS FOR COMMUNITY-BUILDING AND CIVIC ENGAGEMENT

Public libraries have always been more than collections of books and banks of computers; they are "places where individuals gather to explore, interact and imagine" (Edwards et al. 2011). Through their services, their dedication to inclusion and equity, and the connections they foster, public libraries are in the business of community-building (Scott 2011). Libraries thrive on community, and communities thrive when their public institutions are strong and vital; and for public libraries, this means embracing new roles in their communities. In a digital media environment, when individuals have easy access to many of the resources that libraries have traditionally housed, public libraries should embrace their role as a "third place," particularly one that provides a space for creation, collaboration, and community-building (Norman 2012). Partnerships can drive the future of libraries and citizen engagement within these spaces while also expanding the reach of partner organizations. Successful community collaborations "allow each organization to leverage, and benefit from, the resources of their partner" (Saunders and Corning 2020). For media literacy education, these community collaborations expand the possibilities for developing skills and competencies while also affording new connections within and across communities. Within this framework, a civically oriented media literacy framework can inspire creative collaboration and participatory citizenship through the deconstruction and construction of media.

Mihailidis (2018) proposes a media literacy framework that is civically intentional and that prioritizes "bringing people together in support of everyday activism and positive social impact" (159). Mihailidis further argues that civic media literacy should cultivate individual and collective *agency*; should foster a practice of *caring*; should embrace *critical consciousness* as a means of subverting power and reimagining the future; should reject transactional approaches to media literacy in favor of an ethic of *persistence*; and should challenge traditional media forms and structures through the creation of *emancipatory* media (159–62). Beyond the ability to access information and to develop and apply skills, media literacy is a tool that can support collaborative partnerships that will foster community, empower critical thinking, inspire creative voices, and work toward a common good. Civic media literacy is essential to my pedagogical practice, particularly when I have the opportunity to partner with libraries or other community organizations. While not every collaboration that I have been a part of has shared that same vision of media literacy education, I have chosen to highlight several partnerships here that demonstrate the potential and power of civically oriented media literacy.

## Intergenerational Media Literacy
**(Partners: Older Adults Technology Services and Hudson Guild, New York City)**

One of the many interests shared by librarians and media literacy educators is the desire to foster learning as a lifelong pursuit. Public libraries reflect this ethos through the wide range of community members they serve and the many kinds of services they offer. The vast majority of media literacy research and practice, however, focuses on K–12 and undergraduate learners and neglects adults (Rasi et al. 2021). Efforts to extend media literacy opportunities to adults usually prioritize increased online access and digital skills acquisition, with little in the way of media creation, critical thinking, civic engagement, or activism (Dennis 2004). While skills-based, transactional learning is a popular approach to media literacy, especially in adult learning, civic media literacy demands that we attain skills in the service of dialogue, empathy, and social impact (Mihailidis 2018). This approach is vital in a media environment that increasingly caters to echo chambers and confirmation bias and that engenders greater distrust and disengagement, regardless of age. Inter-generational media literacy provides an opportunity for learners of different ages, skills, and experiences to learn from one another and to work together toward purposeful civic outcomes.

The LAMP's educational mission, which prioritizes access for all and sustainable, place-based learning, has provided many opportunities to design and facilitate intergenerational media literacy learning experiences, from family workshops to library makerspaces. Over a number of years, we have partnered with the Hudson Guild and Older Adults Technology Services (OATS) in Manhattan to deliver intergenerational media literacy programs for collaborative communities of teens and older adults. Local teens who were participating in Hudson Guild's youth services joined a group of older adults, who were participating in OATS' technology trainings, at a community center to engage in dialogue about their experiences as media audiences and producers, and to critically examine media representations of teens and older adults and the media structures that target and often disempower both groups. Teens and older adults are two audiences who are heavily targeted by media companies and are also regularly mocked and negatively portrayed in popular media, which created a natural allyship between the two groups in the program. The teens and older adults formed a collaborative community in which they used digital media technologies to critically remix media texts, produce a short documentary, and then design, create, and share a social media activism campaign that challenged negative representations and presented alternative representations of teens and older adults. Both groups were able to embrace and share their own skills and experiences with one another and produce digital media projects that aimed to raise critical awareness, engage public discourse, and work toward positive social change. In addition to their collaborative work, both the teens and older adults also appreciated the opportunity to dispel some assumptions each group had about the other. While this partnership did not include or take place within a library, public libraries present perfect opportunities for intergenerational media literacy experiences because they are spaces in which multiple generations of community members come to explore, interact, and imagine.

## Photography as Activism and PSAs for Social Change
(Partners: Multiple Libraries and Organizations across Kosovo)

While working predominantly in marginalized communities as a media literacy educator, one of the most common media criticisms I've heard from teens is that media don't reflect their realities. For teens in these communities, their relationship with media is often defined by misrepresentation or invisibility, whether it's through the news, advertising, or through entertainment media. Understanding how we use media (and how media use us), how media are constructed, and how we all interpret different media differently are essential media literacy competencies; equally critical, however, is knowing that many stories never get told at all or are distorted for profit and/or power. A civic media literacy framework addresses these systemic inequities while also equipping learners with the tools to explore and share the stories of their own communities, in their own voices. Nearly every group of learners I collaborated with in Kosovo said that they rarely see Kosovo portrayed as anything other than war-torn or dysfunctional, if it's portrayed at all, in Western media, and that local media often neglect the issues that they care about. Through partnerships with the National Library in Prishtina, the Prizren Library, and the Ibrahim Mazreku school in Malisheva, I took these common sentiments as a cue to design and facilitate media literacy learning experiences that connected youth voices, media activism, and civic engagement.

At the National Library of Kosovo, I collaborated with a group of students from the University of Prishtina on a "Photography as Activism" project, in which we explored some of the perceptions we have through the media, especially photographic media, of people and places around the world, and some of the perceptions others might have of Kosovo. We built on this exploration to critically examine why media producers might benefit from perpetuating the negative or reductive narratives and representations of people and places on which we form so many of our ideas about those people and places. Using their smartphones, participants then collaborated on producing their own photographic representations of their communities to form a more positive and complete image of Kosovo. They documented their everyday lives and rituals, their friends and family, their land's natural beauty, and Kosovo's unique cultural blend. These images were used to design and publish a social media campaign with the aim of inspiring other Kosovars to share their own images and to provide a different perspective on life in Kosovo than what the international media usually provide.

I worked with a group of teens at the Prizren Library to create a project called "PSAs for Social Change." The participants investigated advertising messages and the tools of persuasion that advertisers use to target audiences. The teens were then challenged to identify problems within their communities and solutions that they could present to a specific audience in the form of a public service advertisement, or PSA. Collaborating in production teams, the participants designed and produced video PSAs, using the language of advertising to communicate positive messages for social change. Taking their cameras and microphones out into the neighborhoods of Prizren, the teens created PSAs that highlighted a number of issues salient to them and their communities, including protections for Roma and Ashkali families, gender equity, the health risks of smoking, waste being dumped into the river, and air pollution from lignite coal.

In the rural village of Malisheva, I collaborated with students at the Ibrahim Mazreku school at the invitation of a local NGO, Values for a Better Future, which had been founded by a young teacher at the school. With the teacher as co-facilitator, we combined the Photography as Activism and PSAs for Social Change program models to create a multi-week civic media literacy experience that challenged the students to design and produce multimedia campaigns, from photography to video production, aimed at other Kosovars in urban centers to dispel rural stereotypes, encourage tourism in the Malisheva area, and highlight issues facing rural youth in Kosovo. The students developed digital literacy and media production skills, while also working together toward shared civic goals and social impact.

## LESSONS LEARNED FOR FACILITATING MEANINGFUL MEDIA LITERACY PARTNERSHIPS

The partnerships highlighted in this chapter provide a glimpse into the many collaborations that have defined and shaped my practice as a media literacy educator, as well as my interests as a media and education researcher. It has been my great pleasure and good fortune to have been involved in so many meaningful and productive partnerships at home and abroad. However, I have also been involved in a number of collaborations that presented significant obstacles to providing student-centered, media literacy learning experiences. In order to facilitate meaningful media literacy partnerships, whether it's between a library and guest educator or a library and multiple community organizations, there are several lessons I've learned that continue to guide my work:

*Be clear about shared goals.* Each individual or organization entering into a partnership will have their own goals, and it is essential that any partnership identifies what those goals are, where they converge, and where they may conflict. This is especially important when it comes to media literacy, as everyone has a different definition and vision of what media literacy teaching and learning should be. Is your focus on digital skills? Are you more interested in media production? Do you want to encourage citizenship and activism? I've been invited by potential partners to scare young people away from social media. I've been asked by partners to stay away from anything remotely political. While some media literacy practitioners embrace protectionist and apolitical approaches, I believe in an approach to media literacy education that is transgressive, empowering, and civically intentional. Thus, it is important to articulate your shared goals early and often throughout the partnership.

*Engage the larger community.* Partnerships should be about expanding your institution's reach and impact. They should also be about presenting new and challenging opportunities for learners. The most effective media literacy learning experiences involve creative collaboration and community engagement. Challenge your students to go out into their community and engage in conversations. Connect your young learners with your adult learners. Recruit local businesses and organizations for your learners to collaborate with. Make space for learners to present their projects to other community members and local leaders. Utilize the unique affordances of digital media to provide a platform for your learners to engage with a global community.

*Process is more important than product.* My least favorite experiences as a media literacy educator typically occur when partners expect or demand polished media products at the end of a program. Sometimes this expectation is not made explicit, but the partner will express disappointment that the young learners have not produced something more professional after just a few sessions of learning, experimentation, and creation. Media literacy is not an outcome, it is a process. A media literacy partnership should thus prioritize process over product and value experimentation, persistence, and constant reflection over perfecting skills or learning the ins and outs of expensive software or technology.

*Sustainability should be the goal.* Far too many of the partnerships I've been involved in have been "one and done," either because of the particulars of the learning environment, lack of funding, disinterest, or different directions. The most successful partnerships, by far, are those that have been nurtured and developed over time. Partnership sustainability is essential to effective media literacy learning because that type of learning is an engaged, challenging, and lifelong process. Sustainability also depends on continued access because your organization must be able to keep delivering media literacy experiences for your learners. From the perspective of empowering teens, I believe that utilizing tools that learners already have access to and can continue to make use of is essential. Thus, whenever possible, I encourage a bring your own technology (BYOT) ethos in my programming models, or I design learning around what technology is available in a given space. This is especially important when I'm partnering with under-resourced communities and organizations, like those in Kosovo or in many New York communities. This may even require an analog approach to teaching and learning.

*Create a learning environment of hope.* One of the challenges with media literacy education, especially when we are critically investigating questions of power and polarization, is that the media landscape and the potential for change can feel hopeless. Media literacy partnerships that aim to empower teens, especially those who are often disempowered, should prioritize an environment and pedagogy of hope. A civic media literacy framework is helpful in this regard because it directs learning toward community-building, social impact, and the common good.

## CONCLUSION

Partnerships have been vital to the development of media literacy education, in both formal and informal learning environments, and will continue to power the media literacy community as we expand our reach and engage new communities of learners. Media literacy partnerships in public libraries, especially, provide unique opportunities to connect learners of all ages with critical twenty-first-century survival skills in spaces that bridge the past, present, and future of our communities. This chapter has outlined a number of place-based partnerships and programs from my time as a media literacy educator in New York and Kosovo. These partnerships demonstrate powerful connections between communities and organizations and educators and learners in contexts which are very different yet also very much alike in that the communities engaged in the process are disempowered both structurally and symbolically by the media and by the lack of learning resources and opportunities available to them. I've also tried to outline a particular vision for media literacy that moves beyond traditional models toward a framework for fostering lifelong learning, healthy media relationships, and civically intentional outcomes. Media literacy partnerships that work toward shared goals, and that engage with the larger community, while also prioritizing process, sustainability, and hope, can empower learners with meaningful opportunities for both individual and collective expression and agency.

● ● ●

## TEEN REFLECTIONS

**What types of relationships have you built in the community through programs at your library?**

Through Charlotte Mecklenburg Library I developed a supportive relationship with my community. When I was a teenager, I spent a great deal of time in the Teen Loft at the Joe and Joan Martin Center. At this library was a center where the staff would educate youth on everything job-related. When I searched for my first job I went to the library for help. I learned how to format my first resume and cover letter, and personalize them through Canva.com.

On a separate occasion, I attended a program for learning how to create and edit images with Adobe Spark. At the time, I was an intern and was learning about the programming process. I helped show attendees how to use the app and post their creations on social media. Later, I created my program and connected young readers to book kits I assembled. The library was more than a place for books for me; it provided a way to give back to others. I could rely on the library staff because they were always there to support me through programs and educate me on using any available resource. ⏻

—JENEVA CLAIBORNE, former teen patron, Charlotte, NC

I recently participated in the Girls Rock Film Camp through a partnership with the Charlotte Mecklenburg Library. Through Girls Rock I have gained so many new skills, experiences, and friends. Prior to coming to Girls Rock, all of my camp experiences were never truly fun or really something I wanted to do. Because I wanted to be a filmmaker, coming to film camp was actually something for me to enjoy and a way for me to learn many new skills and to meet real women who work in the film industry. Along with the camp being at the library, it provided space for us to edit our films and new settings to shoot our scenes. I wouldn't have some of my closest friends if it weren't for film camp, nor would I have been able to make the connections with people who work in the industry. ⏻

—MAIA McELVANE, 18, Charlotte, NC

● ● ●

## VOICES FROM THE FIELD: Nygel D. White

Nygel D. White is the program production and engagement coordinator at the Hartford Public Library in Connecticut.

### How can library partnerships enhance digital and media literacy programming with teens in urban communities?

It is vital for libraries to work together with community partners of various kinds in order to advance digital literacy programming for community members. Furthermore, in order to enhance digital literacy for teens through programming, a well-rounded resource collective is necessary. This will in turn increase the opportunity for teens to become part of a growing group of digital content creators, as opposed to being consumers only.

Libraries can create well-rounded resource collectives for increasing teen digital literacy by:

- Leveraging partnerships with youth-serving organizations and schools to reach teens who have already formed connections with potential collaborators, and whom libraries are looking to engage. These partnerships can also help develop library resources that support a digital literacy-based curriculum (i.e., space, equipment, programs, etc.).
- Utilizing the skills, business offerings, and personnel of local media and other creative companies to train library staff and patrons, partner on creative projects, and provide internship opportunities for teens.

By allowing themselves to connect with community partners that bring these different variables to the table, libraries can be at the center of circulating and redistributing the various resources that become available to the collective group of organizations and thus to the teens. Libraries in urban communities have a unique opportunity to address inequities in education which most negatively impact inner-city and urban schools. It is imperative that libraries, as the primary center for information in many urban communities, become a distribution center for other resources that those communities have to contribute to the development of digital literacy for their teens. ⏻

* * *

## VOICES FROM THE FIELD: Elis Estrada

Elis Estrada is the senior director of the PBS NewsHour Student Reporting Labs (SRL), where she oversees the development work and content of SRL's growing network of over 160 schools and partner public media stations.

**How can libraries partnering with media companies, journalists, and field experts support media literacy programming and services with teens?**

"Your voice matters" can be powerful words for young people to hear. Spoken in the context of media literacy programming with teens and media professionals, those words have the potential to spark confidence, creativity, and innovation. Libraries partnering with journalists and field experts can enhance media literacy experiences with teens in three key ways. They can meet teens where they are by facilitating conversations between young people and media influencers about how they use media and technology to connect with their peers. These conversations help teens make connections to real-world experiences and build an understanding of the impact of media creation for specific audiences. Beyond learning about the role of journalism from professional journalists, partnering with media professionals invested in building a more diverse industry can also provide invaluable mentorship opportunities for teens interested in pursuing careers in the media. Listening to young people and the issues they care about initiates dialogue that can decrease the cynicism many young people have toward the media because they often don't feel heard. Lastly, partnering with professionals who value youth voices can help create pathways for stories produced by young people to be seen and heard by the bigger audiences. Infusing local and national media ecosystems with youth-centered storytelling can enrich the landscape and empower teens who see in concrete ways that their voices matter. ⏻

## REFERENCES

Dennis, Everette E. 2004. "Out of Sight and Out of Mind: The Media Literacy Needs of Grown-Ups." *American Behavioral Scientist* 48 (2): 202–11.

Edwards, Julie Biando, Melissa S. Rauseo, and Kelley Rae Unger. 2011. "Community Centered: 23 Reasons Why Your Library Is the Most Important Place in Town." *Public Libraries* 50 (5): 42–47.

Katz, Vikki S., Amy B. Jordan, and Katherine Ognyanova. 2021. "Digital Inequality, Faculty Communication, and Remote Learning Experiences during the COVID-19 Pandemic: A Survey of U.S. Undergraduates." *PLoS One* 16 (2): e0246641. doi: 10.1371/journal.pone.0246641.

Mihailidis, Paul. 2018. "Civic Media Literacies: Re-Imagining Engagement for Civic Intentionality." *Learning, Media and Technology* 43 (2): 152–64.

Norman, Mark. 2012. "Frail, Fatal, Fundamental: The Future of Public Libraries." *Public Library Quarterly* 31 (4): 339–51.

Pinos, Jaume Castan. 2015. "Mitrovica: A City (Re) Shaped by Division." In *Politics of Identity in Post-Conflict States*, edited by Éamonn Ó Ciardha and Gabriela Vojvoda, 152–66. Abingdon, UK: Routledge.

Rasi, Päivi, Hanna Vuojärvi, and Susanna Rivinen. 2021. "Promoting Media Literacy among Older People: A Systematic Review." *Adult Education Quarterly* 71 (1): 37–54.

Saunders, Laura, and Sean Corning. 2020. "From Cooperation to Collaboration: Toward a Framework for Deepening Library Partnerships." *Journal of Library Administration* 60 (5): 453–69.

Scheerder, Anique, Alexander van Deursen, and Jan van Dijk. 2017. "Determinants of Internet Skills, Uses and Outcomes: A Systematic Review of the Second- and Third-Level Digital Divide." *Telematics and Informatics* 34 (8): 1607–24.

Scott, Rachel. 2011. "The Role of Public Libraries in Community Building." *Public Library Quarterly* 30 (3): 191–227.

STIKK Kosovo ICT Association. 2019. "Internet Penetration and Usage in Kosovo." Pristina, Kosovo: STIKK. https://stikk.org/wp-content/uploads/2019/11/STIKK_IK_Report_Internet_Penetration_V3-final-1.pdf.

Thevenin, Benjamin. 2017. "Twine as Alternative Media: Video Games, the Culture Industry, and Social Change." *Teaching Media Quarterly* 5 (2): 1–13.

Van Dijk, Jan A. G. M. 2006. "Digital Divide Research, Achievements and Shortcomings." *Poetics* 34 (4–5): 221–35.

Warschauer, Mark. 2003. "Dissecting the 'Digital Divide': A Case Study in Egypt." *The Information Society* 19 (4): 297–304.

# PART II

## Straight Outta the Library

The title of Part II is named after the rap group NWA's debut studio album, *Straight Outta Compton*, released in 1988, which was later the title for the groups' biographical feature film in 2015. This part of the book focuses on successful media literacy programs that have been implemented in libraries or in collaboration. Each chapter focuses on different media formats or mediums for infusing media literacy in programming with teens. The chapters in this section will highlight programs written by librarians, practitioners, and academic scholars from various cities across the United States and will provide insight on how these programs may be replicated at libraries in urban communities to serve teens.

# Traffic JAMS!
## Music and Podcasting

When the whole world is silent, even one voice becomes *powerful*.

—MALALA YOUSAFZAI

**Poetry, music, and other forms of the performing arts have functioned** historically as connectors to people and to the human experience regardless of ethnicity or background. But music specifically has stood out among all forms of art as having an undeniable power. A power that brings people together. A power that is evident in its ability to influence and inspire the lives of individuals who dare to indulge in its intimacy. Whether through its beat or through melodic ballads that mesmerize the mind, music also serves as an escape for teens from their physical reality. As technology has enabled handheld smartphones to download the songs of any artist with just a swipe of a fingertip, music has become entrenched in the everyday lives of teens. Most importantly, music has begun to play a powerful role in teens' lives through personal and communal connections. In a 2015 study published in the journal *Neuron*, researchers highlighted how we humans have a specific part of our brain devoted to processing music (Norman-Haignere et al. 2015). The findings from the study highlight how music has a special function in our biological and physical lives. The study also sheds light on the effect that music has on the brain as we connect with others when we sing in harmony.

Librarians who have used music in their programming, whether as a supplemental resource or as the core focus of the experience, have seen its ability to make connections with teens. Listening to and analyzing song lyrics in a program helps librarians to understand the personal connections that exist between teens and music. Some teens may form connections with the lyrics based on their own personal experiences, while others may find refuge in how the message of a song made them feel. In many cases, the same inspiration that teens get from listening to music may also motivate them to write and express their feelings for others. Writing music encourages storytelling and provides an outlet for expressing pain, joy, heartache, love, confusion, frustration, and all the other feelings and anxieties that teens experience in their everyday lives.

Using music in programs creates an opportunity for librarians to embed media literacy education. Lyric analysis, constructing podcasts, and songwriting all create opportunities to critically evaluate messaging, do research, and understand how musical content has the power to influence the minds of others. Podcasting has become popular with teens and young adults through apps such as Spotify, Soundcloud, Apple, and Google Podcasts. Podcasting was founded by Adam Curry, a former MTV video jockey in the 1990s and early internet entrepreneur; he is known as the "podfather" and has contributed a platform that has given a voice to the voiceless. In this chapter, we will share program profiles that can be replicated at libraries and case studies that have been done with teens in the areas of musical media creation and podcasting.

## 7.1: MEDIA LITERACY AND COMMUNITY CONNECTION: A Profile of Virginia Tech's "Digging in the Crates" Hip Hop Studies Program

by La' Portia J. Perkins, Jasmine Weiss, Jonathan Kabongo, Frederick Paige, and Craig Arthur

Hip Hop Studies at Virginia Tech, or as it is more commonly known, Virginia Tech Digging in the Crates (VTDITC), is a practitioner-focused and student-driven community engagement program that prioritizes experiential and critical service learning (Ladson-Billings 2014). The program is based in southwest Virginia on the campus of Virginia Tech (VT), a public, land-grant university with a student body of approximately 30,000. The main campus library, Newman Library, is the on-campus home of the program. VTDITC was co-created by a diverse transdisciplinary team, and we are now in our fifth consecutive academic year of engagement. The programs hosted have evolved dramatically since VTDITC's origin in fall 2016. The team has successfully hosted over 400 events that have emphasized the essence of hip-hop culture, collaboration, and community. The authors aim to share their program as an exemplar of community-engaged and student-driven initiatives, as well as culturally responsive programming. In this profile, they briefly present the program and, in doing so, focus on its cultural and media literacy foundations. Additionally, they provide examples and accounts of some of the program's contributions to the community it fosters.

The VTDITC program's community mission is as follows: to create learning opportunities among hip-hop artists, fans, practitioners, and scholars in person, digitally, and globally. The program promotes students, faculty, and staff's personal interests as worthy of academic study and publication. In addition, it strives to increase the investment in hip-hop studies' presence on Virginia Tech's campus.

VTDITC builds on a 23-year history of hip-hop-based curricula and roughly 35 years of hip-hop-based co-curricular programming at Virginia Tech. The VTDITC curricular effort predated the official beginning of the VTDITC community. In spring 2003, VTDITC's current director, Craig Arthur, was a student in A. Kwame Harrison's course Sociology 4984: Hip Hop Music, Culture, and Society. In the fall of 2017, Harrison and Arthur co-taught Africana Studies 4354: Foundations of Hip Hop. We have expanded to several additional offerings and a student-authored publication (Harrison and Arthur 2020).

VTDITC's team of a half-dozen "community engagement fellows" (VT undergraduate and graduate students) host the program's regular seminar series events (over two dozen hosted at the time of writing). These events feature compensated hip-hop practitioners and scholars. The fellows also co-teach free workshops for local youth-focused organizations (over 100 taught at the time of writing). For example, the VTDITC community taught a virtual workshop in partnership with a local public library; the workshop concentrated on the intersection of creative writing and MCing. VTDITC's ability to connect and engage with a large number of people (more than 3,500 annually) is a unique attribute of the program and a testament to the power of programming that centers on hip-hop culture. VTDITC's success is a direct result of the dynamic group of hip-hop practitioners who lead the program. They embody the culture, co-create it, and care for it beyond their connection to the university. The VTDITC community is made up of hip-hop artists, practitioners, and scholars from a wide variety of academic disciplines: from forestry to mathematics to library science to anthropology to engineering, the VTDITC community is inclusive and diverse.

VTDITC's media literacy workshops center hip-hop knowledge, sharing, and practice. Arguably these workshops are the community's favorite element of the VTDITC program. Shortly after being hired at Virginia Tech in 2016, Craig Arthur, the program's tenured director, saw many connections between the production-focused hip-hop-based media literacy workshops he had been teaching in the broader New River Valley community and Virginia Tech University Libraries' Digital Literacy Initiative (DLI) (Virginia Tech University Libraries 2021). VTDITC media literacy workshops were initiated shortly after this discovery and by design incorporated numerous DLI learning outcomes; in particular, outcomes related to identity, ethics, creation and scholarship, communication and collaboration, and curation. At the outset of the VTDITC program, the team decided that it was imperative that these learning opportunities would be offered to both students on campus and the larger community.

The media literacy workshops and seminar series are designed to share hip-hop history, creative practices, and tools for hip-hop scholarship, and they create opportunities for hands-on engagement whether it be DJing, rhyme-writing, MCing, beat-making, breaking, creating visual art, or collaborative community-building. An example of one of the hallmark events is the annual beat battle and music production workshop. This starts with an open call for music producers located both in the New River Valley and well beyond the region. Participants are invited to visit the Newman Library to share their strongest aural creations and compete head-to-head. Roanoke-based recording artist Stimulator Jones (currently signed to the legendary record label Stones Throw) served as the guest scholar at the last battle. Members of the VTDITC Leadership Board also provided constructive feedback to the competitors. Ultimately, the winner is always decided by the crowd.

The event offered hands-on training from Jones and concluded with our community having the opportunity to ask him questions. They strive for there to be no end to the synergistic feedback loop of practice, learning, and engagement.

Although COVID-19 has put in-person media literacy workshops on temporary hold, the lesson plans are currently being redeveloped to work in an online synchronous learning environment, and the team is doing as much virtual programming as possible. They have hosted roughly half a dozen virtual workshops, with more to come. Even in virtual learning environments, they utilize an experiential learning approach that connects hip-hop's creative practices to STEAM education. VTDITC learning experiences encourage students to engage in inquiry, dialogue, and critical thinking. While it is difficult to replicate the hands-on experience that utilizes learning technologies such as turntables, records, DJ mixers, samplers, drum machines, digital audio workstations, and microphones, the online environment is well equipped to foster other creative practices and uses them to serve learners well beyond their normal geographic boundaries. For example, the team has been able to use platforms like Twitch, Facebook Live, and Instagram Live to offer weekly DJ mixes, hip-hop storytelling, and information-sharing about various forms of media production to an international audience. They are improving both their virtual and in-person learning experiences to engage with even more aspiring artists in their growing community.

Undoubtedly, the biggest contribution that VTDITC has made is the organization of a community that is far deeper than can be recorded in this brief profile. Hip-hop thrives through an iterative learning process that necessitates reciprocal support. The creative processes inherent to hip-hop involve elements of storytelling and sharing that have the power to unite a variety of communities. In 2005, Virginia Tech created its Principles of Community (InclusiveVT 2021). Hip-hop pedagogy embodies one of these principles: "We affirm the right of each person to express thoughts and opinions freely." In a student-led study on the social and mental health benefits of the program, an undergraduate said: "Digging in the Crates has shown me a community built around Hip Hop, and I have met a lot of creative individuals and just a lot of [people] who want to learn more." Another student, Jon Kabongo, who is now one of our community engagement fellows, stated:

> As an artist, I knew that once I arrived at Virginia Tech I'd be in need of a community of people to share and create music with. VTDITC provided this community for me, and more. Being able to connect with students of different backgrounds increased my knowledge and understanding of various cultures and people, while I also gained more understanding of who I am as a person. Music can do an exceptional job of unifying people, and VTDITC facilitated that process extremely well.

The strength of the VTDITC program unquestionably lies in its ability to bring people together, foster community, and inspire an embodied respect for creativity. The program model provides opportunities for the further development of our co-learners, community engagement fellows, and the Leadership Board. It calls for each of us to learn and relearn to create with people of different backgrounds, struggles, and disciplines.

VTDITC's ability to thrive for half a decade is a direct result of community, both on-campus and more broadly. This program has produced professional recording sound engineers, digital marketing specialists, community managers, graphic designers, and recording artists—and each one of them is an artist and scholar both in practice and at heart. It is their hope that the program continues to evolve so that they can continue to create community-engaged learning opportunities for many years to come.

## 7.2: LET YOUR VOICE BE HEARD:
### Create Podcasting Programming for Your Library
**by Lauren Kratz Prushko**

People enjoy listening to all types of podcasts every day. For example, listening to "Levar Burton Reads" while driving, listening to "NPR Pop Culture" while doing chores, and listening to "Tracks to Relax" before going to sleep. People love podcasts because they can learn something new or connect with an idea or story and end up discovering something about themselves. However, some of the teens at the Studio City Branch of the Los Angeles Public Library don't listen to podcasts as much as adults do, as was found during a teen podcasting workshop held at the library a few years ago during YALSA's Teen Tech Week initiative (now replaced by the nationwide celebration TeenTober).

Teens often state that if they listen to a podcast, it's about true crime, paranormal stories, or discussions about their favorite shows on Netflix. But it doesn't matter if they don't listen to podcasts as much as adults do. They love the process of using their technology skills to create their podcasts and using that medium to let their voices be heard. So podcasting is a perfect media literacy programming idea for you to offer if you want to present programming that empowers teens and teaches them new technology and communication skills.

During a Teen Podcasting Workshop we held in early 2018, teen participants were taught how to create a podcast recording. They received a brief history of podcasting, talked about the definition of a podcast, and listened to some examples of different podcasts. Now, during our podcasting programming with teens and even children as young as eight years old, they already know what a podcast is, and they want to get to hands-on podcast creation immediately. Currently, this is how you can start a program: play an example of a podcast episode, and then break down the different parts of the recording. Is there an introduction? Is there music? What is the podcast's format—an interview, a review of various media, a podcast that features storytelling, giving advice, or sharing local or world news? Asking teens these questions also gets them thinking about what format they want for their own podcast recording.

## What You'll Need: The Nuts and Bolts

Now, what if you decide to use podcasting in your library's programming? Where do you start—especially with the technology and the producing end? The first thing you can do is use your library card and check out some online courses on Lynda.com or what is now called LinkedIn Learning. All you need is access to an iPad. There are also library systems in which you can share and borrow iPads from other departments. There is a free software app, GarageBand, that is pre-installed onto iPads and Mac computers to record podcasts. An exceptional beginner class on LinkedIn Learning for podcasting is "GarageBand: Podcasting" by Garrick Chow, which includes information on planning, equipment, and recording and editing your podcast recordings. A recommendation would be to watch this course with a friend, colleague, or teen volunteer. First, record a sample podcast using GarageBand on your iPad. Then watch the class again and, using the sample recording, follow the steps to edit, split regions, and add music to the beginning and end of the podcast. If you have access to PC laptops, you can download the free, open-source software Audacity, which is similar to GarageBand (figure 7.1).

The first Teen Podcast Workshop that the Studio City Library presented, used what was learned from Garrick Chow's LinkedIn Learning course. Because we had limited technology, with only one iPad and one Mac laptop, the teens worked together to record one podcast episode, interviewing each other about their favorite song or book and why. There

FIGURE 7.1
**Screenshot of GarageBand**

Source: Image provided by Lauren Kratz Prushko

was also a projector to project the GarageBand app from the laptop on a big screen to show the teens how to add music and edit their recording, while taking notes and practicing each step using the iPad. Some of the participants from that first workshop created their podcasts, including Daniella, who has a podcast on iTunes called "Life Told by a Stranger," which is in its third season. She speaks with many different people and asks them the same four questions about life. Through podcasting, Daniella has developed confidence in speaking to large groups of people she may not know. She also secured an internship at a radio station, and this gave her something to mention on her college applications. In addition, she has become an inspiration for me to start a podcast with a children's book club.

But what else do you need to do to make these podcasting workshops engaging and hands-on for teens, tweens, and children? You can research other equipment to use for podcasting. As you know, there are multiple price points for everything. There are all kinds of differently priced microphones, headphones, software, and plug-ins to add to GarageBand and other apps.

Here is a list of what we use for programming:

1. Microphone: Fifine Plug & Play Home Studio USB Condenser ($24.99)
2. DragonPad Pop Filter ($19.99)
3. Edifier H650 Headphones ($29.99)
4. 100 pieces of white, non-woven Sanitary Disposable Headphone Ear Covers ($11.99)

You can record with Skype and the Ecamm recording software when participants are in different locations. (Ecamm recording software: $39.95 one-time payment, all updates are free.)

The following plug-in and web service can also help clean up the audio when recording using a Zoom meeting videoconference:

1. Waves NS1 Noise Suppressor plug-in for GarageBand, which helps get rid of background noise ($39.99).
2. Auphonic.com: a post-production web service for podcasts (two free hours of processed audio per month).

Here are some other tools you can discover and explore with different price points:

1. Talk Sync App: a tool to make high-quality remote recordings.
2. Anchor App: a tool that provides everything you need to record a podcast all in one place.
3. Alitu.com: includes everything you need to record a podcast all in one place.
4. Headliner: a website and app to promote your podcast on social media.

Now, how can you obtain the funding for your podcast program? You may need to write a proposal for a Friends of the Library group or some other grant proposal to get the necessary funding. What's great about podcasting programming is that you can scale the amount of money you will need up or down depending on your funding opportunities and goals. If you try to keep your programming low-cost and aren't worried about editing or uploading your recordings anywhere, all you need is a quiet program space, a microphone, and a pop filter. You can get an inexpensive microphone as long as you have the pop filter. (The pop filter reduces or eliminates popping sounds as people speak into the microphone.) Noticeably, the teens and children will get excited at the experience of using the microphone and DragonPad Pop Filter as they record. You can also ask participants to bring their headphones, which helps with the audio quality; this creates a professional environment that makes this program a memorable experience for everyone.

## Getting Buy-in from Your Library Stakeholders

How do you get the support you need to run your podcast programming? What can you tell your supervisors and stakeholders? First, podcasting is fun and easy and uplifts teens, children, and adults. There is something powerful about speaking aloud, sharing your thoughts, and hearing your voice. This type of programming can provide the usual quantitative data that everyone collects, but more importantly, it can provide qualitative data too. Many pictures from podcast programs have been used for various reports, and the programs also yield quotes from excited participants and their families, telling how they've used the podcast format to design unique projects for school assignments and to record family memories to send as gifts. Podcast programming keeps the library involved in new technology trends and constantly pushes both the library staff and patrons' creativity.

## Podcast Program Ideas

I've served as a public librarian for over ten years, always in an urban environment, first in the Bronx, New York City, and now in Los Angeles, and have presented podcast programming for teens and children of all different backgrounds and origins from ages 8 to 17. One thing I have discovered is that everyone gravitates to programs that combine hands-on technology with working together as a group (or with a partner) and designing something that they can be proud of and share.

FIGURE 7.2
**Lauren and Mphatso at 2019
Maker Faire**

Source: Image provided
by Lauren Kratz Prushko

Here are some podcast programming themes to get started:

1. Interviewing special guests such as authors or community members.
2. Incorporating podcasting into teen council meetings.
3. Participants interviewing each other.
4. Recording poetry and storytelling.
5. Sports announcing and news reports, especially about social justice issues and sustainability.
6. Incorporating podcasting into your summer reading program.

During a DTLA (Downtown Los Angeles) Mini Maker Faire event, there was an opportunity for us to set up a podcast booth. People of all ages stopped by and recorded short podcast episodes and asked questions. The smiles and engagement of each group of participants who stopped by were contagious! You can hold your own show-and-tell podcast event, attract people of all generations to record, and provide patrons with a noteworthy occasion at your library.


## 7.3: PODCASTING THE POSSIBILITIES
by Molly Dettmann

Norman North High School serves about 2,350 students in the ninth through twelfth grades in Norman, Oklahoma. The school has a faculty and staff of almost 200 and two full-time certified school librarians. With such a large student population, there is a wide range of students from all sorts of demographic and socioeconomic levels. One way the library has worked to reach all students and provide equitable access to creative digital outlets is through the podcasting available in the library's makerspace. When I started as a librarian at Norman North High School, I was fortunate to start working in a library where my co-librarian had been working to incorporate more voice and choice in student creations for final projects using podcasting equipment. The library already had a Rode Procaster Broadcast Quality Two-Person Podcasting Kit setup, and this was one of the most popular methods for students to share what they had learned in the form of a professional sound quality podcast. The recording software used with the podcasting equipment was a web and app-based podcasting studio called Anchor (https://anchor.fm), on account of its ease of use and the fact that it was free. Students could quickly create an account on Anchor with their school Google accounts and with minimal buttons yet many editing options. It was by far the best tool to use when getting students started with podcasting.

During my first year, we implemented an appointment request system using Google Forms so students could use the podcasting equipment not only for class projects but for passion projects as well. A group of freshman students immediately started to make regular appointments to record their podcast about the video games they were playing while they also played their video games. Within the first year of working with students and podcasting in classes and individually, over 100 individual appointments for podcasting were fulfilled. Because of the demand, we sought grant funding for an additional setup, which resulted in the Podcasting the Possibilities program, in which students recorded episodes highlighting YALSA's Teens' Top Ten book nominees. Our teen podcasters started with high school students who had read any of the books on YALSA's Teens' Top Ten list. A librarian was also interviewed about the books on the list and what she thought of them.

Our library expanded by showcasing and teaching podcasting in more intentional ways. Instead of simply having the equipment available and helping individual students, when librarians were introducing methods of digital creation during units with classes, they started hands-on showcasing the possibilities of podcasting. They would get volunteers, practice outlining a short podcast episode, and would get at least two volunteers to record it, and then show how easy it was to polish and edit the podcast in Anchor. These strategies expanded the potential of the librarians' work with courses and were effective with all grade levels and with subjects ranging from English to psychology, special education, science, and more. For individual appointments, ninth graders would book the most appointments because they had on-campus lunch and would use the podcasting equipment during their lunch hour. Additionally, the librarians worked with students on various ways they could edit their podcasts with their own original logos and music, and showed them how they could find copyright-free images or music to incorporate in their work. After the librarians started implementing these concepts in their teaching on a more regular basis that school year, podcasting requests doubled before the COVID-19 pandemic came and the school shut down.

## Challenges

The biggest hurdle to providing this programming for students was meeting the demand in general and scheduling appointments accordingly, when we had several groups of students all wanting to use the equipment at prime times (like before school or lunch). The library also started to run out of quiet space for groups to podcast within the library because there were only two study rooms and a makerspace as quiet space, and sometimes there were as many as three groups working at once. Currently, the biggest challenge to teaching and offering podcasting to the teens is that staff have to be creative while socially distancing and limiting appointments in accordance with COVID-19 precautions, and keeping the equipment sanitized without damaging it.

## Replicating the Program

This program could easily be replicated by other teen librarians (in schools or public libraries) with any device that can record audio. While the Rode Procaster setup is top quality, staff have also had students record podcasts using just their phones or computers. Library staff were most successful after they had actually showed students how to podcast, so re-creating the example podcast and walking teens through the process would be the best method in re-creating this as a successful public library program. Including other experts from the community in the program would also elevate this method of teen creation for students at any library.

## Podcasting the Possibilities Program: Lesson Setup

The following are the procedures for creating an introductory program for teens on podcasting:

- Time: 30-40 minutes, depending on how many examples you go through with the teens.
- Equipment needed: Computer, sound recording equipment (if available and/or computer cannot record audio); a large monitor to show the recording and editing process (can be a SMART Board, monitor, projector and screen, etc.); and a whiteboard (or something to write on and display to teens).

Begin by explaining the podcasting setup to teens and how they could use the library's particular equipment or space. Then have the teens listen to some clips or other short examples of professional podcasts (or other teen examples if you have them).

Practice outlining a podcast script with the teens. Start by establishing a topic and who is going to ask the questions and who will answer (or if there will be a mixture of both). Work with a volunteer teen to outline the flow of the example podcast. Use a whiteboard to write everything out as you work with the teens.

If there are two teen volunteers, one of them can be the host asking questions and the other can be the expert talking about whatever topic was outlined, or else the librarian can be the host. Start recording with the library's equipment, following the outline prepared at the beginning of the program. Walk the teens through connecting the equipment to record directly using Anchor (or another recording software if preferred), and then let the podcasting magic happen.

Then listen to the podcast. There is always some laughter here because listening to one's own voice can be a little awkward. At this point, the librarian facilitator would then show how easy it is to edit in Anchor (or whatever software is used) by taking the raw recording and applying the editing options in the software (such as editing out any mistakes or adding music).

Let teens take turns trying out the equipment and editing their own creations. Reiterate how teens can utilize the library's podcasting setup and space to do this after the program is over.

## REFERENCES

Harrison, Anthony Kwame, and Craig E. Arthur. 2020. *The Foundations of Hip-Hop Encyclopedia*. Blacksburg, VA: Virginia Tech Publishing.

InclusiveVT. 2021. "The Principles of Community." www.inclusive.vt.edu/
Programs/vtpoc0.html.

Ladson-Billings, Gloria. 2014. "Culturally Relevant Pedagogy 2.0: A.k.a. the Remix." *Harvard Educational Review* 84 (1): 74–84. https://doi.org/10.17763/
haer.84.1.p2rj131485484751.

Norman-Haignere, Sam, Nancy G. Kanwisher, and Josh H. McDermott. 2015.
"Distinct Cortical Pathways for Music and Speech Revealed by Hypothe-
sis-Free Voxel Decomposition." *Neuron* 88 (6): 1281–96.

Virginia Tech University Libraries. 2021. "Digital Literacy." https://lib.vt.edu/
research-teaching/digital-literacy.html.

# City Blue PRINTS
## Books and Print Literature

**When most people think of libraries, they don't think of them without** having printed materials. And it's likely one would be hard-pressed to find a library where these materials don't exist. Whether it's books, graphic novels, or literature, some form of the written word is considered foundational to the library. Because these resources are so woven into the fabric of what a library is, we may often forget that they too are just various forms of media. In other words, it's not just "books" and "everything else." Like other forms of media, the printed word can help develop various literacy skills and engage a myriad of readers. "If, as the research indicates, there is a strong relationship between leisure reading and school achievement, it only makes sense that educators develop an understanding of leisure reading habits" (Hughes-Hassell and Rodge 2007). The kind of reading that is not required but is done voluntarily is considered to be leisure reading.

The other day a group of teens visited my library, and the leader asked them to each pick out a book. They could choose from shelves of fiction, nonfiction, magazines, comics, graphic novels, and manga. After most of the group had made their selections, checked them out, and started reading, one teen male broke the silence by loudly exclaiming, "This is so boring and these books are stupid!" I don't think he necessarily spoke for everyone in the group, but it was a pretty powerful statement. There could have been many reasons that led to his declaration, but many of us would probably appreciate a glimpse of the bigger picture: how exactly are youth reading today?

While it is true that the reading habits of youth have changed, especially with the pandemic, "there are still plenty of young people reading. It just might be through different mediums than physical books. When readers can download books from online to their device and access them immediately, a paperback or hardcover is no longer necessary to read" (Reavis 2021). This is key to understanding how youth interact with media, particularly the printed word. Because we ourselves may have experienced the magic worlds beyond our own by reading books, this doesn't mean that teens today—especially urban teens—are somehow deficient because they're engaging with media in another way or form.

As educators and librarians, it's important to be aware of any messages—overtly or unintentionally through body language—we're sending which might signal this bias and figure out how we can change that into something more positive and dig deeper into our own creativity to make those connections. For example, if we work in a school library, we may be able to increase the amount of time that youth have to engage in voluntary reading. At a public library, we may have more opportunity to solicit the opinions of youth as to what materials the library should purchase—especially magazines. "If we want urban students to engage in leisure reading, perhaps the first thing we need to do is expand our definition of reading" (Hughes-Hassell and Rodge 2007). The program examples included in this chapter will inspire and hopefully show new ways to support the literacy development of teens today.

## 8.1: Alt RA: Looking Beyond Books in Readers' Advisory
by Heather Love Beverley and Cyndi Hamann

Readers' advisory is a fundamental library service that aims to connect readers to books that match their interests. Traditionally, this has been done by asking readers about other books they have enjoyed and then building recommendations based on those books.

Some teens thrive with traditional readers' advisory service because they are avid readers and have no trouble listing books they have loved or hated. Some teens, however, are not readers, and focusing on books as the only source of inspiration can leave them out of readers' advisory conversations. If a teen has not actually read a book since elementary school, they may be reluctant to admit this and might give the title of a book they have neither read nor enjoyed, or they may check out of the conversation entirely. However, if the conversation is expanded to look beyond books, and focus on other media that the teen already enjoys—media like video games, internet videos, music, TV shows, movies, and more—the possibilities become endless. Traditional readers' advisory skills and methods can be modified to connect any teen to books that will match their interests. If library staff can connect a teen to a book based on the media they already enjoy, they can potentially create a reader and open a world of exciting new books to them.

## Appeal Factors

The core of readers' advisory lies in finding the appeal factors that a reader is looking for in a book and then finding books with those same factors. The main appeal factors are character, story line, pace, genre, and tone. While these appeal factors are the basis of readers' advisory for books, they are also what draws many into other types of media. Most forms of media have characters and story lines—movies, TV shows, and video games are clear examples, but music, videos, and other forms often have elements of character and story line as well. Tone and pace are consistent across media—even GIFs have tone. The way a teen talks about a character or story line they love may sound the same whether they are describing a book, a movie, or their favorite video game. The trick to readers' advisory for non-book media is discerning which of these appeal factors is the main draw for that teen; that answer is the key to successful advisory service for teens.

## Character, Story Line, and Pace

Characters are the people (or animals) who drive the action of any media, while the story line is what happens to them. Does the teen talk a lot about their favorite characters? Character is most likely the main appeal. When they discuss their favorite movie or video, is their speech littered with "and then, and then, and then"? If so, story line is likely the main appeal. Pace is the speed of the action in any imaginative work. The way the teen describes their favorite work, either with lots of action verbs or meticulous attention to detail, will help pinpoint their pace preference; pace is hidden within contextual clues.

## Genre and Tone

Genre is often the easiest appeal factor to identify; every piece of media has a genre; even musical styles often have a set genre feel to them. Genre is the broad category that the media fits into, such as romance, fantasy, science fiction, true crime, horror, and so on. Tone is the feel of the media—the feelings one may have while experiencing the media and the overall mood of that work—whether it is heartfelt, funny, serious, dramatic, or something else entirely. Genre and tone can sound similar; for example, we say, "they're scary" to describe horror movies, and these are a genre, while we say, "it was scary" to describe a particular mystery novel is a tone appeal. It is important to know the genre of the media that the teen enjoys in order to be able to properly differentiate genre from tone.

## Your Mileage May Vary

While these appeal factors exist in each media, the teen likely won't care about all of them. They might like characters who love to hate each other but not care about the story line or pace at all, so long as the characters kiss by the end. Another teen might not care at all about characters, but loves fast-paced action media. Be sure to listen to how the teen describes the shows they enjoy. Teens may not didactically tell the librarian that they want a serial killer-based horror book, but if one listens to the way they describe the media they enjoy and what they focus on, these requests will become clear. Base your readers' advisory suggestions on the appeal factors that the teen focuses on. If the teen doesn't mention certain appeal factors of the works they love, it is not necessary to consider those factors as you choose books to match their interests.

Tone is the exception among appeal factors, though, and should always be considered in readers' advisory. Identifying tone is extraordinarily important; it is the difference between *Law & Order: SVU* and *Brooklyn Nine-Nine*. The story lines and plot sound the same for those TV shows, but the tone is vastly different. Ensuring that your suggestions match the tone of the media the teen enjoys is key to a successful readers' advisory interaction.

## Finding the Books

Once library staff have a feel for what the teen is most drawn to in their chosen media, they can start a search for books that have those very same appeal factors. They might know many books right off the top of their head, but if not, they can consult other sources. Novelist (www.ebsco.com/novelist) has extensive facet features in which you can search precisely for the appeal factors you have identified. If the media is popular enough, there might already be booklists out there for recommended readalikes; sites like BuzzFeed (www.buzzfeed.com) and BookRiot (https://bookriot.com) often feature lists of books to read based on current media obsessions. Looking through Goodreads (www .goodreads.com) can also help pinpoint potential readalikes through their user-generated lists, which often focus on highly specific appeal factors.

## Teen-Centered Readers' Advisory Tips

Start any readers' advisory conversation by asking the teen what they like or are into, and go from there. Keep in mind that being asked about books can be embarrassing for teens who may struggle with reading, so let them lead the conversation. If they want to talk about music and video games, let them, and wait until later to bring up books.

Try to be aware of diversity within popular media, even if the teen does not directly reference it. They might bring up that they enjoy a show with an LGBTQ+ character while not expressly stating that they like the LGBTQ+ representation. They may code their requests for diverse representation by mentioning another work that has similar representation. Beyond the diversity that is written into media, also be mindful of any hidden subtext in the conversation you are having with a teen. Some shows and videos games are well known for a subculture that explores LGBTQ+ or diverse themes, even though LGBTQ+ and/or diverse characters are not expressly written into the canon. While it is impossible to know the ins and outs of every media, spend some time dipping into various fandoms to learn about these hidden topics and appeal factors.

Many pieces of media have multiple appeal factors. Focus your attention on the specific aspects the teen mentions; two teens might find different elements appealing in the same show or any other form of media.

Finally, when trying to connect a teen to a book based on their media interests, be sure to leave the conversation open. Let the teen know that you are focusing on finding items that *they* are interested in and that you will try to help them find just the right book to meet their interests, even though you might not get it perfectly right the first time around. Just knowing that a trusted adult and librarian is willing to keep trying, keep listening, and keep helping until they get it right is reassuring and can build trust.

## 8.2: THE EDUCATION OF BLACKS IN CHARLOTTE, AN ONLINE YOUTH EXHIBITION
by Pamela McCarter and Jimmeka Anderson

"The Education of Blacks in Charlotte (1920–2020), An Online Youth Exhibition" was a project created to capture the educational experiences from 1920 to 2020 of Black children in Charlotte, North Carolina. With high school students serving as digital archivists and curators of its digital print content, this invaluable initiative bridged history with critical media pedagogy to build understanding and empower action in the community of Charlotte. The project was a collaboration between the University of North Carolina at Charlotte's Urban Education Collaborative, the Charlotte Mecklenburg Library, I AM not the MEdia, Inc., scholar and historian Pamela Grundy, and educators/coordinators from five local middle and high schools in Charlotte.

## Why Capture History Through the Media?

Charlotte has an interesting and rich history involving education, specifically with that of Black children, that is both triumphant and disheartening. The initial idea for holding the exhibition came from a newspaper article published on September 5, 2018, in the *Charlotte Observer*. The article highlighted how high-poverty neighborhood high schools serving predominantly Black and Hispanic teens were experiencing a significant decline in graduation rates. This article, along with national data in the United States showcasing how Black students consistently perform the lowest on academic assessments compared to White students, sparked the interest of media literacy educator Jimmeka Anderson to explore and unveil the story of Black education in Charlotte with the help of a team of high school students. Jimmeka had served as the founder and executive director of I AM not the MEdia, Inc., for ten years and was also a doctoral student at UNC Charlotte at the time.

Jimmeka's studies in the field of urban education had revealed additional factors that contributed to disproportionate rates of school discipline enforced upon Black students. According to the Civil Rights Data Collection website, in 2015 Black students made up 72 percent of out-of-school suspensions in Charlotte Mecklenburg schools. Around this time, Jimmeka saw a need to foster conversation that would connect the past to the present and could create potential remedies for the future. She also believed that creating awareness around history and the disparities of the current time would be critical toward building social capital that could empower economic mobility for Black children when they grew up. Thus, the "Education of Blacks in Charlotte Youth Exhibition" was born. A small grant from the North Carolina Humanities Council supported the development of the project and funded workshops for the youth participants. The resulting exhibition was completely virtual and was launched in September 2020, with a final exhibit showcase presented to the community in February 2021.

## The Library's Investment in the Exhibition

The Charlotte Mecklenburg Library works to connect youth to reading and information so that young people can satisfy their curiosity, explore their interests, and discover their passion. It was essential that the library collaborate on the exhibition project by sharing access to its archive of historical information about the Black community in Charlotte.

By utilizing the library's vast online image collection, as well as an online digital photo album highlighting the experiences of Black people in the city from before the 1950s, online newspaper articles, and selected school publications and yearbooks, the outreach librarian collaborating with the project gathered a great pictorial and print collection of Charlotte's history, allowing new narratives of the Black community to emerge with regard to teens. This collection provided a visual story of the experiences of young Black students and what shaped their lives. The library has a role in helping young people learn about historical research; in the process, young people see themselves connected to local history and become aware of what impact they can have on the story of their community. Helping teens become active members of our community is key to the longevity of local history.

## Program Overview

The team of partners worked collaboratively to assist students in capturing historically marginalized students' educational experiences of the past and explore today's educational system through print literature and digital media. This initiative encompassed weekly historical workshop sessions for students led by historian Pamela Grundy. Archival research sessions were led by Charlotte Mecklenburg Library to locate newspaper articles from the past and local school yearbooks dating back to the 1920s. Community interviews with students, administrators, educators, and school board members past and present were booked and scheduled by the program partners and the program coordinator, Jimmeka Anderson. A partnership was formed with the Carolina School of Broadcasting wherein its students volunteered to record and edit all of the video interviews conducted by the students. Digital media workshops were conducted by I AM not the MEdia on using the Wix web development platform to upload, edit, and post the project's content to the exhibition's website. After the completion of the workshops, students developed that website with newspaper clippings, photographs, audio interviews, and digital artifacts that captured the educational experience of Blacks in Charlotte from 1920 to the present day with the goal of educating the community. An overview of the weekly workshops is provided below.

### Workshop 1: We Are Here (1920–1955)

In this workshop, teens explored the history of education in Charlotte and learned about the Brooklyn community, a Black community that has been erased from Charlotte's history. Students discovered the first Black high school in the city, First Ward High School, the history of West Charlotte High School, and Johnson C. Smith University, one of the oldest Black colleges in the United States. Students recorded their video reflections on the lesson to go on the exhibition website. This session was facilitated in partnership with Charlotte Mecklenburg Library. (Pre-assessments were also taken at this session to evaluate students' knowledge of Black history in Charlotte.)

### Workshop 2: We Are Equal (1955–1990)

In this workshop, students learned about Charlotte having served as a leader in school integration nationally through its busing plan and through the case of *Swann v. Charlotte-Mecklenburg Board of Education*. Through interviews with guest speakers, students explored the challenges that Black students experienced with integration during this time and their sentiments at having to leave their neighborhood schools (as part of the desegregation effort using busing). These interviews were recorded and added to the website.

## Workshop 3: We Are Worthy (1990–2020)

In this workshop, students discovered the introduction of magnet schools and the events that led to the ending of mandatory busing in Charlotte in 2001. Additionally, they explored the ramifications of the end of busing in Charlotte and a new era of resegregated schools. Students reflected on their own experiences in education by blogging on the website. This session was facilitated in partnership with Charlotte Mecklenburg Library.

## (Week 5): We Can Explore

This workshop session was facilitated in partnership with Charlotte Mecklenburg Library to discover online resources that could be used for the online exhibition. The students learned several resource tools with which to gather information and artifacts for the project.

## (Week 6): We Can Imagine

During this workshop, students experienced a creative mapping exercise led by I AM not the MEdia to begin brainstorming their ideas for the digital photo project. Students completed a mock sketch and layout of their projects and collected digital artifacts. All digital artifacts and content was uploaded to each participating high school's Google folder.

## (Weeks 7 and 8): We Can Develop

In this workshop, students conducted interviews and began constructing the content for the online exhibition. In addition, all digital artifacts and content were uploaded to each participating high school's Google folder.

## (Week 9): We Will Create

In this workshop, the students' final reflections on the overall program were recorded, and students uploaded all the required content for their exhibition projects to the website. (Post-assessments were taken at this session to evaluate how much the students had learned from the project.)

## (Week 10): We Will Inspire

Students met virtually with all of the participating high schools to review the final website and rehearse their speeches for the exhibit launch.

## (Week 11): We Will Lead the "Exhibit Launch"

Students led a live panel discussion for the community on Facebook to formally present the "Education of Blacks in Charlotte Online Youth Exhibition." Awards and recognition of all participants were done during the live viewing of this event.

## Outcomes of the Program

The online exhibition is available to view at www.blackeducationclt.com. When the exhibit was complete, the youth began to reflect and write about their experiences in the program. Here are a few reflections that were posted on the exhibit's website.

● ● ●

### TEEN REFLECTIONS ────────────────────────────

The painting I contributed to the exhibit depicts what classrooms looked like in the 1970s. During this time, people were fighting for equality between African American and whites, so segregation was slowly coming to an end. The schooling system at that time was unfair: Black schools were shabby, while white schools were pristine. Many people complained about how unfair it was that the schools were so different, and sooner or later there were some changes. You can see from the painting that the ratio of white to Black students was severely unbalanced. Also, even when the Black students came to the white schools, they were not treated kindly by most teachers and students. The students more than likely didn't know any better because they were only doing what they had been taught, but the teachers did; therefore, the students are represented as pawns in the painting. The pawns in chess can go straight or attack if they are used in that way; however, when they reach the other side, they can become any of the other pieces, making them very valuable. It is similar for children because though they may be young, they are our future, and what you teach them will impact how life will be for them later on. ☼

—RACHEL EDMONDS, 17

For years, we have learned about famous African Americans. Yet we never imagined that some of those great men and women lived in the same city that we live in. I always thought I had sufficient knowledge of Black history to appreciate and respect the trailblazers of Black education, but in doing this research, appreciation would be an understatement. I am inspired by the zeal and passion expressed by both the teachers and the students of that era. They truly valued the use of education despite the challenges and obstacles they faced in acquiring it.

I am grateful for the things that I learned from this project. It gives me a fresh outlook on education in general. The thing that stuck with me the most is to prize and cherish the opportunities that are granted to me because those who made it possible did not have the same access but created the possibility for me to have access. I was inspired by all of the information that I learned from this research and deeply appreciative of those who blazed the trail for better opportunities for those of us who would follow them.  ⏻

—ARIAH CORNELIUS, 17

The "Education of Blacks in Charlotte Online Youth Exhibition" is a great example of how librarians can bridge history and critical media literacy in a program. A total of twenty teens participated in the program and learned how to access archival data, photos, and newspapers through the library's digital resources. Serving as curators of content, the teens also were taught how to identify the difference between primary and secondary resources. The interviews, art, and poetry created by the teens enabled them to become journalists and artistic media creators in their own right. Partnerships with the university, a local historian, media organizations, and the library were vital to the success of the program. This program is one that should definitely be replicated at libraries in other urban communities to unveil the history of marginalized groups, exalt their voices, and use media to educate teens in those communities and impart knowledge that is transformative and liberating.

## 8.3: THE ZINE CLUB
by Liz Allen, Nicole Rambo, and Kristine Tanzi

A zine is a self-published work print work consisting of text and images that can be either original or borrowed from other sources. A zine usually takes the form of a small booklet or pamphlet, whose text and images have been cut and glued together to form a sequence from page to page.

Zines are a low-cost, versatile medium and a natural complement to hands-on creative programming. These self-published, do-it-yourself (DIY) magazines can be about anything and everything, and they are a great addition to low-budget programming as they require minimal supplies to create; at the very least, a piece of paper and a writing utensil will do just fine. At the Middle Country Public Library (on Long Island, NY), our first venture into zine programming came about in 2018 when we received a YALSA Summer Learning Resources Grant to offer "The Zine Project," which allowed us to build a zine collection and offer programming based on zines. We felt that this type of programming lent itself well to many types of teen interests: art, social interaction, collaboration, and media literacy, as well as English learning and practice. The Zine Project soon transitioned into the Zine Club. We will treat both programs in this section.

## Description of the Population Served

The Middle Country Public Library serves 63,000 residents of the Middle Country Central School District, a largely blue-collar, middle- to lower-income community that lacks a central "downtown." The community is culturally, economically, and racially diverse, with a steadily growing Hispanic and Latino population. The New York State Education Department's 2019–2020 report card shows that 40 percent of students in the school district are economically disadvantaged. The Zine Club specifically targets middle and high school students in the sixth to twelfth grades in the Middle Country Central School District, which has two middle and two high schools.

## Grant-Funded Zine Project

At the start of the Zine Project, twenty examples of zines were made available before the project began to show teens the wide array of zine styles from which they could draw inspiration. This strategy for starting the program was adopted by the program coordinators after attending the feminist Zinefest at Barnard College, where they purchased zines that were suitable for a young adult audience. They also purchased the books *Stolen Sharpie Revolution* and *Whatcha Mean What's a Zine?*, which are two great guides for zine-making. The Zine Project was structured as a five-week workshop for teens in the seventh to twelfth grades for two hours each Tuesday night. Nicole Rambo, one of our youth services librarians, along with a local professional artist, facilitated the workshop. Together they emphasized a safe space environment and encouraged the teens to express themselves however they desired. At the first session, the facilitators defined what a "zine" is for any teens who were not already aware of the form. Then teens received a short history lesson on zines, learned how to fold and lay out a zine, and learned tips on self-publishing and copyright. Then they were on their own to create, with guidance if needed.

The project culminated with a Zine Showcase, in which teen participants were provided with a table to present their zines and had the artistic control to set up their space in a way that would best reflect their personalities and the theme of their zine. Friends and family attended and the show was very well received. After the show, we recognized that more of this unique type of programming combining art, writing, and self-awareness created by young people was needed, and so the Zine Project transitioned into the Zine Club.

The main focus in running the Zine Club is not only to provide a safe space for creative expression, but also to allow teens to sit in the driver's seat in terms of what their meetings focus on and what projects they take on. The staff really want to encourage teens to think about setting their own goals in this informal, creative environment so they can feel comfortable trying new things and expressing themselves. In this way, we let the teens lead the Zine Club while the staff act as facilitators and provide guidance. We also encourage the sharing of techniques and ideas among the teens, letting them be the experts and teach one another.

At each meeting, the teens typically do a mini-zine activity facilitated by youth services librarian Liz Allen. They fold their own mini-zine with one sheet, and Liz provides the group with a topic as a starting point, such as a fanzine, a DIY zine which teaches the reader how to do something, a doodle/art zine, or a quick mini-comic. While they make their mini-zines, the group chats about art, school, and what they have been watching/reading. The librarian allows time for sharing at the end of the session. Another great addition to the Zine Club meetings is the incorporation of a "zine swap." Over the course of several weeks, each teen creates at least one complete zine to contribute to the swap, and then the teens submit their completed zines to the librarian. Copies of the zines are made and sent to the club members via snail mail, and the packages include fun little swag such as washi stickers, pens, pencils, and so on. The club members always look forward to this activity so they can share their work with others and receive fun surprises in the mail.

FIGURE 8.1
**Zine Club teen Zakariyah**

Source: Middle Country Public Library

The open format of zines encourages teens to pursue a creative outlet that may not be available during the school day. Zine-making provides them with an avenue to showcase their art and sketches or bring the idea for a comic they've been imagining to life. They can take the photos off their phones for use in a zine, or they can express their love for their favorite topic in a fanzine. If a teen does not know where to begin or feels overwhelmed, having a collection of zines for teens to browse may help jump-start their ideas.

## Successes and Challenges

Due to their versatility, zines are the perfect medium to explore different avenues of teen creativity and development. Themes that have been explored in the club include civic participation, #ownvoices, and LGBTQ+ pride and allyship, in addition to art and creative writing. The Zine Club's sense of ownership goes beyond the creative process—the staff regularly add Zine Club members' zines to the library's circulating zine collection in the teen space. Seeing their names in the library catalog and their work on display is a huge confidence booster and adds to the teens' enthusiasm for the club.

The past two years have been a challenge transitioning from in-person club meetings to a virtual format. Keeping the same group of teens engaged while at home required more work and communication. However, during the pandemic, the online club meetings enabled staff to provide teens with a creative outlet and a place to talk with friends, which helped combat the lack of socialization they were experiencing during quarantine and online classes. This challenge turned the Zine Club experience into a positive support at a time when many teens began to face mental health issues—a phenomenon that has been reported through both educator and community feedback.

## How the Program Can Be Replicated by Teen Librarians

Zine-making is very minimalist; at the most basic level, copy paper (8.5 × 11 or A3) and permanent markers can be provided. This makes it easy for libraries of any size to offer this type of program, either active or passive, and is also something that teens can easily re-create outside of the library. After-school programming with zines is an excellent opportunity to spark unique partnerships with artists and creators right in the community; this can elevate the program to the next level, allowing students to focus on certain aspects of zine-making such as drawing and painting techniques. Jumping right into a recurring program dedicated solely to zine-making, like the Zine Club, might be a bit daunting or hard to sell to coworkers or communities that aren't familiar with the format. Luckily, zines can be incorporated into many different types of events or projects; for example, making fanzines as part of a program during Comic Con, or in celebration of a favorite book series, or as part of a book club activity—zines and fandoms go hand in hand! Zines are also a great partner to civic engagement. There are a number of ways to introduce the concept of zines in a civic setting, such as identifying and expressing opinions and views on various social justice issues, or building a sense of community through a collaborative zine about the area the teens reside in. It is also easy to incorporate zines into any educational programming. As part of the NASA@MyLibrary program series, the Middle Country Public Library offered a "Moon Zine" program, where participants were shown fun videos and discussed facts about the moon and the solar system. Then teens were asked to create their own zines about what they had learned. Library staff have found that the versatility and simplicity of zine-making lends itself to all kinds of program formats and themes, as a tool to engage participating teens in creative expression about any given topic while teaching media creation.

### REFERENCES

Hughes-Hassell, Sandra, and Pradnaya Rodge. September 2007. "The Leisure Reading Habits of Urban Adolescents." *Journal of Adolescent & Adult Literacy* 51 (1): 22–33. doi: http://dx.doi.org/10.1598/JAAL.51.1.3.

Reavis, Allyson. 2021. "Reading Habits of Young People Are Changing." *The Daily Gamecock*, University of South Carolina. www.dailygamecock.com/article/2021/01/young-people-students-reading-2021-reavis-arts-culture.

# SCREEN Doors
## TV, Film, and Broadcasting

Freedom is *power*. To live a life untamed and unafraid is the gift that I've been given, and so my journey begins.

—**HALLE BERRY** in *Catwoman*

**When ImaginOn, a public library branch dedicated to youth, opened** in the early 2000s in Charlotte, North Carolina, the originators of the building had the forethought to include a blue screen as part of the design in the teen space. A blue screen allows visual effects to be added while filming—in much the same way that a green screen does when viewing the weather as part of a newscast. The mission of ImaginOn was (and still is) to "bring stories to life through extraordinary experiences that challenge, inspire, and excite young minds" (Charlotte Mecklenburg Library 2018). The library branch's creators saw the concept of film and video as another type of storytelling—in addition to the books on the shelf. This was seen as innovative at the time. Now it is not uncommon to see libraries with spaces for filmmaking or renting out film equipment—and of course, this is not just limited to public libraries.

Someone would be hard-pressed to argue that creating and editing videos isn't a valued skill set. How many times has a marketing department sought out folks in the community with the ability to take a concept and translate it to the digital medium of film? They likely want someone who can tell a concise story, catch the public's attention, and sell the product or idea quickly. This is not always an easy feat.

**143**

In the mid-2000s, a survey was conducted by the Pew Research Center on how American teens use their time. Not surprisingly, it found that "the biggest chunk of teens' daily leisure time is spent on screens: between 3 hours and 4 hours average" (Livingston 2020). This figure has held steady over the past decade, according to the survey. Also worth mentioning is that the pandemic in 2020 saw a marked rise in the amount of time that teens spent viewing screens. "The pandemic triggered a rise in the use of electronic devices among American children under 13 and teenagers, with screen time now double that of what it used to be across all age groups" (Johnson 2021). Among the most popular video platforms, Netflix and YouTube reigned supreme among teens, which the pandemic was shown to have done little to shift that. Teens are attracted to content that is relevant to their interests and which also provides a sense of community.

While teens many may be struggling with how to make catchy TikTok videos (a video platform that is increasingly popular), librarians can learn teens' interests and not discount videos as a viable storytelling medium to transmit information. It's important to understand that teens are much more than consumers, and producing their own videos and films is a great way for them to get their message across to an audience. They can be provided with tools on how to do this (and maybe even have them market some of the library's materials along the way) through programming and community partnerships.

## 9.1: GIRLS ROCK FILM CAMP: The Future of Film
by Lonna Vines

Girls Rock Charlotte (GRC) is a nonprofit organization in Charlotte, North Carolina, that is dedicated to amplifying the voices of girls, women, and gender-diverse youth through music and film. It is just one chapter of the Girls Rock Camp movement, which has seventy-five chapters located throughout the United States, mostly in large urban centers.

FIGURE 9.1
**Girls Rock Charlotte Film Camp logo**

Women today are still underrepresented in the film industry compared to men.

> Of the indie films screening at U.S. festivals in 2019–2020, women fared best as producers (40%), followed by directors (38%), writers (35%), executive producers (33%), editors (28%), and cinematographers (16%). (Women and Hollywood 2020)

Motivated to address the numbers that show women grossly underrepresented in the film industry, GRC became one of the first Girls Rock Camp chapters in the nation to add a film camp dedicated to changing the statistics of women's roles in film. Charlotte is a very diverse city, and one of the priorities for this camp was to have that diversity represented on the camp roster. The camp partnered with Charlotte Mecklenburg Library (CML) as a host location in 2019. Of the campers who attended camp at the library that year, 47 percent were youth of color, 15 percent identified as LGBTQ+, and 50 percent of the campers received scholarships. In the span of just one week, thirty-two campers learned the roles of director, camera operator, editor, art director, lighting, sound, and more. They filmed, edited, and premiered four three-minute short films with the assistance of library staff and local women filmmakers.

When searching the terms *libraries and film* online, one will see that filmmaking is a media that is already being explored in libraries across the country. However, if filmmaking or editing software is unavailable (or unfamiliar) to a library, the idea of starting a film camp or film-related program might seem overwhelming. The partnership model between GRC and CML outlined here is a great way to serve a need in the community, by providing a free programming space to a nonprofit with similar goals as the library with regard to media literacy, and it can also provide library staff with opportunities for professional development. This crucial component of the partnership will empower your employees to create similar filmmaking programs in the future at the library.

As a host location for Girls Rock Charlotte, Charlotte Mecklenburg Library provided a staff member, designated as the "library liaison," who attended all the trainings and workshops during the camp and in the months leading up to the camp. The support provided by this liaison included everything from a reminder of site rules, to facilitating communication between library staff and camp leadership, to supervising the campers in library spaces while filming. The biggest challenge presented throughout the partnership was maintaining communication between camp planners and library staff at multiple branch locations. That is why the role of the liaison was so crucial to the success of the partnership. This individual was there during the planning of the camp to ensure that the plans were safe, doable, and able to be executed without interrupting the daily operations of each library branch.

The programming portion of the partnership began at the Independence Regional branch of CML several months before the camp, with a series of Screen Writing 101 workshops. The programs were facilitated by camp leadership and local script writers, and library staff were invited to attend. This was the staff's first opportunity to learn from the camp partnership, and it empowered them to create similar library-led workshops in the future. Each teen, of any gender, who attended the screenwriting workshop had the opportunity to submit their script to the camp for filming consideration.

In the weeks before the camp, the library paid for Adobe Premier editing software to be installed on library computers for use during the week of camp. Local filmmakers led a workshop attended by both camp leadership and library staff to learn the software. The camp leadership

FIGURE 9.2

**Campers receive hands-on training with state-of-the-art camera equipment from industry professionals**

Source: Girls Rock Charlotte

used their knowledge to teach campers, and library staff now knew how to assist teens with the software should campers or other teen filmmakers come to their location for editing.

During the week of camp, the home base for campers was the Imag-inOn Library's Teen Loft in uptown Charlotte. The campers met there each day before the library opened to the public to ensure the safe and timely arrival of each camper. Each day began with a series of morning round-up activities, such as Tuesday morning's local improv troop that led team-building activities. The start of the day was also when campers reviewed the daily schedule and the site's rules. Campers were then split into four film crews, and each day they had to complete tasks such as script review, storyboards, location scouting around uptown Charlotte, compiling a shot list, gear prep, wardrobe, filming, and editing. Each film crew was led by local female filmmakers, such as Jolly Dale, who is well known for her role as a producer of *The Walking Dead*. Dale had this to say about the camp's partnership with the library:

> Girls Rock Charlotte's Film Camp is about many things—media literacy, storytelling, technical knowledge, sisterhood. Our partnership with Charlotte Mecklenburg Library means the camp

participants and leaders have a safe and familiar space to start
the process of combining these concepts. They get access to tools
they might not have at their schools or homes (computers with
state-of-the-art editing software, for example), they have a built-in
resource for reference materials, and they get to come to the library!
It has added value in ways we probably haven't even fully realized!

During lunch, camp leadership brought in women speakers who
work in the media industry. From local journalists to sound editors,
these women inspired teens to pursue their dreams despite entering
a highly male-dominated industry. The daily "lunch and learns" were
yet another educational opportunity for library staff. On the final day of
camp, campers were furiously completing final edits at the library and
getting ready to "walk the red carpet" to showcase their films for library
staff, camp leadership, volunteers, family, and friends. Most empowering
of all, the ImaginOn Teen Loft is a teens-only space to which campers
can return again and again to continue their passion for filmmaking.

Because the Girls Rock Camp organization has so many chapters
across the country, our partnership with them could easily be replicated
at other urban libraries. It starts with something as simple as a phone
call or e-mail. Every chapter is different, so invite them to your library

FIGURE 9.3

**Film camper behind the
camera on set at Charlotte
Mecklenburg Library**

Source: Girls Rock Charlotte

FIGURE 9.4
**Maia McElvane marking the slate for scene, shot, and take on set**

Source: Teen reflection author

space to discuss things, and focus the conversation on the mutual benefits a partnership like this could potentially provide.

In 2020, due to the COVID-19 pandemic, Charlotte Mecklenburg Library halted all in-person programs, and Girls Rock Charlotte took its film camp virtual. However, the library and the camp leadership hope to continue a partnership in the future that serves their shared goal of inclusion in media and media literacy.

To learn more or see behind-the-scenes footage from the camp, check out the following resources:

- Girls Rock CLT (www.girlsrockclt.org)
- Girls Rock Camp Alliance (www.girlsrockcampalliance.org)
- Vimeo Girls Rock Charlotte (https://vimeo.com/channels/1291690)
- Women and Hollywood (https://womenandhollywood.com)

## 9.2: KEEPIN' IT REEL: Black Girls Film Camp
by Deneen S. Dixon-Payne and Jimmeka Anderson

Black Girl Magic is a rallying call of recognition. Embedded in the everyday is a magnificence that is so easy to miss because we're so mired in the struggle and what society says we are.

—AVA DUVERNAY

To "liberate" means that one must be bound or confined, so there is a desire to be set free. For Black girls, emotional and mental liberation is needed because there aren't many spaces dedicated to addressing their unique needs. Black girls are often trapped in a continual pattern of navigating the misrepresentation of themselves in the media. They are often at the intersection of identity and girlhood in society.

Moreover, there are few spaces whose sole intentions are to promote Blackness and collectivism among Black girls. Thus, spaces dedicated to this purpose are needed. Patricia Collins asserts that Black girls who experience racialized gendered oppression in their daily lives require spaces with educators that foreground and honor their lives (1995). Collins's book *Black Feminist Thought* leans in on the notion that Black females have a unique standpoint from which they see and understand the world—one that is different from those of Black men and other women. It is through these experiences that Black females have had to counteract many forms of oppression.

In 2013, Cashawn Thompson coined the term "Black Girl Magic," which subsequently became a hashtag and refers to the significant, positive achievements of Black girls and women. This global hashtag has come to be associated with the celebration of the unique experiences that Black women share and their brilliance.

> This movement is for every black woman—the ratchet girls, the hood girls, the trans girls, the differently-abled girls. Black Girl Magic is for all of us. (Flake 2017, par. 8)

According to Jones (2021), informal programs for Black girls have a legacy of supporting their development, healing, and resilience, allowing the full realization of their "magic." Informal learning spaces, such as the Black Girls Film Camp, which perpetuate Black girl joy, liberation, and magic, are paramount to the mental and emotional survival of Black girls.

## Lights

*If I didn't define myself for myself, I would be crunched into other people's fantasies for me and eaten alive.*

—AUDRE LORDE

Why a Black girls film camp? There is a need to foster holistic spaces for Black girls' identity development, healing, and joy (Price-Dennis et al.

2017). The Black Girls Film Camp served as a counter-space to resist the deficit notions of Black girls in the media by offering a liberating space for Black girls to self-define and thrive. This camp set the stage for the critical work of challenging the plethora of negative depictions of Black women in the media by enacting a process of liberation for Black girls through filmmaking. The Black Girls Film Camp encouraged the girls to be authentic and share their perspectives on Black girlhood. There are many ways to be a Black girl, and no individual set of behaviors should be expected or demanded of them as a prerequisite for equal access to opportunity (Epstein, Blake, and González 2017). It is essential that Black girls self-define and write their own stories in an oppressive society that offers little space for their self-definition. This oppression is often exacerbated by their intersectional identities as both racialized and gendered beings (Collins 1995).

The representations of Black girls in the visual media often offer a narrow perspective of them. It is important to note that the reinforcement provided by positive visual media images matters. There is value in the portrayal of Black girls on the page and on screen. Furthermore, how they are depicted on screen often influences the ways they are treated in real life (Price-Dennis et al. 2017). Thus, the Black Girls Film Camp reinforced the message of art imitating life. There was a clear message throughout the camp that self-definition is important. There are many ways of being a Black girl, and the authentic representation of Black girlhood on film matters.

The Black Girls Film Camp also valued the importance of community as it relates to the positive identity of Black girlhood. When Black girls interact with one another, it gives them permission to be themselves. It also gives them space to explore their complex identities as Black girls, as these are not monolithic (Price-Dennis et al. 2017). Black Girls Film Camp was attentive to honoring the unique differences among the girls. Essentially, this film camp was dedicated to the wholeness of Black girls and sought to create a liberating space for them to reimagine their Black girl magic.

## Action

*The only thing that separates women of color from anyone else is opportunity.*

—VIOLA DAVIS

The theme of Black Girls Film Camp was triumph over trauma. This theme was befitting of the title "keepin' it reel." The girls were given the freedom to create authentic short films that defined Black girlhood. Unfortunately, in our society Black girlhood is often reminiscent of resilience. This suggests that at some point in the journey, trauma was there. Black girls are more likely to experience trauma than their white peers (Crenshaw et al. 2015). For many of the girls, their short films describe some aspect of resilience. Other girls' short films focused on unique aspects of theirs that are not often portrayed in the media, such as Black girls in nature or Black girls who play video games.

In 2021, the inaugural year of the Black Girls Film Camp, the camp hosted ten high school-aged girls for a free virtual experience. The camp was generously paid for through grants and sponsorship from the Urban Education Collaborative, UNC Charlotte; the UNC Charlotte Chancellor's Diversity Fund; and the Women + Girls Research Alliance and Civitas Education Management, LLC. The virtual four-week camp met on Saturdays for four weeks in April and May for four hours each week. Camp creator Jimmeka Anderson's ultimate goal for the camp was to create a safe space that centered authentic Black girlhood through filmmaking. It was important to create this space of self-definition because many of society's definitions of Black girlhood are cast from a deficit perspective. During the weekly Saturday sessions, the girls were introduced to many aspects of filmmaking, such as storyboarding and the importance of capturing b-roll footage.

Professional Black women from the film and TV industry were another highlight of the camp. The girls had the opportunity to hear from these Black women and their journey to and through the industry. The girls had the chance to listen to inspirational guest speakers who reaffirmed the value of Black girl joy and liberation. A powerful team of twenty Black women volunteered as film editors, mentors, and film crew. The film crew helped the participants curate their short films outside of camp hours. According to Cayleff et al. (2011), mentoring relationships can help build self-esteem, self-actualization, and confidence in Black girls. They can also help improve one's physical and mental health. Participants were gifted with a camp tote bag that contained essential tools to help with their film concepts. Each girl's tote bag consisted of a T-shirt, digital tablet, ring light, tripod, wireless microphones, and a camp workbook with handouts. These aspects of the film camp ensured that the girls had the skills to complete a short film and feel a sense of support. A formal virtual community film screening took place to culminate the film camp. In addition to the virtual film screening, the girls received awards such as ones for "most impactful film" and "most original story." The films were judged by a separate group of judges outside of the camp volunteers. Participants were also able to walk the virtual red carpet and receive a "people's choice award" from the camp's private Instagram participants for best dressed during the livestreamed event.

## Impact

When I liberate myself, I *liberate others*. If you don't speak out, ain't nobody going to speak out for you.

—FANNIE LOU HAMER

Liberation, joy, and authentic voices were focal points of the Black Girls Film Camp. These words, thoughts, and actions resonated throughout the weekly camp sessions and were portrayed through the girls' films. One strength of the camp was the liberating and supportive environment. The girls were surrounded by supportive Black women mentors, editors, and guest speakers. This environment reassured the girls that they were supported and that their voices would be heard and honored. The camp's goal was to provide a safe space for Black girls to express creatively what Black girlhood meant to them and to develop creatively as filmmakers. Ladson-Billings (1995) argues that only Black women can truly understand what it means to be Black women, and their experiences and conversations with each other are the basis for their knowledge claims.

Black women construct meaning from experiences of self-discovery and self-definition (Muhammed and Haddix 2016). The impactful, liberating experiences from the Black Girls Film Camp will leave a lasting impression on the girls. This camp encompassed Black girl magic as it showcased and celebrated the unique experiences that Black girls share, along with their brilliance. The films created by the participants are available to view at www.blackgirlsfilmcamp.com.

## 9.3: GIRLS ON THE BEAT @ CHARLESTON COUNTY PUBLIC LIBRARY
by Darcy Coover

Girls on the Beat is a summer journalism camp for girls in grades 6 through 12 from the Charleston, South Carolina area. Led by women working in the field, the camp's attendees learn about journalism from the ground up, including print, broadcast, and web-based media. They explore the tenets of accurate, fact-based reporting; practice identifying unbiased, informative pieces; and engage in group activities—all with a special focus on the particular challenges faced by women in journalism. The program's leaders have included local print and broadcast journalists, investigative reporters, photojournalists, news editors, social media managers, and more. The attendees range from 12 to 18 years old and come from all over Charleston County. Their home communities range from urban neighborhoods in downtown Charleston and North Charleston to the more rural areas of the county.

Girls on the Beat was held twice during the summer of 2019: at Charleston County Public Library's (CCPL's) Main Library in downtown Charleston and again at the Wando Mount Pleasant branch, which serves suburban and rural communities in the northern part of the county. The camp was highly successful in engaging young women to think critically about journalism and the way that information is presented to the public. Each day featured one or two local journalists from news organizations in the Charleston metro area. These journalists guided the attendees through introductions to their particular fields, shared activities and exercises to help the attendees explore things in more depth, and answered questions about what it's like to work in the media.

On the last day of the camp, the participants enjoyed a hands-on day where they worked in small groups to produce a print or broadcast news piece, with the guidance and assistance of the journalists.

## Day 1: Journalism 101 and Photojournalism

The participants spent the first half of day 1 learning about the basic tenets of professional journalism from a local news anchor and discussing the power for change that quality reporting can have. They were presented with a selection of real broadcast pieces to analyze as examples, and they learned about basic story structure, how to anticipate the questions that the public will have about a topic, and how to use clear and concise writing to present information in a straightforward manner.

The participants spent the second half of day 1 with a local photojournalist, who spoke to them about the impact that visual media can have in telling a story. They studied news photographs and learned about both the events behind them and the effort involved in getting the perfect shot. The journalist in question spent a great deal of time covering the Mother Emanuel shooting and the arrest and trial of Dylann Roof, so the young women had a chance to ask questions and learn about what it takes for a professional photojournalist to cover events in a way that communicates the emotional experience of the people involved.

## Day 2: Investigative Journalism and Digital Journalism

After covering the basics on day 1, the participants worked with a local investigative journalist to learn about the importance of engaging with their communities to find the stories that are important to them. They learned how to conduct research using online and government resources, as well as how to construct investigative interviews with members of the public and with subject experts. Through a series of group activities, they practiced using digitized government records to find information and draw reasonable conclusions about hypothetical topics. The participants also viewed a number of news stories and identified ways in which the language used might create viewer bias surrounding the subjects.

Later on day 2, the participants met with the digital engagement editor of the local newspaper to learn about how a news organization works to make sure the public is engaged with the work being produced by journalists. They discussed digital marketing, journalism in the age of social media, and the way that news stories are visually packaged and presented to the public in an era of smart devices and constant connectivity.

## Day 3: Broadcast Journalism

Participants spent a full day learning about broadcast journalism with a former news reporter and weekend anchor who now works for CCPL. She walked them through a typical day for a news reporter acting as a "one-woman band" in the field; that is, conceiving of, researching, filming, and editing a piece from beginning to end. The participants learned about the different parts of a broadcast news segment and practiced presenting and interviewing on camera after writing sample scripts and questions. They also learned some rudimentary film editing techniques and got some insight into how editing can shape the public's perception of a story.

## Day 4: Features Writing and Sports Journalism

To learn more about more niche fields of journalism, participants spent day 4 first with the features editor of the local newspaper and then with a sports reporter from a local news station. Though these two fields are of course very different, both speakers provided additional insight into the ways that the participants might translate their personal passions and interests into a career in journalism. The features editor began her career as a news clerk and worked her way up through the ranks over the years, and so she had an incredible wealth of experience to share with the participants about different types of print media jobs. The sports reporter has worked for a number of years in what has traditionally been a very male-dominated field, and she had some great insights to share about working in an industry where one might find oneself in the minority.

## Day 5: Hands-on Projects

Participants began with a Skype chat with national correspondents Christine Brennan and Soledad O'Brien, and then spent a hands-on day working on the project of their choice—either a broadcast news segment or a written article. Both Brennan and O'Brien had incredible insights to offer the participants about the trajectory of their own careers, the challenges they've faced, and the impact they've tried to have with their work. The girls were energized about spending the rest of the day working on their projects—about half of them created a news broadcast segment, and the other half worked on written articles, all focusing on events occurring in and around the library that day. A number of CCPL staff members who are former journalists came to help the participants get started on their stories, assist them with technical issues, and provide editing help after their pieces were complete. Each participant was able to leave the camp with a polished piece of work that showcased what she had learned over the week of lectures, discussions, and activities.

## Pandemic Plans

In 2020, the COVID-19 pandemic forced the Girls on the Beat program into the virtual realm, which presented both challenges and new opportunities. While attendance was limited to those young adults with access to a device and an internet connection, it did provide the opportunity to include attendees and presenters from outside of the Charleston metro area. The program followed the same basic outline as in 2019, but the participants got to have some unique experiences that were not possible before. For example, they were able to take virtual studio tours with a number of news anchors from different stations, giving them a behind-the-scenes look at what working in a news studio is like. The usual hands-on day was replaced with a lesson on using free apps and other resources to record and edit interview and news pieces, and the participants were encouraged to find a local story in their own community that they could safely report on in the midst of the pandemic.

## CONCLUSION

The aim of Girls on the Beat was to familiarize young adults with the various career options open to them in the field of journalism and to highlight for girls in particular the challenges that women have historically faced in this profession. However, we found that a secondary outcome was the incredibly thorough knowledge the participants gained about how the media packages and presents information to the public. The insights they gleaned from working with professional journalists over the course of the week allowed them to look at the media they consume in new ways and to analyze the information they take in with a new eye toward accuracy and potential bias.

### REFERENCES

Brinkman, Britney G., Samantha Marino, and Lauren Manning. 2018. "Relationships Are the Heart of the Work: Mentoring Relationships within Gender-Responsive Programs for Black Girls." *Journal of Feminist Family Therapy* 30 (4): 191–213.

Cayleff, Susan, Melissann Herron, Chelsea Cormier, Sarah Wheeler, Alicia Chávez-Arteaga, Jessica Spain, and Cristina Dominguez. 2011. "Oral History and 'Girls' Voices': The Young Women's Studies Club as a Site of Empowerment." *Journal of International Women's Studies* 12 (4): 22.

Charlotte Mecklenburg Library. 2018. "About ImaginOn." www.imaginon.org/about-imaginon.

Collins, Patricia Hill. 1995. *Black Feminist Thought: Knowledge, Consciousness, and the Politics of Empowerment.* New York: Routledge.

Crenshaw, Kimberlé, Priscilla Ocen, and Jyoti Nanda. 2015. "Black Girls Matter: Pushed Out, Overpoliced, and Underprotected." African American Policy Forum and Center for Intersectionality and Social Policy Studies at Columbia Law School. www.atlanticphilanthropies.org/wp-content/uploads/2015/09/BlackGirlsMatter_Report.pdf.

Epstein, Rebecca, Jamilia Blake, and Thalia González. 2017. "Girlhood Interrupted: The Erasure of Black Girls' Childhood." Georgetown Law Center on Poverty and Inequality. www.law.georgetown.edu/poverty-inequality-center/wp-content/uploads/sites/14/2017/08/girlhood-interrupted.pdf.

Flake, Ebony. 2017. "As #BlackGirlMagic Turns Four Years Old, CaShawn Thompson Has a Fresh Word for All the Magical Black Girls." Blavity, February 12. https://blavity.com/as-blackgirlmagic-turns-four-years-old-cashawn thompson-has-a-fresh-word-for-all-the-magical-black-girls?category1 =trending&category2=news.

Johnson, Joseph. 2021. "U.S. Children & Teens' Daily Screen Time COVID-19 2020." Statista, May 6. www.statista.com/statistics/1189204/us-teens-children -screen-time-daily-coronavirus-before-during/.

Jones, Sosanya Marie. 2021. "Not by Magic: Perspectives on Creating and Facilitating Outreach Programs for Black Girls and Women." *Journal of African American Women and Girls in Education* 1 (1). doi: https://doi.org/10.21423/ jaawge-v1i1a25.

Ladson-Billings, Gloria. 1995. "Toward a Theory of Culturally Relevant Pedagogy." *American Educational Research Journal* 32 (3): 46.

Livingston, Gretchen. 2020. "The Way U.S. Teens Spend Their Time Is Changing, but Differences between Boys and Girls Persist." Pew Research Center. www.pewresearch.org/fact-tank/2019/02/20/the-way-u-s-teens-spend -their-time-is-changing-but-differences-between-boys-and-girls-persist/.

Muhammad, Gholnecsar E., and Marcelle Haddix. 2016. "Centering Black Girls' Literacies: A Review of Literature on the Multiple Ways of Knowing of Black Girls." *English Education* 48 (4): 299–336.

Price-Dennis, Detra, Gholnecsar E. Muhammad, Erica Womack, Sherell A. McArthur, and Marcelle Haddix. 2017. "The Multiple Identities and Literacies of Black Girlhood: A Conversation about Creating Spaces for Black Girl Voices." *Journal of Language and Literacy Education* 13 (2): 1–18.

Weiston-Serdan, Torie. 2017. *Critical Mentoring: A Practical Guide.* Sterling, VA: Stylus.

Women and Hollywood. 2021. "2020 Statistics." https://womenandhollywood .com/resources/statistics/2020-statistics/.

# Bridges, Tunnels, and City CONNECTIONS
## Social Media, Information, and News Literacy

In a world of complex threats, our security and leadership depend on all elements of our *power*—including strong and principled diplomacy.

—**BARACK OBAMA,** 2014 State of the Union Address

**One notion that is certain is that the world and humans survive on** information. Around the world, information and technology literacy inequities exist in areas with high poverty and limited access to technology. The United States is not an exception. The possession of both physical access to technology and information literacy skills is now a necessity for those attending higher education institutions and entering the workforce. The term *information literacy* was coined in 1974 by Paul Zurkowski and was adopted by library professionals with the seal of approval from the American Library Association in 1989. Information literacy is the ability to distinguish fact from opinion and to analyze content or messaging (Gunton et al. 2014). Information literacy proficiency in the twenty-first century also involves knowing how to search and locate information on devices, and evaluate the quality, perspectives, and factuality of the sources. The need for media literacy education has assumed increasing urgency in the political sphere with the spread of mis- and disinformation during the COVID-19 pandemic. While the circulation of misinformation has intensified in recent years, its reach and seriousness reached new heights during the pandemic, and in the

**161**

aftermath of the 2020 presidential election. Alternative facts and false claims—and the confusion and distrust they spread—have not only undermined the health measures taken by the public in response to the pandemic, but they also have now begun to threaten the very foundations of democratic government itself in the United States.

Given the global impact of social media on news and information-sharing, the role of educators in teaching media and information literacy skills has become more urgent (Gretter and Yadav 2016). In 2013, UNESCO proposed media information literacy (MIL) for citizens as a required competency for living in an informative global society. *Media information literacy* is an umbrella term created by UNESCO that joins *media literacy* with *information literacy* while emphasizing the importance of critical analytical skills (Wilson et al. 2013). In this framework, UNESCO highlights the importance of computing technologies for media and information literacy in today's globalized and connected world. Media and information literacy also aligns with media creation and is contingent upon knowing certain basic skills, such as how to download content from the internet, how to send e-mails from mobile devices, and how to share MP3 music files. Some additional media and information literacy skills are needed to thrive in a post-truth era, such as knowing how to access credible news posts on social media and how to collaborate in online communities. In this chapter, we will profile several programs and case studies that have been carried out with teens in the areas of social media and information and news literacy.

## 10.1: THE JOURNALISTIC LEARNING INITIATIVE
by Ed Madison, Ross C. Anderson, and Rachel Guldin

Libraries can cultivate curiosity, strengthen college and career readiness, and prepare students for democratic participation. However, librarians and their teacher-colleagues can sometimes feel ill-equipped to implement media literacy programming with urban teens. Better preparation is critical during our current highly politicized era, when truth and trust in public institutions are questioned. Politicians' attacks on mainstream media intensify confusion. These issues have added urgency to the need to develop youths' writing proficiency, as well as their information and digital literacy skills. Students are intrinsically motivated to write about current events and their lived experiences, an inherent characteristic of journalism. Using a journalistic learning approach can inspire and empower teens to become agents of meaningful discourse and social change, while also developing their writing and information literacy skills (Guldin, Madison, and Anderson 2021).

The approach *journalistic learning* was designed collaboratively by a University of Oregon research team based on the observations of innovative educators at Palo Alto High School (Madison 2012 and 2015) and has been developed, researched, and refined in diverse secondary schools in recent years (Madison, Anderson, and Bousselot 2019). The Journalistic Learning Initiative (JLI) is a research-based media literacy and writing program that aims to empower teen voices, encourage self-directed learning, foster a love of writing, develop respectful discourse, and strengthen news literacy skills through research and production. The JLI approach aims to engage underrepresented teens' *voices*, build *agency*, produce original *publications*, and foster *reflection*.

## Why Integrate Journalism?

The practice of *journalism* might itself have become a source of controversy in the current political climate. Social media, memes, fake news, and viral videos are just some of the rapid and disruptive changes to the media landscape that are fragmenting audiences and flooding our devices with unvetted news and information. But it's not all bad news: despite imperfections, journalism remains remarkably resilient (Madison and DeJarnette 2018). Journalists maintain a constitutionally protected watchdog role in society that is designed to help the public make sense of the world and keep political power in check.

Youth-produced publications are ubiquitous in secondary schools. They have empowered thousands of young people to find and express their voices and have provided youth with opportunities to develop the communication skills that are vital for any career path. Student journalists learn to develop and defend story ideas; approach and interview experts and unsung heroes; and research, write, edit, and publish their discoveries.

Youth with publication experience earn better grades and test scores in high school and college than their peers (Dvorak and Choi 2009); first-year college students with prior high school publication experience outperform their peers in writing (Dvorak 1988); and journalism students are known to make fewer errors in their writing than AP English and honors students (Blinn 1982). Outside of traditional journalism classes in high school, our research found that journalistic learning experiences integrated into other content areas may provide some of those same benefits to a broader group of students.

Unfortunately, only a small percentage of students take elective journalism courses in high school. Opportunities and access to these courses are limited in many schools. However, public libraries and school libraries can support students' participation in journalistic learning outside a standard publication structure.

## What Is the Journalistic Learning Initiative?

At its heart, a journalistic learning approach aims to empower student voices, encourage self-directed learning, foster a love of writing as a tool for respectful discourse and evidence-based perspective-taking, and improve academic engagement and outcomes. Now entering its sixth year, the Journalistic Learning Initiative (JLI) currently works with educators and students in eighteen secondary schools in Oregon and California. The JLI approach was piloted at a middle school in a conservative, rural Oregon community after the 2016 presidential election. Since then, the process has been adapted to different contexts, including large and diverse middle and high schools in Los Angeles and San Jose, California.

In designing the JLI framework, researchers modified a successful journalism program's methodology to support historically underserved and rural schools and students in Oregon and California, with the intent of spreading these resources nationwide. Traditional secondary-school journalism courses are often electives. By contrast, the JLI program can be embedded in English language arts and social studies courses or modified for non-classroom settings. Journalistic learning makes use of new yet accessible digital technologies. Librarians can collaborate with teachers or modify the journalistic learning approach to fit library electives or after-school programming.

Very little of the youths' writing produced in the JLI program resembles the campus-focused student news publications found in many secondary schools. Journalistic learning engages youth who may be classified as "reluctant" readers and writers by tapping their intrinsic interests and providing them with a sense of purpose to effect positive change in their communities. In teams, youth originate and research topics ranging from their personal interests to social justice themes. The approach harnesses students' natural curiosity in order to engage them in complex subjects and the writing craft. The youth practice information literacy and research skills by identifying and engaging with news texts, assessing their credibility, and identifying information gaps and missing perspectives in them.

Using JLI's framework, educators coach students to identify and invite community experts to engage in live interviews, either in-person or via videoconferencing. The interviews have included scientists, doctors, veterans, artists, activists, thought leaders, world-class athletes, and local heroes. The youth develop their oral communication and note-taking skills, and learn to synthesize their findings by writing and editing articles. Teens further develop their digital literacy by using word-processing software and online platforms, like blogs or the school or library's website, to publish their pieces so that authentic audiences can access and read them; this is a critical component of the program (Madison 2012 and 2015). Journalistic learning provides flexibility as well—students' writings can vary in length and include audiovisual components, like photographs or explainer videos. The JLI approach emphasizes analysis, criticism, and production in developing news, information, and digital literacy.

## What Is the JLI Core Framework?

A four-year process of research and development established the JLI framework. The four quadrants emphasize *voice, agency, publication,* and *reflection.* (See figure 10.1.) *Voice* acknowledges that students have perspectives that matter; students acquire and exhibit *agency* when they realize that their voices can influence others; *publication* amplifies their influence with authentic audiences; and *reflection* completes the process by expanding awareness, exploring the significance, and interpreting

FIGURE 10.1
**JLI Core Framework**

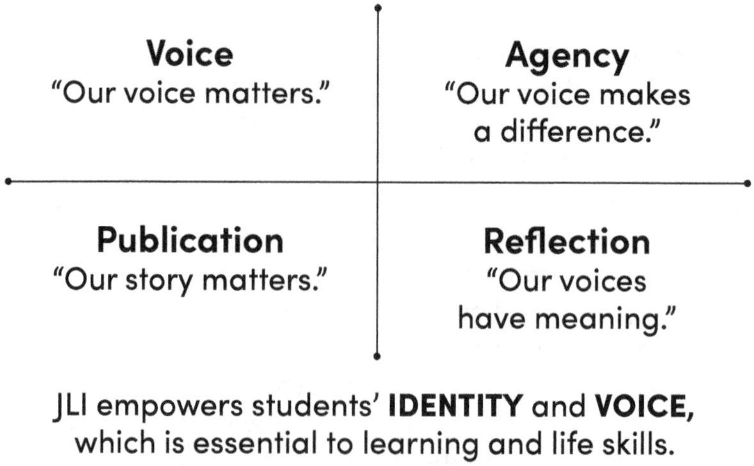

| | |
|---|---|
| **Voice** <br> "Our voice matters." | **Agency** <br> "Our voice makes <br> a difference." |
| **Publication** <br> "Our story matters." | **Reflection** <br> "Our voices <br> have meaning." |

JLI empowers students' **IDENTITY** and **VOICE**,
which is essential to learning and life skills.

Source: 2021 Journalistic Learning Ventures

meaning. Publication is a critical aspect because youth bring forth their best effort when their work reaches an authentic audience (Madison 2012 and 2015).

The JLI framework provides a philosophical lens designed to inform rather than restrict student learning. Its principles ensure that youth complete a journalistic learning experience with confidence, skills, pride in their work and its impact, and a greater understanding of how they can think, process, and write about challenging issues. In a school setting, the approach can inform and supplement the existing curriculum; in a community setting, the method can be modified to reflect patrons' needs and interests.

## Where Has Journalistic Learning Worked?

After its pilot in rural Oregon schools, a developmental evaluation of the JLI program revealed that students perceived improvements in areas related to their willingness, interest, and ability to use journalistic research and writing as a means of empowerment. Students reported that their self-direction, intrinsic motivation, state of flow in learning, and self-efficacy in writing improved with journalistic learning. They also reported improved critical thinking about issues, improved perspective-taking of others, and improved relational support from educators and peers. Importantly, students' sense of agency and empowerment to share their voices with the world and become agents of change did not just happen because they were given a chance. The results of the work reveal that students must feel capable, respected, and supported while developing the thinking and social-emotional skills to carefully approach sensitive and complex topics and respect the different perspectives of others.

In a later study of the JLI program carried out at an urban school, Latinx students in a socioeconomically isolated Los Angeles middle school dove into their journalistic learning experience with a passion for social justice topics, including immigration, racism, gun violence, and LGBTQ rights. A recent study found that students gained a much greater awareness of issues that affected their community and the world (Guldin, Madison, and Anderson 2021). They developed and published stories to share with their community. Many students reported a greater sense of agency to effect positive change by critically thinking and writing about seemingly intractable challenges. Journalistic learning encouraged students to research and write on issues and topics that resonated with their interests, life experiences, and cultural perspectives. The experience demonstrated promise for empowering young people with new understanding and writing skills to initiate and contribute to respectful discourse. JLI is currently developing and piloting Effective Communicators, a new journalistic learning course.

The journalistic learning approach can be adapted to fit programmatically with the goals and resources of public libraries and school libraries that aim to empower student voices and engage their critical thinking and literacy skills with local and global issues. It can develop students' sense of purpose and possibility in their research and writing.

## Resources for More Information

- Journalistic Learning website (www.JournalisticLearning.com)
- JLI Facebook (www.facebook.com/journalisticlearning)
- JLI Instagram (www.instagram.com/journalisticlearning)

- JLI Twitter (www.twitter.com/journlearning)
- Contact JLI with questions at info@journalisticlearning.com.

## 10.2: AN INTRODUCTORY LESSON PLAN IN NEWS MEDIA LITERACY FOR YA LIBRARIANS
by Michael A. Spikes

"Like drinking from a firehose" is a common phrase used to describe the task of trying to make sense out of all the different types of media that are created, shared, and consumed online. Many teenagers spend large parts of their time online, consuming, creating, and curating media content on social media (Auxier and Anderson 2021). While misinformation and disinformation—terms for false information that is spread without and with the intent to mislead, respectively (Wardle and Derakhshan 2017)—take up much of the current conversations about the use of media online, it is even more important for young people to understand the effects of media messages, the intentions of their practitioners, and the responsibilities that come along with sharing information with large groups of people. This section will outline a lesson adapted from a model of news media literacy, developed by the Center for News Literacy at Stony Brook University, and will briefly discuss the use of the lesson with various practitioners, who then customized it for use with young people. To do so, we will first discuss news media literacy as a learning domain, then outline the particular lesson's objectives, and outline the skills that lead students to proficiency with those objectives, by presenting sample activities with suggestions for adaptation. The section includes a lesson plan with online links to resources that provide additional information for engagement with different audiences. Readers are encouraged to review these resources while reading this section. The resources are also suggested for use with young people to better engage with the concepts covered in the lesson.

## Background

*News media literacy* (NML; also known as news literacy) is a subdiscipline of media literacy that focuses on building critical media-viewing skills and knowledge by using the lens of journalism (Ashley 2019; Tully et al. 2021). In doing so, it teaches students how to distinguish news as a product of journalism among different genres of media, how to verify claims with evidence, and how to evaluate sources of information, among other skills, by using news media as a platform for both modeling these skills and practicing them. A major objective of NML is to drive regular, active engagement of news media content with real-time evaluation through a process of "deconstruction"—in which media messages are continually analyzed for their veracity during consumption (Hornik et al. 2018; Spikes and Haque 2014).

In various learning environments, NML has been used to build the skills that students need in order to counter the effects of mis- and disinformation. The approach highlighted in the lesson emphasizes a constructivist approach, which builds skills and knowledge by utilizing learners' previous knowledge and everyday experiences as part of the process of learning (Johnson 2009; Zittoun and Brinkmann 2012).

## NML Lesson: Know Your Neighborhood

The concepts covered in this lesson, "Know Your Neighborhood," are adapted from a model of NML that comes from the Center for News Literacy, a nonprofit organization based at Stony Brook University that has been building and distributing NML learning materials since 2007. The lesson has been used in classrooms from the primary to the postsecondary level in schools and universities, along with libraries, both public and academic. The lesson provides an introduction to NML by presenting the challenges that today's consumers of news and information face, followed by techniques for distinguishing different "information neighborhoods"; that is, the genres of media in which information may be distributed. For an example of how different "information neighborhoods" are distinguished, we can look at the differences between a YouTube video that demonstrates the use of a product that is produced and posted by the company that made the product, and a video review (again distributed on YouTube) of the same product that comes from an outlet that conducts product reviews independently, such as Consumer Reports. In this example, the first video would be identified as a promotional piece for the company, and the second, as a piece of news. These distinctions are defined in the taxonomy of information neighborhoods provided in the online resources at the end of this section.

Highlighted in this lesson are the ways in which the lines between media genres may blur, creating amalgams of media that borrow from the techniques of other genres in order to deliver a message, which make the intentions of the creator unclear to the viewer. Consider the contemporary genre of "infotainment," a media genre that blends the presentational style of entertainment with the perceived importance of news (Lilleker 2006, as cited in Thussu 2007). Television programs such as *Last Week Tonight* and *Full Frontal with Samantha Bee* are prominent examples of infotainment, in that they use current events information as material for satire and assert opinions in the service of creating a show that is entertaining and current. These programs provide viewers who would not otherwise tune into a news program with an entertaining approach to learning about current events. However, from an NML perspective, it is important for the viewers of these kinds of programs to obtain their knowledge of current events from more independent sources before finding themselves being persuaded toward the particular framing of an issue by a captivating and humorous presenter.

Past uses of this lesson in libraries have included adapting the taxonomy of information neighborhoods (see the online resources at the end of this section) into a printed form for reference use by students. These printed forms have included small cards with the different genres that were passed to students and then used as reference as part of a media genre identification game. Another use of the taxonomy has been in poster form for public use; this is an easy-to-use resource for determining when the lines blur between media genres and what to be aware of. Yet another use of this lesson has been as part of online LibGuides that have presented basic media literacy skills to patrons along with tools in an easy-to-follow format (see the online resources for an example).

Young adult librarians are encouraged to review the lesson and resources and think of ways that they may be able to customize parts of it to engage patrons—especially those in formal library programming, where librarians deliver information, or facilitate discussion or activity among the group—in ways that draw on their existing knowledge and experiences. Examples of this may include noticing that a young patron frequently posts replies to posts from the library's Instagram or other social media channels, or asking about young people's general use of social media. You may wish to post questions such as "Where do you get your information?" or "What's a piece of information you used to complete a goal today?" These can help students think about their own information-seeking needs and their dispositions toward them.

Another suggestion is to make connections to the uses of media in fiction, such as the use of broadcasting battles between teenagers in *The Hunger Games*, the hugely popular young adult fiction series that deals with issues involving media effects, similar to those introduced as part of the lesson on information neighborhoods (for further details, see *Media Literacy in the Library* in the online resources at the end of this section).

In conclusion, it is important to consider that while this lesson can lead to greater confidence in one's use of media and news, it is far from being the only tool that a person needs to understand the confusing and overwhelming media environment that we find ourselves in. Librarians are encouraged to continue thinking of themselves not only as professionals who help guide patrons through the uses of their library's collections but also as "information navigators" who can play a vital role in helping patrons gain a better understanding of their own uses of different media and information, both in library spaces and beyond.

## ELEMENT TYPES FOR DESIGN

### Lesson Outline: Introduction to News Media Literacy/ Information Neighborhoods

NOTE: See the online resources at the end of this section for supplemental material and the slide presentation.

### Essential Question

What are the challenges in getting information, and how do I distinguish sources?

### Introduction to NML Learning Objectives

- Identify the four (4) main challenges of our new information age (provided in the slide presentation in the online resources).

*(cont'd)*

*Elements Types of Design (cont'd)*

### Information Neighborhoods Learning Objectives
- Identify the five (5) information neighborhoods presented in the lesson.
- Explain the characteristics of each of the 5 information neighborhoods.
- Describe the three traits that define journalism as explained in the course (verification, independence, and accountability).
- Apply the three traits of journalism to a specific event or story.

FIGURE 10.2
## Lesson Vocabulary

| News Media Literacy Lesson | Associated Vocabulary |
|---|---|
| Introduction to News Literacy | • filter failure<br>• publisher/consumers<br>• reliability<br>• information overload<br>• informed action<br>• reliable news<br>• blurring of the lines<br>• news literacy |
| Information Neighborhoods | • advertising<br>• promotion<br>• raw information<br>• open platform<br>• reverse image search<br>• influencers<br>• propaganda<br>• verification<br>• independence<br>• accountability |

## Delivering the Lesson: Understanding the Challenges of the Digital Age

1. Introduce students to the four major challenges in the information age (see the slides in the resources section), but focus on blurring of the lines. Ask students to summarize the meaning of "blurring of the lines."
2. Introduce definition of *news literacy*—briefly discuss reliability and credibility.
   a. Ask students to define *reliability*.
   b. Ask students to define *credibility*.

## Delivering the Lesson: Identifying Information Neighborhoods and Their Characteristics

Beginning the lesson:

1. Use different pieces of media, including a Twitter post, a Facebook post, and a Google search, and the students to ink-pair-share what they would do with each of the pieces. Give them 2 minutes to compose their thoughts and 2 minutes to share their thoughts with a partner.
   a. Bring the students back together and do a whole-class sharing of thoughts. Highlight parallels and patterns in the students' thoughts.
   b. Transition to information neighborhoods.

2. Introduce students to the information neighborhoods
   a. Hand out the taxonomy of information neighborhoods.
   b. Ask students to define the neighborhoods' characteristics.
      i. Highlight an example and how it aligns with the criteria that place it in a category. Engage students in a full-group discussion of how the example might "blur" the lines between categories.
   c. Have students then go back to the initial media examples presented at the beginning of the lesson and define the category of media they belong to by identifying the goal, methods, creators, and intended outcome of one of the examples.

Have the students in groups work out the example's characteristics. 5–7 minutes.

3. Introduce the definition of *news/journalism*.
   a. Ask students to define verification, independence, and ac-
      countability (VIA).
   b. Hand out the new taxonomy.
   c. Using a piece of preselected media, ask students to identify
      if it meets VIA. Reengage with the topics and definitions as
      needed. If time permits, have the students find their own
      piece of media, and apply VIA to it.

## Online Resources

- Taxonomy of Information Neighborhoods: https://bit.ly/
  nlinfoneighborhoods2
- Google Slides Deck: https://bit.ly/33c4NWc
- Note Taking & Assignment Worksheet: https://bit.ly/3vEN85w
- Supplemental Video Lesson: http://drc.centerfornewsliteracy.org/
  content/know-your-neighborhood-part-1
- Huntsville-Madison County Public Library Online LibGuide:
  https://guides.hmcpl.org/c.php?g=790569&p=5656591
- "Media Landscape and Economics," in *Media Literacy in the
  Library: A Guide for Library Practitioners*, 16–19: www.ala.org/tools/
  sites/ala.org.tools/programming/medialiteracy

## 10.3: ANALYZING THE NEWS THROUGH INFOGRAPHICS
by Mark J. Davis

The Barrington Public Schools district (in Rhode Island) has invested in
library and media spaces with highly certified teachers in each of its six
buildings. At the Barrington Middle School, there is a two-story Library
Media Center that includes a makerspace with prototyping tools and
a global classroom with advanced videoconferencing. The Barrington
Public Library and the school library department frequently collaborate
on community projects.

Students at Barrington Middle School are divided into clusters for grades 6 through 8. The curriculum is unique by offering frequent cross-curricular collaboration between teaching teams and specialists. Media literacy is embedded in all subjects and is facilitated by partners, including the library media specialist and library assistant, the digital literacy teacher, the video production teacher, and the physical education and health department teachers. The goal is to ensure that all students will receive frequent opportunities to engage in contextualized media literacy learning.

Students were engaged in units focusing on digital citizenship skills involving news and media literacy informed by the Common Sense Media curriculum. The students discussed propaganda in the news, commercials, and printed publications. The entire learning community frequently engages in facilitated dialogue around the social issues emphasized in media literacy. The district's goal is to design culturally responsive teaching units to engage in challenging conversations around race, gender, and related social issues.

## Successes and Challenges Experienced

All classrooms established norms around respectful attitudes, responsible statements supported by evidence, and equal opportunities to voice ideas. A protocol for drawing attention to violations of the norms consists of nonverbal cues, facilitated dialogue between teachers and students, and careful resolution of uncomfortable statements.

Families are notified of the lesson and the norms prior to the start of the curriculum. Although most of them are supportive, occasional incidents of disapproval are expressed in private settings. Anecdotal investigations demonstrated that some parents were concerned about skewed faculty perspectives and the possibility of suppressed viewpoints. In response, the lessons were observed by media researchers and educational and media consultants, and they were discussed with the school administration. The collective determination was that the district was taking a proactive approach that encouraged multiple perspectives and equity for divergent opinions.

One notable lesson was focused on the production of narrative infographics. The intention was to have students collect data and produce an infographic poster with a specific perspective. The goal for students was to use what they learned in the previous lessons about propaganda and apply it to a new visual medium. Writing through narrative infographics would enable the students to focus their attention on captivating a reader while incorporating data literacy.

The topic of data literacy was unpacked through a series of examinations of existing narrative infographics. Students worked in a think-pair-share activity using multiple examples of infographics. Throughout the paired discussions, the students analyzed the characteristics of an infographic using simple, self-selected codes. The resulting codes were shared with the whole class and discussed. At the end of the discussion, a simple rubric for evaluating the depth of infographic design was created. The rubric would be used for guidance in the independent creation of a narrative infographic researched data.

Students learned to use an online infographic design program and imported their research into data visualizations. The teacher addressed different forms of data visuals and their purpose in order to add greater comprehension to the task. The students produced drafts of their narrative infographics and submitted them digitally for peer review. Each student gave three students anonymous feedback about their design informed by the class-created rubric.

Revisions of the narrative infographics were completed by students, and then copies of the infographics were printed for public display. Students invited other teachers, peers, and their families to a gallery showcase of their work. A plan was in place to use augmented reality to embed an author's introduction with each infographic, but this idea was tabled for future lessons to minimize the bias of the author regarding design choices.

The response to the infographic unit was overwhelmingly positive. Students expressed pride and empowerment stemming from the creation process. Teachers were impressed with the depth and perspective of students, as well as their willingness to demonstrate evidence and analysis for challenging topics. Families were impressed with the creativity and craftsmanship of the students. Consequently, differentiated forms of the lessons continue to be incorporated into a content-area curriculum.

## How the Program Can Be Replicated by Teen Librarians

The curriculum used existing and self-created resources to complete the lessons. The most supportive material involved the Mind Over Media (www.mindovermedia.us) text and companion resources. Mind Over Media's author, Renee Hobbs, provides practical lessons that develop rapport with students, mini-lessons for unpacking multiple modes of media, and lessons that connect to the contemporary world. The visual aids were curated from public sites, including the Internet Archive (https://archive.org/details/classic_tv_commercials_emperor), iSpot.tv (www.ispot.tv/browse), and YouTube.com.

The development of infographic instructional resources required connecting numerous sources together. One resource worth highlighting is Nicole Edwards's infographic unit designed for the Educating for Democracy in the Digital Age (EDDA) organization. Edwards's "Analyzing and Creating Infographics" curriculum map (http://eddaoakland.org/analyzing-and-creating-infographics/) outlines an adaptable practice for teaching adolescents. Librarians should also consider "School Library Infographics: How to Create Them, Why to Use Them," by Peggy Milam Creighton, for context and resources. A number of online resources for designing infographics are available with both free and paid subscriptions, including Piktochart (www.piktochart.com), Infogram (www.infogram.com), and Visme (www.visme.co).

REFERENCES

Ashley, Seth. 2019. "News Literacies." In *The International Encyclopedia of Media Literacy*, edited by Tim P. Vos, Folker Hanusch, Dimitra Dimitrakopoulou, Margaretha Geertsema-Sligh, and Annika Sehl, 1–11. Wiley Online Library. https://doi.org/10.1002/9781118978238.ieml0173.

Auxier, Brooke, and Monica Anderson. 2021. "Social Media Use in 2021." Pew Research Center. www.pewresearch.org/internet/2021/04/07/social-media -use-in-2021/.

Blinn, J. R. 1982. "A Comparison of Selected Writing Skills of High School Journalism and Non-Journalism Students." Ohio University.

Dvorak, Jack. 1988. "High School Publications Experience as a Factor in College-Level Writing." *Journalism Quarterly* 65 (2): 392–98. https://doi.org/10.1177/107769908806500219.

Dvorak, Jack, and Changhee Choi. 2009. "High School Journalism, Academic Performance Correlate." *Newspaper Research Journal* 30 (3): 75–89.

Gretter, Sarah, and Aman Yadav. 2016. "Computational Thinking and Media & Information Literacy: An Integrated Approach to Teaching Twenty-First Century Skills." *TechTrends* 60 (5): 510–16. https://doi.org/10.1007/s11528-016-0098-4.

Guldin, R., E. Madison, and R. Anderson. 2021. "Writing for Social Justice: Journalistic Strategies for Catalyzing Agentic Engagement among Latinx Middle School Students." *Journal of Media Literacy Education* 13 (2): 71–85. https://doi.org/10.23860/JMLE-2021-13-2-6.

Gunton, Lyndelle, Christine Bruce, and Kate Davis. 2014. "Information Literacy Research: The Evolution of the Relational Approach." In *Library and Information Science Research in Asia-Oceania: Theory and Practice,* edited by Jia Tina Du, Qinghua Zhu, and Andy Koronios, 82–101. Hershey, PA: IGI Global. https://doi.org/10.4018/978-1-4666-5158-6.ch006.

Hornik, R., J. Anzalone, and M. A. Spikes. 2018. "GetNewsSmart: A Guide to Understanding the Key Concepts of News Literacy." Center for News Literacy, Stony Brook University. https://bit.ly/382PbHP.

Johnson, G. M. 2009. "Instructionism and Constructivism: Reconciling Two Very Good Ideas." *International Journal of Special Education* 24 (3): 90–98.

Madison, Ed. 2012. "Journalistic Learning: Rethinking and Redefining Language Arts Curricula." University of Oregon.

———. 2015. *Newsworthy: Cultivating Critical Thinkers, Readers, and Writers in Language Arts Classrooms.* New York: Teachers College Press.

Madison, Ed, Ross Anderson, and Tracy Bousselot. 2019. "Self-Determined to Write: Leveraging Interest, Collaboration and Self-Direction through a Journalistic Approach." *Reading & Writing Quarterly* 35 (5): 473–95.

Madison, Ed, and Ben DeJarnette. 2018. *Reimagining Journalism in a Post-Truth World: How Late-Night Comedians, Internet Trolls, and Savvy Reporters Are Transforming News.* Santa Barbara, CA: ABC-CLIO.

Spikes, Michael A., and Yousuf S. Haque. 2014. "A Case Study Combining Online Social Media and Video to Teach News Literacy." *Journal of Educational Technology Systems* 43 (1): 99–116. https://doi.org/10.2190/ET.43.1.g.

Thussu, Daya Kishan. 2007. *News as Entertainment: The Rise of Global Infotainment.* London: Sage.

Tully, Melissa, Adam Maksl, Seth Ashley, Emily K. Vraga, and Stephanie Craft. 2021. "Defining and Conceptualizing News Literacy." *Journalism* (April). https://doi.org/10.1177/14648849211005888.

Wardle, Claire, and Hossein Derakhshan. 2017. *Information Disorder: Toward an Interdisciplinary Framework for Research and Policymaking.* Strasbourg, Fr.: Council of Europe.

Wilson, Carolyn, Alton Grizzle, Ramon Tuazon, Kwame Akyempong, and Chi Kim Cheung. 2011. *Media and Information Literacy Curriculum for Teachers.* Paris: UNESCO.

Zittoun, Tania, and Svend Brinkmann. 2012. "Learning as Meaning Making." In *Encyclopedia of the Sciences of Learning*, edited by N. M. Seel, 1809–11. New York: Springer US. https://doi.org/10.1007/978-1-4419-1428-6_18.

# City Zip CODES and Community PLAYgrounds
## Tech, Gaming, and Coding

**"At the most basic level, video game play itself is a form of digital literacy** practice. Unlike television, books, or any other media that came before them, video games are about a back-and-forth between reading the game's meanings and writing back into them" (Steinkuehler 2010). Online gaming and mobile apps can enable youth to have an immersive experience with media and help build community.

Some librarians often like to compare the benefits of printed materials versus games—with games usually taking the back seat amidst claims that they are contributing to declines in the reading of printed material. This doesn't have to be an either/or decision, though: we can have both books and video games in our libraries and recognize that each serves a niche in supporting media literacy. We're not likely to replace books with movies, or replace laptops with smartphones, and games wouldn't be any different. Each of these media plays a role in the lives of teens, the majority of whom now have a smartphone. According to 2018 survey data from the Pew Research Center, "some 95% of teens now say they have a smartphone or have access to one" (Anderson and Jiang 2021). This represents a 22-point increase from the 73 percent of teens who said this in 2014–15. Smartphone ownership is now nearly universal among American teens of different genders, races and ethnicities, and socioeconomic backgrounds. However, as pointed out in several places throughout this book, high-speed access to the internet is still not universal, which is an important point to keep in mind when serving the community.

As stated in 2020 statistics reported by YPulse, a leader in youth research and insights, Generation Z and millennials are spending an ever-increasing amount of time on mobile and video games. COVID-19 and quarantines have certainly played a role in increasing the time spent gaming, the report shares as well. According to their 2020 report, "59% of 13–39 year-olds are playing games on their phones daily," and "that's up from 48% who reported playing games daily on their phones in 2019" (YPulse 2020).

Fortunately, if online gaming is where teens are at, there can be many ways for the library to connect with them through this medium. In their book *The Library as Playground: How Games and Play Are Reshaping Public Culture*, Leorke and Wyatt "explore the way games and play are reshaping the social, cultural, spatial and temporal milieu of public libraries" (2022). While our own personal experiences or concepts of gaming might be a bit limited, this book illustrates programs that show the changing and ever-relevant landscape of games in libraries which goes far beyond manipulating characters on a screen with a controller but looks at the very structure of the library and how it can encourage play. This is a focus well worth exploring as we seek to expand our own implementation of gaming as a service for and with teens in libraries.

We offer a great variety of approaches to gaming in this chapter that will engage teens with the library and its after-school programming. From role-playing to coding, libraries from across the country share their successes and how-to's in this chapter so that you can try new ways of connecting with teens.

## 11.1: DEWEY AND DRAGONS (DUNGEONS AND DRAGONS FOR TEENS): Connecting Teens with Technology at the Library

by Laura Vallejo, Jamey Rorie, and Chris Spradlin

In 2017 the Allegra Westbrooks Regional Library, a branch of the Charlotte Mecklenburg Library (CMC) (in Charlotte, NC), initiated a program for teen patrons to play the tabletop role-playing game Dungeons & Dragons at its facility. This program, Dewey and Dragons (or Dungeons and Dragons for Teens), was made available for teenagers in grades 6 to 12. The Dewey and Dragons program had its start at the Allegra Westbrooks Regional Library (formerly Beatties Ford Road) when teen customers reached out about creating a Dungeons & Dragons group of players. The program proved a success, but in 2020 Dewey and Dragons, along with all other CML programming, moved to the virtual realm due to the COVID-19 pandemic. Teen programming staff reached out to Wizards of the Coast, a role-playing game company, about its Digital Club Support Program, which provides kits to help displaced Dungeons & Dragons groups transition to virtual gaming. With their help, we were able to not only continue offering Dewey and Dragons, but expand the program to other age groups such as preteens (9–11) and adults (18 and up) with new players each month.

The process of moving Dewey and Dragons to a virtual platform began with Wizards of the Coast (https://company.wizards.com/en), a role-playing game company offering a Digital Club Support Program to help displaced groups that could no longer meet at schools, libraries, community centers, or other places where gaming is used as an enrichment program. The library's teen staff reached out to Wizards of the Coast and were provided with a digital key code to unlock a "Legendary Bundle" on the website D&D Beyond, which is the official digital toolset and game companion for Dungeons & Dragons. The Legendary Bundle supplied access to the D&D Adventures, core rulebooks, characters, and new player guidelines. Groups used free virtual tabletop platforms to meet with their players online such as Roll20, Foundry VTT (Virtual Tabletop), and Discord; the players could access and update their character sheets from D&D Beyond as the game progressed. The platforms Roll20 and Foundry VTT allow the Game Master and players to manipulate graphics such as character and creature tokens, maps, and various handouts.

Once members of our teen staff had investigated the online resources, the next step was a trial program. In May 2020, teen staff reached out to an existing group of teens aged 12 to 14 who had previously attended our in-person programming and asked them to join the online pilot of the first virtual Dungeons & Dragons program after the state of North Carolina issued an official stay-at-home mandate. Teens who participated in the pilot had to create a free account on the virtual tabletop platform Roll20, as well as have access to the internet and a basic Chrome OS computer. Players sent in their character sheets via e-mail or image text, and teen staff uploaded a digital copy that attached to a character token the players could manipulate around the platform. Five teens took part in a short campaign titled "The Pale Codex." The game was created by Jamey Rorie of the Allegra Westbrooks Regional Library and was transferred to an online platform. This short campaign, which was perfect for new players, was made for a Level-1 adventuring party of 4–6 players:

> Deep beneath the Grand Library lies an ancient building known only to a few. Known as The Black Library, it was once the lair of an evil and powerful necromancer. Long forgotten by most, it contains many dark tomes guarded by servants to a long dead master. Amongst all the vile materials is the most dangerous of them all, the Pale Codex. (Rorie 2020)

Before starting the game, the Game Master reviewed the basic rules of Dungeons & Dragons and the game's Rules of Conduct with the group. Players were able to quickly grasp the basics of the game, as well as learn how to navigate the platform as the story progressed. The teens were excited to participate in the pilot and asked to be updated on other online programming pilots they could take part in. Based on the success of the pilot Dungeons & Dragons program, we were able to expand more in-person teen programs to an online format.

Several community resources aided in the success and expansion of these virtual programs. In June 2020, Charlotte Mecklenburg Library reopened to the public through a multiphase plan, though its programming remained exclusively online. The reopening plan aligned with planning and guidelines from Mecklenburg County, the state of North Carolina, and the CDC (Centers for Disease Control and Prevention). During this time, the district's schools transitioned to remote learning and offered students the opportunity to take home a Chromebook and sign up for a hotspot, a portable device to access the internet. Internet service providers were also offering discounted plans to families that had students enrolled in classes during the stay-at-home mandate. Charlotte Mecklenburg Library supplied rental Chromebooks and hotspot devices for a period of one week with no additional charge, using a library card. All library locations offered free wireless internet access (Wi-Fi) for use with personal devices during normal library hours.

The Charlotte Mecklenburg Library's shift to virtual programming coincidentally aided the expansion of the online Dungeons & Dragons program from the Allegra Westbrooks Regional Library to other library branches. In July 2020, CML expanded its online programming from the central library to include branch-managed programs. This policy increased its online program offerings while ensuring that various branches were not competing for an audience. Teen department staff members used an internal online calendar so staff could see what programming was being offered. Branches that had an existing audience could continue to meet online as needed. This change allowed teen department programmers to reach a demographic of teens who had previously not participated in person, as well as increase participation in multiple online programs offered by various library branches. Because CML's programming was exclusively online, our Dungeons & Dragons programs grew, and some branches were able to divide the player groups by age range. For example, the South Boulevard Branch Library divided its group into two campaigns with six players each: one group for pre-teens aged 9–12 that met on Tuesdays from 3:30 to 5:30 pm, and another group for teens aged 13–18 that met on Thursdays from 5:30 to 7:30 pm.

The sessions typically began with an orientation that allowed players to create their characters on the D&D Beyond website. The orientation also covered the general layout of the virtual tabletop platforms Roll20 and Foundry VTT. Both tabletop gaming platforms give players the option of virtual dice and allow users to add an additional Chrome extension that works with D&D Beyond, allowing players to participate with no additional costs. The South Boulevard groups met for two hours each week, and players could decide to participate as they felt comfortable. Options included using the camera and audio on Zoom or using the chat and audio on Discord. Both options let teens interact with one another while the Game Master narrated the adventure of the day.

The Game Master can decide which virtual tabletop platform to use, depending on what works best for their players and the style of campaign they plan to run. Game Masters who plan to facilitate a short session, two hours or less, must allow time for new player orientation, technical issues, a last session recap, and player updates. For inexperienced players or younger players, Foundry VTT works best because it limits the users' ability to move through a game pause function and encourages users to learn the turn order in the game. For more experienced players, the Game Master can use the Roll20 or Discord platform channels. Both of these platforms allow the Game Master and players to engage in a "theater of the mind" and participate in collaborative storytelling and world-building, where the use of imagination is key in the role-playing game of Dungeons & Dragons.

Dungeons & Dragons helps teens foster imagination, acute problem-solving, quick math, communication, and teamwork. For teen programmers who are thinking about starting their own Dungeons & Dragons group in their library, free campaigns continue to be uploaded on the D&D Beyond website; the link to register a group with the Digital Club Support Program also remains on the D&D Beyond website. Teen programmers can reach out to their local game shop to ask for volunteer Game Masters to co-host virtual campaigns, or they can reach out to experienced players in their current campaigns to see if they would like to lead a quest. Online programming allows teens to interact with each other in a safe environment during the COVID-19 pandemic. Teens have expressed their passion for the game by sharing portraits of their characters using both traditional and digital media and by dressing as their characters. Charlotte Mecklenburg Library continues to encourage players to participate as they feel comfortable and is excited to see an increase in new players as its online programming continues to expand.

## 11.2: BOSTON PUBLIC LIBRARY: Teen Technology Mentor Program

by Brianne Skywall and Christopher Jacobs

The Teen Technology Mentor (TTM) program is an invention of the library staff of Teen Central, the Boston Public Library's teen-exclusive space. Teen Central is co-coordinated by a full-time staff of 6.5 employees, two of whom—the teen technology coordinator and the teen tech specialist—maintain and create programming germane to two smaller spaces within Teen Central. These two spaces are the "Lab," a well-outfitted computer lab equipped with 10 high-performance computers (5 Windows and 5 Mac) equipped with Adobe Creative Cloud, as well as two 3D printers and other hands-on STEAM materials; and the "Lounge," a slightly smaller area with lounge seating, two 60-inch TV screens, and a range of current-generation video game systems. The giant glass walls that separate the Lab and Lounge from the remaining sections of Teen Central are meant to encourage an "open-concept" relationship among the spaces, though the tech areas are more limited in terms of their hours of operation.

The Teen Tech Mentor program was conceived to develop a variety of twenty-first-century digital and STEAM-oriented literacies within a limited cohort of paid teen workers (the "mentors"), who in turn are directed to use their acquired skills to enrich the lives of patrons within the library. Though the position requires no prior job experience, its parameters are comparatively rigorous: prospective mentors commit to a 2-day, 5-hour per-week work schedule that runs for a term of no fewer than 35 weeks, in direct accordance with the Boston Public Schools' academic calendar (September–June). They must be actively enrolled in an area high school, be participating in equivalency training, and be in good academic standing. The schedules are identical for all cohort members from week to week and are meant to take into account the academic needs of all teens as well as the business hours of the library.

Much like academic curricular road maps, the TTM work calendar operates on a cycle of training and practicum that prioritizes training and research in the fall "semester" followed by programming and project-implementation in the spring. That said, the TTM program sees teens interacting with patrons from an early start, both in prescribed meetings as well as unstructured "Open Lab" sessions in which they are encouraged to explore, ideate, and "mess around" with STEAM materials/technologies with other teen patrons.

Ultimately, all of the work conducted by the teen tech mentors, or TTMs, throughout their year (a total of 175 work hours) will fall under one or more of the following categories:

*Training.* This category includes any activity or event that involves the imparting of specific hard skills and/or content knowledge. These mainly consist of software trainings relevant to the Lab and Lounge spaces, but they also include internal and external visits to STEAM-relevant community spaces and private organizations.

*Mentoring/Programming.* The TTMs' primary role is to serve in a mentor capacity to the patrons of Teen Central—specifically other teens (ages 12–18) and tweens (ages 8–11). While some of this will be achieved through the facilitation in existing Open Lab contexts, a significant portion of that duty involves both assisting with and creating audience-centered programming predicated on the mentors' own research and training.

*Research.* The TTMs use some of their work time to explore technological and demographic trends by conducting online and off-site research, as well as through more local, in-house data collection.

*Personal Passion Project.* As the hard skills of the TTMs become more well-rounded and the teens begin to establish propensities for specific tech realms, they embark on a more independently driven "Personal Passion Project" (PPP) in their spring semesters. Not unlike a summative academic assessment, the PPP represents a culmination of significant portions of the teens' learning throughout the work term. The PPP is directed at

> » serving the needs of the library's young patrons in an informed way, while
> » encouraging the mentor to make "geeking out" something that drives their personal and professional pursuits.

Much like an open-ended project in an independent study course, a PPP could take many forms: a library program (or series), tutorial videos, an app, a redesign of the Lab or Lounge's aesthetic, and so on. It is largely left to the individual TTM to put forth a proposal to be approved by the Tech Team staff. Because the PPP will be self-determined, differentiation is built into the assignment.

It is essential to note that, as of the time of writing, an implementation of the Teen Tech Mentor program as described above has been limited by the COVID-19-induced closure of Teen Central as a public space. As readers will note in the ensuing sections, however, the Teen Tech Team has stuck as closely as possible to the original plan, with some highly encouraging results.

## Description of the Population Served

In all of its iterations, the Teen Tech Mentor program was designed to serve a broad teen population: namely, the daily in-house patrons of Teen Central, the teen library space of the Boston Public Library's Central location in downtown Boston. Demographically, Teen Central patrons are drawn largely from area public schools, with a majority being BIPOC students on the older end of the 12–18 (or grade 6–12) age spectrum. Before the pandemic, Teen Central would regularly see over 100 teens per weekday (significantly fewer on weekends), though it is also important to note that only a relatively small portion of those teens (between 10 and 20 percent) would electively partake in Lab and Lounge provisions and services, which themselves were available primarily during after-school hours. A portion of the TTMs' weekly time was also scheduled to provide bridge STEAM programming for Children's Library patrons ages 9–12 (affectionately dubbed "Tween Time").

Because Teen Central was closed due to COVID-19 in March 2020, the TTM program for the 2020–21 academic year shifted its attention to working with virtual teen and tween audiences, whose demographics have been harder to determine due to technical constraints and a decreased sample size. In general, however, the Teen Services sector has observed some shifts from its in-person demographics, with notable decreases in the proportion of BIPOC teens served and increases in the number of virtual patrons residing outside of the city.

Despite being few in number, the mentors are themselves greatly served by the TTM program because they can build skills in the realms of STEAM, education, and public service that can serve as a vital antecedent to all sorts of rewarding work opportunities. Though the onset of COVID-19 precluded our capacity to draw from our base of existing teen patrons (because we didn't have a functional database of teen patron e-mails at the time of our closure) for interviews, our recruitment for the mentor positions took into consideration our strong desire for diversity, equity, and inclusion in our teen staff and relied almost exclusively on responsiveness and alacrity from staff within the Boston Public School system.

## Successes and Challenges Experienced

Despite the dramatic changes driven by the impact of COVID-19, there have been some decided successes within the "virtual" mentorship program, alongside some unique challenges. A concise explanation of each of these is given below:

*Interviews.* The advent of the "Zoom videoconferencing era" since the COVID-19-forced closures enabled us to see the advantages of conducting remote interviewing for the Teen Tech Mentor positions. Common online tools such as Google Forms and Slides helped create consistent and dynamic experiences for each applicant and helped us determine some of the applicants' core technical literacies early on. We will most likely keep one or more interview rounds virtual in all future iterations of the program.

*"Tween Time."* With weak virtual connections to teen populations, our partnership with the Boston Public Library's children's librarians helped give early purpose to the TTMs' positions by providing a consistent and eager audience for STEAM programs: a biweekly session called "Tween Time." The tweens provided an opportunity for TTMs to practice their mentorship skills on patrons who were less likely to challenge their authority, and Tween Time was named the favorite fall-term activity by both of our 2020–21 mentors.

*Adaptations and Record-keeping.* The stark differences between our intended and resulting program year (due to the pandemic) have motivated us to keep stronger tabs on the activities we have conducted, what has worked, and how live program elements have been adapted to a virtual format. We also implemented a regular "video diary" assignment in our program curriculum in order to keep records of how our mentors are experiencing their work. Our hope is that future cohorts will benefit from this information.

*Tech Equity.* Without access to a common physical space to level the playing field, technological equity has become a limiting factor in determining the viability of virtual mentorship. Just as virtual programs must be constructed with these inequities in mind, so too must the program director understand the inequities that might exist *within* a cohort. We were fortunate to be able to afford providing our current cohort of mentors with "work laptops" to ensure that they were capable of the same trainings because there were sufficient differences in their home setups to frustrate those processes.

*Full Schedules.* Because we intentionally selected high-performing, academically focused rising juniors, we expected them to be busy. However, we were disillusioned by how little they were able to take us up on interesting and diverse opportunities to work outside of their five hours per week. Additionally, a mid-semester course opportunity arose through these teens' school that impacted their ability to commit to their existing schedule. As our cohort grows, we will remain mindful of how lateness and absence will need to be accommodated, considering the rigor of the program as a whole.

*Budgeting.* Despite the nature of the TTM program, it has proven far more challenging to find ways to spend money on virtual—as opposed to in-person—programming. Though we have found some ingenious ways to reallocate funds to benefit patrons, such as prizes, kits, and software licenses, the lack of a physical space has left us with a dearth of opportunities to purchase content which has a lasting value.

## How the Program Can Be Replicated by Teen Librarians

The depth and breadth of the TTM program relies on its status as a paid work opportunity for the mentors, which would surpass the typical budgetary constraints of most teen libraries or librarians (including that of Teen Central). Though certain parameters (i.e., weekly hours, length of tenure) can be modified to mitigate these limitations, most library staff who are looking to subsidize a paying version of this program should seek out a dedicated funding source, such as an internal (re)allocation or an external grant. Most urban centers should have departments at the city level devoted to providing workforce opportunities for youth, particularly when they are of a STEM/STEAM nature; they may also provide access to invaluable networks of local and national grant applications. For reference, the current cohort of the TTM program was funded by a grant from a local nonprofit, with plans for future iterations of the program involving funding from local and national tech organizations.

In addition to financing, libraries that are seeking to build programming involving STEAM will need the technological resources to serve both the mentors and the teen patrons. Teen Central's existing Lab and Lounge spaces exist to provide suitable collaborative spaces for current and future cohorts, and we were fortunate to be able to allocate mobile library resources to our mentors for little cost upon the realization that we would likely not be reopening our physical spaces during their tenure.

Though there are low- or no-cost alternatives to many of the more popular software options in the realms described above, librarians should work backward from their program's desired goals (for both the TTMs and teen patrons alike) to determine the cost of software access needed to run the program and whether specific trainings for that software will be necessary. Alternatively, you may consider letting both the mentors as well as your teen patrons determine the needs of your specific library, as it is likely that (1) some mentors may enter their positions with software experience that they may share in the form of training, and (2) your teen mentors have a stronger sense than you do of what teen patrons are looking to create, learn, and experience.

Though it is important that the librarians directing the mentor program be tech-savvy and even tech-forward, they needn't possess mastery in all of the software, games, and experiences the TTM program will purport to confer at the year's outset. Part of the beauty of this program is the degree to which teens and mentors are given agency over their own experiences and the pace of their own learning. This is not to imply that a program plan should not be rigorous—indeed, rigor and enthusiasm form much of the facilitators' contributions—but the teens who earn these positions should already harbor a degree of passion for STEAM and/or mentorship as part of their own ambitions.

Despite these flexibilities, the design and implementation of a year-long curriculum, as well as the recruiting, hiring, and training of part-time staff, are heavy loads for a small team, let alone individual employees. Staff and managers should anticipate the need for a 2-to-1 hourly investment in the planning and execution of any Teen Tech Mentor program, particularly in its first iteration. In the end, the success and growth of this type of program is contingent upon staff who are afforded the time and resources not only to implement it, but also to record and assess its continued effectiveness.

For additional information on the TTM program, you can view this article: Ally Dowds, Catherine Halpin, and Jess Snow, "Teen Leadership Development through a Teen Gaming Program," *YALS Journal* 15, no. 4 (2017): 33–38, http://yalsjournal.ala.org/publication/?m=53337&i=460559&p=35&pp=1&ver=html5.

## 11.3: THE BEAUTY OF S.T.E.M.
by Andrea McNeil and Shimira Williams

"The Beauty of S.T.E.M.," a series created and implemented by Shimira Williams, provided innovative programming opportunities for the tweens and teens who congregate at the Carnegie Library of Pittsburgh (CLP)-Homewood. The Beauty of S.T.E.M. is a studio series that integrates technology with the design and fabrication of clothing fashions. The youth participating in the studio sessions are introduced to basic electronics, e-textile materials, and wearable technology. They become familiar with common fashion-industry terms and acquire experience with the tools of the industry through the fabrication or repurposing processes needed to create their garments. The youth are provided with materials to design and fabricate their very own pieces to be modeled in a fashion show. Youth also participate in "lunch and learn" activities that introduce career opportunities in fashion technology, the technology sector, and the fashion industry.

Shimira is a lifelong library lover, and the library is always the first place she visits when she is developing an implementation plan to bring her ideas to reality. Libraries foster a collaborative community through sharing ideas and storytelling. Plus, the library can offer access to the tools to construct a prototype of your vision. But the real magic is the people at the library. They are essential community connectors of knowledge, resources, and tools.

The Beauty of S.T.E.M. was a windfall of innovative programming opportunities for tweens and teens who congregated at the Carnegie Library of Pittsburgh-Homewood because the youth services librarian Andrea McNeil believed in what was possible. Andrea's ability as a youth librarian to see what the youth in the community desired and weave this into the library's services fostered the collaboration with The Beauty of S.T.E.M. and host the culminating fashion show.

## The Partnership

Andrea McNeil first met Shimira Williams in June 2013 when Andrea transferred from the Hill District branch to the Homewood branch of the CLP. She organized a luncheon to introduce Shimira to some of the movers, shakers, and stakeholders who were advocating for changes that could lead to a better future for children in Homewood. Shimira knew that, like her, Andrea was a product of this underserved and under-funded community in the eastern part of Pittsburgh. The very same library that has employed Andrea for the past ten years was the library she grew up in. Her childhood librarian, Miss Franklin, would save at least twenty books for her each week to read. Andrea won the summer reading contest at the library by wide margins three straight summers while devouring the books she'd set aside to read. To come full circle and empower young people to be their best selves, just like Miss Franklin did, has added to Andrea's passion for working in this field. After many conversations with Andrea, Shimira revealed that CLP–Homewood is a very special place to her as well. It was her childhood library too!

In 2013, CLP–Homewood became the site for The Beauty of S.T.E.M. program. In the program's weekly sessions, Shimira empowered children and teens with the information and skills necessary to create technology based fashions through weekly sessions. Some weeks' participants would start anew on their designs, and some would be finishing up a project. Teens worked at their own pace and level of understanding. In mid-August 2013, a fashion show was presented featuring the finished designs and creations of the participants.

## Media Literacy + Social Justice + Fashion

The Carnegie Library of Pittsburgh's Children and Teen Services had been studying and conducting research on best practices to integrate media literacy and digital learning into its programming and collections. CLP Teen Services moved from studying to implementing programming that would help develop the digital literacy skills needed by young people in the twenty-first century. Andrea liked to say that "we were on the cusp of change."

Shimira's ability to take abstract thoughts and turn them into reality has fostered an innovative approach to media literacy with teens, and her efforts have extended beyond just The Beauty of S.T.E.M. program. For example, the CLP participates in Remake Learning, an organization that supports innovative learning projects and practices throughout southwestern Pennsylvania and northern West Virginia. In another example, the library needed an impactful project for teens to work on in the summer of 2018. Initially the idea was to make Light Up Hoodies because in 2012, Trayvon Martin was murdered in the dark in his neighborhood by an overzealous watch member who didn't recognize him as a part of that community. Shimira needed conductive thread, lights, and other technical devices to enable the hoodies to light up. Additional supplies, including the hoodies, were provided by the CLP's Office of Programs and Partnerships, a new library department that the coordinators, the digital learning librarian, and library leadership developed to formalize and streamline library services in the digital realm. The Light Up Hoodies project gave the library an opportunity to connect with the teens on an empathetic level. It gave teens a safe environment to talk about the racial and social implications of the Trayvon Martin incident among their peer group. The Light Up Hoodies project was a success.

## Challenges of Being Part of a Large Consortium Implementing Individual Programming

Money is always an issue. The CLP's digital learning librarian in the spring of 2012 was Corey Wittig. One of his responsibilities was to identify grant opportunities for resources, programming aids, and tools. The pilot program The LABS@ CLP was designed to educate and immerse teens in digital literacy programming. The digital learning librarian supervised part-time mentors who would have weekly open labs and skill acquisition at four CLP regional locations and the Main Teen location at the Oakland branch library. The other fourteen CLP neighborhood libraries were not part of the pilot for regular weekly services. We could schedule a mentor and plan a S.T.E.M. digital literacy-related program once every three months.

Like any sapling in the shade of a mighty oak, we needed the light for S.T.E.M. to grow. The Beauty of S.T.E.M. was that outlet of creativity. A place to collaborate and implement imaginative and innovative programming with a for-profit organization in a public space. Under Shimira's leadership, TekStart, the company that operates The Beauty of S.T.E.M., gave us the chance to supplement weekly sessions in the areas of S.T.E.M. and digital literacy.

Shimira's programming for the youth in her community created a much-needed opportunity for the youth of Homewood to experiment with emerging technologies and S.T.E.M. activities. CLP–Homewood, a nonprofit, didn't have the money to implement or pay Shimira for what the program was truly worth. It was a solution to an equity and access issue for teens in the eastern most region of the CLP's service area.

The digital learning lead librarian, Kristin Morgan, was supportive of the efforts. The teen services coordinator, Kelly Rottmund, was an excellent coordinator, was supportive, and made sure that equity of resources and services reached all library branches and Allegheny County. These librarians had a shared goal of giving the teens space to be. They found resources, money and/or equipment, and opportunities to support the work.

In conclusion, Shimira's reach has been beyond conducting workshops for teens. She brought together national talents in the world of sewing for a conference and lecture. She organized local cutting-edge entrepreneurs to talk with teens about the financial windfalls that can occur when someone creates a product that people find to be useful and how this can turn into revenue.

Andrea is grateful Shimira wanted to use a place that holds such special meaning to her. She recognizes the public library's ability to provide resources and connectivity to help young people figure out what they want to do with their lives. She helps them see S.T.E.M. in their community. Andrea is also grateful that through the years they have not stayed stagnant and just done the same programs over and over. Andrea respects and values that, like the technologies, The Beauty of S.T.E.M. is evolving and takes on new meaning for them and the participants. It also gives younger children who attend programming at CLP-Homewood the chance to have their turn at creating, implementing, and seeing The Beauty of S.T.E.M. become a reality.

## 11.4: BLISSFUL CODING CLUB
### by Anusha Bansal and Maisy Card

Anusha Bansal, a high school junior in Livingston, New Jersey, founded the nonprofit organization Blissful Us in 2017 to focus on several issues that citizens face: hunger, poverty, social inequality, and education gaps. Anusha had been volunteering since 2010, leading several food drives and fundraisers for underprivileged communities by working with organizations such as the Covenant House and United Way. She serves on the board of the Teen Leadership Council at Community Food Bank where she has engaged in many projects to serve her community. As a student leader, Anusha found ways to build a strong connection with youth in underserved communities and their families. As a student in a school's remote learning environment due to the coronavirus, she learned that peer-to-peer learning for teens and youth is an effective way to enhance the overall learning, engagement, and motivation of kids from all backgrounds. Our society's youth, especially in underserved communities in urban centers, and in low-income and first-generation immigrant families, is at risk of losing touch with STEM fields, even though computer science is the language of the future. These youth may also not have a readily available mechanism by which they can express their views in an educational setting without being judged. At the same time, the widening income divide carries the risk that the younger generation will lose awareness of those others in society who face challenges when it comes to education and access to resources.

## Program Overview

Anusha founded the Blissful Coding Club in 2020; this online club is specifically designed to teach STEM and coding skills to kids from underserved, inner-city, and low-income communities. With this project, Anusha hoped to achieve three major objectives: (1) to engage kids in underrepresented communities across America to participate in STEM, (2) to give them a strong platform in STEM-related skills in the hopes of bettering their economic prospects in the future, and (3) to provide a volunteer platform for college students to give back to the community.

The Blissful Coding Club was the first class of its kind to be offered to both girls and boys by the Newark Public Library, with lessons in a coeducational setting, using a peer-to-peer training model, and providing age-appropriate classes for students from grades two and up. Anusha reached out to professors at Carnegie Mellon University to get help with the program's curriculum. She reached out to professors at local universities to recruit computer science college students as volunteers to help teach the program. She made hundreds of phone calls to set up the program with volunteers, libraries, and organizations that believed in her mission. So by the time the first Blissful Coding Club classes were offered, Anusha had been able to recruit fifteen college students from Carnegie Mellon University and the New Jersey Institute of Technology to serve as volunteer tutors. She created the class's curriculum using CMU Computer Science Academy, Code.Org, MIT Scratch, the Creative Computing Curriculum from Harvard, and other well-known open sources. The instruction in the Blissful Coding Club is once a week for six weeks, followed by an extra help session once a week to encourage information retention as well as concept reinforcement. The classes are highly engaging with a 1:5 instructor-to-student ratio and with copious volunteer support provided to the students.

The Blissful Coding Club's online lessons came as a relief to many parents during the COVID-19 pandemic and were the perfect opportunity for their children to learn computer coding while using their summers productively. Anusha and her volunteers' biggest challenge while teaching was that many students took classes on their phones—some didn't have working computers, let alone microphones, speakers, or cameras, and they could not share their screens. Moreover, some students lacked support at home due to COVID-19 disruption in their families, and other students had jobs and joined the classes just to "listen in" and learn.

## Program Success

From these humble beginnings, the Blissful Coding Club has expanded greatly, and Anusha and her dedicated team of 105 college volunteers have now served a total of 4,000 students with 25,000 reached from more than 30 countries, including France, India, and countries in Africa. Blissful Us has evolved its curriculum and has changed it to work on phones, tablets, and personal computers in an effort to extend this educational opportunity. In order to encourage attendance during each session, the club hands out certificates and small gift cards to students with the best projects. Anusha keeps her focus on curriculum development and spends a lot of time raising donations and grants in order to reach more students, while her hard-working staff makes every student feel welcome and have fun in the classes. Anusha has been able to procure valuable partnerships with libraries, organizations, and universities to help her volunteers find a purpose and give back to the community. She says, "I have learned that perseverance and ability to learn from mistakes and keep moving forward despite hurdles and discouragement is the only way to keep advancing my organization's mission."

Anusha and the Blissful Coding Club's team were invited to present their lessons to military families, along with First Lady Jill Biden, at the Military Child Educational Summit in November 2020. They received extremely positive responses from parents in these communities, and several of the students have returned to learn more advanced skills in coding.

Anusha says that it was difficult, at first, to put a successful coding program together. "As we all know, remote and virtual learning, especially a program free of cost, doesn't always tend to retain student attention. However, with the help of all our partners, mentors, and incredible volunteers, we are able to build a fun, engaging method to not only provide access to STEM education, but to make it enjoyable for students. We wanted every one of our students to feel the urge within them to join again for our next session and to pursue STEM and computer science in their free time."

The issue of gaps in media literacy skills involves more than just computer science education. In Anusha's words: "Students my age (including myself) need to feel the confidence within ourselves such that we actually believe that any goal we put ourselves to can be matched. Sharing our thoughts, emotions, expressions, and more is critical within our society today: to be heard. To address these challenges, I want to empower the student community to lead this effort themselves for our peers. I am grateful to the communities and urban libraries that foresee the challenges of media education and are investing in their teens through programs like ours." (Anusha can be reached at info@blissfulus.org regarding partnerships or bringing the Blissful Coding Club to your library or town.)

As Anusha progresses with her mission of media and STEM awareness, she has received significant support from the Military Child Education Coalition, National Military Family Association, Blue Star Families, Google for Nonprofits, United Way Worldwide, Girls Inc., the Jersey City Free Public Library, Kearny Public Library, Newark Public Library, Microsoft TEALS CS programs, and several universities like Carnegie Mellon University, the New Jersey Institute of Technology, Rutgers University, Fairleigh Dickinson University, Stanford University, and the University of Michigan, along with other foundations.

## Library Collaboration

Anusha started the club with the cooperation of Maisy Card at Newark Public Library. In Maisy Card's past experience of working as a middle school and high school media specialist, as well as a teen services librarian in an urban public library system, she's had the opportunity to lead both coding clubs and classes. As a teen services librarian at the Newark Public Library, she managed the volunteer-led Girls Who Code club for three years. Card was comfortable going through the basics of HTML and CSS, as well as very basic JavaScript, but that's where her knowledge ended. The library did have a wonderful volunteer from Google who was able to not only teach introductory lessons on Python and JavaScript but also arranged an annual tour of the Google offices in New York, where the students met with women software engineers. But even with a qualified and dedicated volunteer, maintaining consistent student attendance was always challenging. Teens, especially those who are in high school, have a multitude of extracurricular activities, and this often meant that their attendance would drop off once another activity, like sports season, began. They would return the following fall to the Girls Who Code Club but find that they had forgotten many of the lessons and had to begin at the introductory level again. Technology was also an issue. The Newark Public Library had about twelve available desktop computers in its technology training lab, but enrollment would sometimes reach more than twenty, forcing some teens to double up, which had both benefits and drawbacks. Moreover, our talented volunteer eventually had to leave to attend to other commitments, leaving Card with the difficult task of finding someone who was both knowledgeable in computer science and comfortable working with teens and meeting them on their level.

So when Anusha Bansal reached out to Card, offering to lead a coding club online, Card was excited at the opportunity and readily accepted. Teaching in a virtual environment was new to Card, but Anusha had had previous experience teaching both her peers and younger children online. Moreover, Anusha was familiar with a number of programming languages, and Card thought that Anusha's experience as a student learner gave her firsthand knowledge of the kind of support novice coders need to progress beyond their introductory knowledge. Card had witnessed many students participate in the early weeks of coding clubs, but their attendance would begin to slip once the lessons got too challenging.

Once Card began advertising the Blissful Coding Club to library patrons, she was surprised to find that there was even more interest than when the library had offered coding clubs in person. One reason for this was that the students no longer faced the challenge of finding transportation to come to the Main Branch Library. Instead, they were able to use their own desktop computers or laptops at home, and even those without computers could participate by using their smartphone. Because of the number of registrants, Anusha reached out to colleges for support. She was able to recruit Carnegie Mellon computer science students to act as teachers. At the end of the summer, Card saw the results of the added support from these volunteers, who had held virtual office hours for students who needed help beyond the club sessions. When the students presented their final coding projects, Card saw that they had progressed more in one summer than many of the students she'd previously worked with had managed in a year of participating in in-person clubs. What made the program truly unique was the volunteers' engagement. Instead of relying on one volunteer, Anusha had created a program that brought together a large number of volunteers to provide intensive support to young learners. The student-to-teacher ratio, the extra tutoring outside the virtual classroom, and the extra assignments that students completed on their own and submitted to Google Classroom for feedback made the program on a par with for-profit coding bootcamps. The experience was also valuable to the volunteers, all of whom were computer science undergrads who were able to gain valuable experience teaching and mentoring students.

## Social Media Links

- Instagram: Blissful Coding Club, www.instagram.com/blissfulcodingclub
- Twitter: Blissful Us, https://twitter.com/BlissfulUs
- LinkedIn: Blissful Us, www.linkedin.com/company/blissful-us

## Websites

- Blissful Coding Club, www.blissfulcodingclub.org
- Blissful Us, www.blissfulus.org

FIGURE 11.1
**Logo of
Blissful Us**

## 11.5: AFTER-SCHOOL CODING AND TECHNOLOGY CLUBS

by Ally Doerman and Pamela Jayne

After-school coding and technology clubs developed and led by librarians targeted teens at middle schools. These coding, technology, and 3D printing clubs were started to provide students who were curious about coding or technology a way to experiment and explore, as the schools were not providing as many classes at that time. In these clubs, teens learned about computer coding and 3D design, and they explored skills they might not have otherwise been able to build. During club meetings, discussions would take place about what could be done with this technology and skill, and how the teens might want to use tech in their futures. Teens were also tasked with collaborating as a team and working through critical thinking and problem-solving skills in order to improve their code or design.

### Coding Clubs

*Use multiple sites.* At the club's first meeting, introduce the website(s) that will be used in the club. Use several websites to provide different experiences, depending on the students' skill level, interest, or goal. While you may want to have the teens all working on the same website, one challenge was experienced with conducting the coding club this way. The librarians discovered that some teens didn't enjoy the site used and became frustrated or bored. So offering multiple options is preferable because it allows the teens to have more power over what they'd prefer to learn and thus increases their engagement.

*Avoid downloadable software.* We chose websites that did not require a download, as staff were unable to download anything to the school computers. This also helps if the exact same computers aren't able to be used each time because all the teens need to log in to their accounts on the website. In addition, this allows teens to work in their free time, if they so choose.

*Allow time to explore.* After introducing the different websites, allow the teens the rest of the meeting time to explore each of them so they can decide which one they will want to work on, while reminding them that they can change their mind at any time. The websites used were:

> » *Code.org:* This website is often used for an introduction to coding and utilizes drop-and-drag blocks for coding, and instructional videos to watch. It also has a full coding course for a variety of age groups, all self-paced. Also included is a link to CS Unplugged, a source for offline lessons, which are especially useful if you have only a limited number of computers available.
> » *Codecademy:* This is a great site for those who want to learn more in-depth coding (HTML, Python, JavaScript, etc.); however, they offer a Pro course that requires users to pay. This might be confusing for students because the majority of the courses are now Pro.
> » *Scratch* (https://scratch.mit.edu): G Scratch is great to challenge students to create stories or games. It uses drop-and-drag blocks and provides several tutorials.
> » Other websites to consider:
>> – Code with Google, https://edu.google.com/code-with -google
>> – Google Codelabs, https://codelabs.developers.google.com
>> – Girls Who Code, https://girlswhocode.com

Working through a few lessons on each site is helpful but not necessary. Encourage the teens to help each other and work through the problem with staff, especially if their skill levels vary. During the remainder of club meetings, teens will work through the lessons on the websites or work on their stories and games. You can bring books from the library that will provide more information about the languages they are learning and reaffirm their skills for how to look for information. Try to encourage the teens to work together to help each other when they run into roadblocks. If students are frustrated, help them brainstorm ways to find solutions for their problem. If a school develops its own coding curriculum for the students, you may find that students will lose interest. If so, try to incorporate other coding/technology opportunities, or try running the club for a shorter amount of time.

## Technology Club

The technology club was developed after students started losing interest in the original coding club, especially after the integration of more coding in the school curriculum. While the coding club met only once a week during the school year, the technology club met twice a week for six weeks.

In a few meetings, students worked with coding through Code.org and Codecademy, and they also worked with Spheros, which the public library purchased through grant funds. For most of the meetings, however, students worked largely in TinkerCAD. This is a free, online 3D-modeling program that enables users to construct designs and models for 3D-printable items. A model constructed by someone using TinkerCAD can then be converted into a 3D physical object by 3D printing technology.

In the technology club, the students' learning was mostly self-guided with the training provided by TinkerCAD. TinkerCAD does not need to be downloaded to any computer, but students will need to create their own accounts. TinkerCAD requires participants to be thirteen or older to create an account, or have guardian permission. When starting this club, staff worked with the school librarian to create a permission form for students to take home. As of this publication, a classroom can be created, which will allow students access to TinkerCAD without having guardian permission. Teens are able to access their account from any computer with internet access. The NKY Makerspace, which is part of the school district, visited the club and discussed different careers that use coding. At the end of the six weeks, images were printed of their designs and the entire school voted on their favorite. The winner had their design 3D-printed by the NKY Makerspace. If there is no access to a 3D printer, look to partner with an organization in the community with one.

## 3D Printing Club

In contrast to the technology club, the 3D printing club, as its name implies, focused exclusively on the acquisition of design and modeling skills for 3D printing. The club was created as a partnership between the library and the NKY Makerspace, which is part of the school district. With a grant from the Greater Cincinnati STEM Collaborative, a 3D printer was purchased that could be easily transported to different schools, and the collaborative provided the training and curriculum.

During the club meetings, students would show up a bit late to the program. This was completely understandable because they were waiting for transportation. Instead of moving forward with the lesson or work for the day, staff decided to start each meeting with a critical thinking/logic activity that would help students start looking for solutions in different ways, which is helpful when designing in TinkerCAD.

### First Meeting

The initial meeting of the club introduces the teens to 3D printing and design. This includes finding out what they already know and watching videos about the various things that can be created using 3D printers. After each video, you should have a discussion about how this technology might disrupt the industry and if that is a realistic alternative to what we use currently. Then, introduce the purpose of the club—what are they working to create? This can be something general, like an invention to solve a real-world problem, or something service-oriented that might help a person or organization in the community. Before the end of the meeting, help the teens create a TinkerCAD account. Create an account for yourself with a teacher code so their designs can easily be seen. Once they create an account, they should work through the TinkerCAD tutorials.

## Remainder of Club Meetings

The remaining meetings will vary based on what the goal is for the students to make; however, the first few weeks should focus on research and design. Students should learn more about what they are trying to create, sketch their designs, and receive feedback from fellow students or staff. If they are trying to create something that's for a specific person or community, they should interview the people who will potentially be using the object they're designing and get feedback from them. The teens should be able to explain why they chose their design and why it would be better than existing products.

As students submit their designs, they will need a way to print them. This will require purchasing a 3D printer or partnering with another organization that can print them for the club. This may not always be possible for everyone. Submitting the item for a business to print for the club might be one option. In order to reduce the printing costs, running a contest and only printing the design that is voted the best with an accompanying type of rubric, similar to what was done in the technology club, is a great alternative as well.

## Overcoming Challenges with Space

The space did not always have enough computers for everyone. In order to accommodate this, the staff would split the group in two and have part of the group working on the computers and the other half working on offline activities or sketching. The students would switch halfway through the meeting. For some projects, the staff had them work in teams, which also reduced the number of computers ultimately needed.

## REFERENCES

Anderson, Monica, and Jingjing Jiang. 2021. "Teens, Social Media & Technology 2018." Pew Research Center. www.pewresearch.org/internet/2018/05/31/teens-social-media-technology-2018/.

Leorke, D., and D. Wyatt. 2022. *The Library as Playground: How Games and Play Are Reshaping Public Culture.* Lanham, MD: Rowman and Littlefield.

Rorie, Jamey. 2020. "The Pale Codex." Dungeon Masters Guild, August 20. www.dmsguild.com/product/325105/The-Pale-Codex.

Steinkuehler, Constance. 2010. "Video Games and Digital Literacies." *Journal of Adolescent & Adult Literacy* 54 (1): 61–63. www.jstor.org/stable/20749077.

YPulse Inc. – Youth Research and Insights. 2020. "4 Must-Know Stats on Young Consumers & Gaming." www.ypulse.com/article/2020/08/20/4-must-know-stats-on-young-consumers-gaming.

# CONCLUSION
## The Takeaways

**While wrapping up the writing of this manuscript, we're still in the middle** of the pandemic. Libraries across the country are offering varying degrees of programming, from virtual to in-person yet outdoors. The media is full of stories and opinions regarding the vaccine, wearing masks, ending or extending the eviction moratorium, and more. It's a patchwork for sure. It's hard enough to stay adequately informed as information professionals. What about urban teens?

Lillian Mayer, a colleague of ours, recently shared in her monthly report that "J," a teen who had frequented the library when it was fully open, felt disconnected due to the pandemic. He said that the library is a place that "keeps him on track." Now that he knows the library is back open, he assured her that he'd return and that her mentorship was important to him.

Library workers (and workers in many other professions) don't always hear how much of a difference their services can make in teens' lives. Trust that they do. Especially in urban communities. The "power lines" in the title of this book and that Jimmeka explains so well in the "Introduction" are our incredible opportunities to help make sense of a world that is sometimes confusing, unfair, and even ominous. There's still so much possibility and need even if it feels like progress isn't being made. Find where change is needed in empowering teens through media literacy—and then be relentless and make it happen.

This book was designed to provide librarians with insight into the challenges experienced by teens in urban communities and offer pathways for implementing media literacy to connect, liberate, educate, and exalt their voices. But this work is null and void without action. It is imperative for you to apply the information found in this book and begin making change in your library and community. But before you do, take these next steps to learn more about your teens and community.

*Take a walk or drive and explore.* Step outside your comfort zone in the library building and go outside, literally, to get to know the faces and spaces in your community. Schedule time on your work calendar to take a one-hour drive or walk one day and pay attention to the buildings, the businesses, and the people that you pass by. Make a mental inventory of the construction, graffiti, and signage you encounter. What are the stories behind the words, landscaping, and buildings in the neighborhoods? How do these stories capture the experiences of the people? And most importantly, who are those people?

*Research the history.* Do you know the history of your community? Most urban communities are rich in history that has been bull-dozed down and covered up with skyscrapers and buildings. When urbanization began in cities across the United States in the early twentieth century, many communities, especially Black communities, were displaced or even destroyed. Urban communities have evolved over time with arts culture, the migration of people, and even devastating historical events that redesigned their architecture and aura. These communities change and evolve with the ebb and flow of new residents, and with new construction implemented by urban planners. Gentrification has also contributed to the closing of notable and historical small businesses in cities that have been replaced with new businesses, which are not owned by or aim to serve the people in urban communities. Use your library's resources to learn more about the history of the community where you work.

*Observe and evaluate.* In chapters 4 and 5, you were provided with strategies for creating space and building relationships with teens from urban communities. Chapter 4 specifically identified and addressed the barriers that exist to serving historically marginalized teens in libraries. After reading this book, you should try to observe how the policies, interactions, and services at your library influence the teens you serve daily. Remember that systems of oppression are perpetuated in policies and procedures that don't serve the best interests of those who are marginalized by them daily, and instead protect those who are privileged by their existence. Evaluate the policies and practices that are present in your library's daily operations that may serve as barriers for teens. Explore the possibilities for revamping those policies and the benefits this would provide for your patrons, and then share this with management. By doing so, you will be taking an important step to becoming an advocate for equity and sparking change in your library.

*Pursue professional development.* While this book has provided you with detailed information about media literacy—particularly chapter 3, written by the directors of the National Association for Media Literacy Education (NAMLE)—there is still so much more to explore! You can seek out opportunities to join librarian and educator associations that focus on media literacy, such as NAMLE or the International Society for Technology in Education. YALSA and the ALA have also begun investing in media literacy education and have created resources to support librarians in their work. Attend conferences in the fields of urban education and media literacy to learn more about effective strategies and programming. In the appendix, a list of associations, conferences, and resources is provided to help jump-start your professional development journey in the field.

Now that we have provided you with strategies and programs to better serve teens in your community, you are well equipped to begin implementing the knowledge you have acquired. But first, reflection is key before critically pursuing media literacy education with teens. So grab a notepad and pen, or a tablet, whichever you prefer, to reflect on the following questions and what you have gathered from your reading of this book:

1. What did you learn about teens in urban communities that you didn't know before?
2. What biases did you (or do you) have about Black and Hispanic teens and people from urban communities?
3. How have your biases influenced the interactions you've had with patrons in the past?

4. Based on your reading of chapters 1 and 2, how can you approach media literacy through a critical lens with historically marginalized teens?

5. How can you create a safe space for teens in your library to engage in media literacy?

6. Who can you partner with in your community (or virtually) to collaborate on media literacy programming at your library?

7. What would you like to achieve by implementing media literacy programs in your library with teens?

# APPENDIX
## Collection of Resources for Continued Learning

**Several lists of resources are provided below to support continued** learning in both the fields of urban education and media literacy. Any concise list could not do justice to the extensive number of valuable resources that are available. These lists are only intended to serve as launching points for further exploring how to better serve teens in urban communities and teach media literacy.

## 10 WEBSITES WITH MEDIA LITERACY CURRICULUMS, ACTIVITIES, HANDOUTS, FILMS, OR GAMES

1. Media Smarts. "Privilege in the Media." https://mediasmarts.ca/ digital-media-literacy/media-issues/diversity-media.
2. The Representation Project. "The Representation Project Films and Curriculum." https://therepproject.org/films.
3. Critical Media Project. "Critical Media Project Playlist." https:// criticalmediaproject.org/playlists.
4. U.S. Department of State, Global Engagement Center. "Breaking Harmony Square Game." https://harmonysquare.game.
5. News Guard. "Do You Know Your News? Quiz." www.knowmy news.com/en-US.
6. The Getting Better Foundation. *Trust Me Documentary*. www .trustmedocumentary.com.
7. News Literacy Project. "Checkology." https://get.checkology.org.

8. Stanford History Education Group. "Civic Online Reasoning." https://cor.stanford.edu.
9. Common Sense Media and Cornell University. "Social Media Test Drive." www.commonsense.org/education/social-media-test -drive.
10. Bad News. "Bad News Game." www.getbadnews.com/#play.

## 10 PROFESSIONAL DEVELOPMENT WEBSITES

1. American Library Association. "Media Literacy Education in Libraries for Adult Audiences." www.ala.org/tools/programming/ MediaLiteracy.
2. PBS. "Media Literacy Educator Certification." https://edu-landing .kqed.org/certification.
3. National Association for Media Literacy Education. https://namle .net.
4. The Media Education Lab. https://mediaeducationlab.com.
5. International Society for Technology in Education. www.iste.org.
6. International Conference on Urban Education. www.theicue.org.
7. Action Coalition for Media Education. https://acmesmartmedia education.net.
8. Critical Media Literacy Conference of the Americas. www.project censored.org/critical-media-literacy-conference-of-the-americas.
9. Culturally Sustaining Teaching Certificate. https://continuinged .uncc.edu/culturallysustaining.
10. Social Justice + Media Symposium. www.sjmsymposium.org.

## 10 BOOKS AND ARTICLES ON SERVING TEENS IN URBAN COMMUNITIES

1. Cervantes Soon, C. 2017. *Juárez Girls Rising: Transformative Education in Times of Dystopia*. University of Minnesota Press.
2. DiAngelo, R. 2018. *White Fragility: Why It's So Hard for White People to Talk about Racism*. Beacon.

3. Freire, P. 1970. *Pedagogy of the Oppressed*. Continuum International, 2000.
4. Kay, M. R. 2018. *Not Light, but Fire: How to Lead Meaningful Race Conversations in the Classroom*. Stenhouse.
5. Ladson-Billings, G. 1994. *The Dreamkeepers: Successful Teachers of African American Children*. Jossey-Bass.
6. Landsman, J., and C. Lewis. 2011. *White Teachers/Diverse Classrooms: Creating Inclusive Schools, Building on Students' Diversity, and Providing Educational Equity*. 2nd edition. Stylus.
7. Lopez, W. D. 2019. *Separated: Family and Community in the Aftermath of an Immigration Raid*. Johns Hopkins University Press.
8. Love, B. 2019. *We Want to Do More than Survive: Abolitionist Teaching and the Pursuit of Education Freedom*. Beacon.
9. Moore, J. L., and C. Lewis. 2012. *African American Students in Urban Schools: Critical Issues and Solutions for Achievement*. Peter Lang.
10. Wilson, W. J. 1990. *The Truly Disadvantaged: The Inner City, the Underclass, and Public Policy*. University of Chicago Press.

## 10 BOOKS AND ARTICLES ON CRITICAL MEDIA LITERACY AND MEDIA LITERACY EDUCATION

1. Alvermann, D. E., J. S. Moon, and M. C. Hagood. 2018. *Popular Culture in the Classroom: Teaching and Researching Critical Media Literacy*. Routledge.
2. De Abreu, B. S. 2019. *Teaching Media Literacy*. 2nd edition. American Library Association.
3. Hobbs, R. 2021. *Media Literacy in Action: Questioning the Media*. Rowman and Littlefield.
4. Kellner, D., and J. Share. 2019. *The Critical Media Literacy Guide: Engaging Media and Transforming Education*. Brill.
5. McArthur, S. A. 2016. "Black Girls and Critical Media Literacy for Social Activism." *English Education* 48 (4): 362–79.
6. Mihailidis, P. 2014. *Media Literacy and the Emerging Citizen: Youth, Engagement, and Participation in Digital Culture*. Peter Lang.

7. Morrell, E., R. Dueñas, V. Garcia, and J. López. 2013. *Critical Media Pedagogy: Teaching for Achievement in City Schools*. Teachers College Press.

8. Morrell, E. 2012. "21st-Century Literacies, Critical Media Pedagogies, and Language Arts." *The Reading Teacher* 66 (4): 300–02.

9. Price-Dennis, D., and Y. Sealey-Ruiz. 2021. *Advancing Racial Literacies in Teacher Education: Activism for Equity in Digital Spaces*. Teachers College Press.

10. Robertson, L., and J. Scheidler-Benns. 2016. "Critical Media Literacy as a Transformative Pedagogy." *Literacy Information and Computer Education Journal* 7 (1): 2247–53. https://doi.org/10.20533/licej.2040.2589.2016.0297.

# ABOUT THE AUTHORS AND CONTRIBUTORS

**JIMMEKA ANDERSON** received her PhD in urban education and is an author, media literacy educator, advisor, and consultant for several national organizations such as the American Library Association, Women's Sports Foundation, New America, U.S. Department of Education's Office of Education Technology, and WestEd. Currently, she serves as a project manager for the Cyber Citizenship Initiative with the National Association for Media Literacy Education (NAMLE) and is an Education Policy Program Fellow at New America. She is the creator of the Black Girls Film Camp and the founder and executive director of I AM not the MEdia, Inc. Jimmeka has been featured in *WIRED* magazine, the *Washington Post*, on NPR 1A, and in the *Trust Me Documentary* that was released in 2020.

**KELLY CZARNECKI** is the teen library manager at the ImaginOn branch of the Charlotte Mecklenburg Library. She also served as the 2021–2022 president of the Young Adult Library Services Association (YALSA). Czarnecki has developed, implemented, and managed new library programs serving the Charlotte Mecklenburg community in North Carolina. Some of her programs have earned national recognition from YALSA. She has also contributed extensively to the literature on teens and libraries, particularly with technology as a focus. Czarnecki earned both MSLIS and EdM degrees from the University of Illinois at Urbana-Champaign. She has also worked for more than twenty years with people experiencing homelessness who are sheltered.

LIZ ALLEN is a youth services librarian who specializes in school-age and teen program development. Her work is motivated by a passion for providing a safe, familiar space for youth to explore their creative voices and develop new interests and skills.

ROSS C. ANDERSON holds a PhD in education leadership from the University of Oregon. He is principal researcher at Inflexion, an associate scientist at the Oregon Research Institute, and the cofounder of the Creative Engagement Lab. His research focuses on agentic, artistic, and creative development in educators and the young people they teach.

CRAIG ARTHUR is an assistant professor and the head of community engagement at the Virginia Tech University Libraries. He's also been paying dues and working on his craft as a DJ since 1997. He cofounded VTDITC: Hip Hop Studies at Virginia Tech shortly after starting work at his alma mater in 2016.

ANUSHA BANSAL, a high school senior, is the founder of the Blissful Coding Club, an initiative to spread STEM and media awareness. Her work has been featured in *School Library Journal, Scholastic*, and other publications. She is the editor-in-chief of *The Blissful Pursuit* magazine, and she provides scholarships for Scholastic and the Alliance for Young Artists & Writers.

R. ALAN BERRY is a media literacy educator, researcher, and advocate based in Maine, where he is completing a PhD at the University of Maine. He was formerly the education director at The LAMP, a media literacy organization in New York City, and a Fulbright scholar in Kosovo.

HEATHER LOVE BEVERLEY is the assistant manager of children services at the Cook Memorial Public Library District in Libertyville/Vernon Hills, Illinois. She was a 2012 ALA Emerging Leader and a 2019 *Library Journal* Mover & Shaker.

MAISY CARD is a school library media specialist and author of the novel *These Ghosts Are Family*. She previously worked as the teen services librarian for the Newark Public Library. Her writings have appeared in *School Library Journal*, the *New York Times*, and other publications. Card lives and works in Newark, New Jersey.

DARCY COOVER is the teen system coordinator at Charleston County Public Library (CCPL) in South Carolina. She left a background in education to pursue a career in librarianship, and she served as the CCPL's assistant manager of young adult services for seven years before becoming the teen system coordinator there in 2019.

MARK J. DAVIS, PhD, is a digital literacy educator and advocate with eighteen years of public service. He is a doctoral candidate focusing on infographic literacy education and serves as a researcher for the University of Rhode Island's Media Education Lab. His wife and two children reside with him in Massachusetts.

BELINHA S. DE ABREU, PhD, is a global media literacy educator. She served as an international expert for the Forum on Media and Information Literacy for UNESCO's Communication and Information Section. De Abreu's focus is on the effects of the media and technology consumed by K–12 students on their learning and on providing students with viable, real-life opportunities to engage in various technological environments while also encouraging them to be creative users of technology and media. De Abreu is the president of the International Council for Media Literacy and teaches at Sacred Heart University.

MOLLY DETTMANN, MLIS, is a teacher librarian at Norman North High School in Norman, Oklahoma. She has worked in school libraries since 2018, having previously worked in public library teen services since 2014. She is highly active in the Young Adult Library Services Association and is also actively involved in the Oklahoma Library Association.

DENEEN S. DIXON-PAYNE is a doctoral candidate in K–12 education (urban education) at the University of North Carolina-Charlotte. Her research interests include addressing equity, diversity, inclusion, and justice centered around Black girlhood, and she is focused on gifted education and STEM in PK–12 urban school settings.

ALLY DOERMAN began working in libraries in 2006 and later went on to graduate with a master's degree in library science in 2016. She currently works for the Dayton (Ohio) Metro Library System as a teen services librarian.

RACHEL GULDIN, PhD, earned her doctorate in communication and media studies from the School of Journalism and Communication at the University of Oregon. She researches neoliberal capitalism and racism in media literacy education and takes a critical cultural approach to analyzing popular culture. Guldin is a certified elementary school teacher.

CYNDI HAMANN is the collection supervisor at Arlington Heights Memorial Library in Illinois. She previously worked as a teen librarian at the Crystal Lake Public Library. She was a 2019 ALA Emerging Leader.

CHRISTOPHER JACOBS is a Boston native and a former high school ELA teacher who joined the Boston Public Library system in 2019. He and Brianne Skywall comprise the Teen Technology Team at the Central location of the Boston Public Library. Both of them help to run Teen Central, a teen-exclusive community space equipped with robust technological resources.

PAMELA JAYNE is a youth services librarian at the Boone County Public Library in Florence, Kentucky. She has worked in libraries for thirteen years and received her MSLIS degree from Drexel University in 2014. She has spent most of her career focused on youth services, specifically teen services.

JONATHAN KABONGO holds a bachelor's degree in creative writing and is a graduate student in English at Virginia Tech. Kabongo plans to focus on a comparison analysis between rapper Kendrick Lamar's album *DAMN* and John Milton's *Paradise Lost* to show the strong similarities between them, despite the obvious differences.

ABBY KIESA is the deputy director at CIRCLE, a national nonpartisan research center that uses research to illuminate and find solutions to systemic gaps in young people's access to civic learning and engagement. CIRCLE's research informs policy and practice for healthier youth development and a more inclusive democracy. The research center is part of the Tisch College of Civic Life at Tufts University.

CHANCE W. LEWIS is the Carol Grotnes Belk distinguished professor of urban education at the University of North Carolina at Charlotte. Additionally, Lewis is the executive director of the Urban Education Collaborative.

MICHELLE CIULLA LIPKIN is the executive director of the National Association for Media Literacy Education (NAMLE) and an adjunct lecturer at Brooklyn College where she teaches media literacy. She has helped NAMLE grow to become the preeminent media literacy education association in the United States. Lipkin launched Media Literacy Week (now in its seventh year) and restructured the governance and membership of NAMLE. She has overseen five national conferences and made countless appearances at conferences and in the media regarding the importance of media literacy education.

ED MADISON is an associate professor at the University of Oregon's School of Journalism and Communication and has affiliated faculty status with the College of Education there. He is the author of *Newsworthy: Cultivating Critical Thinkers, Readers, and Writers in Language Arts Classrooms* (2015).

PAMELA McCARTER is an outreach coordinator and equity initiative lead at Charlotte Mecklenburg Library. She has more than twenty-five years' experience working with teens and adults in educational, recreational, and detention settings, as well as working with individuals experiencing homelessness. McCarter has been active in equity and inclusion initiatives at the local and national levels, including work with Mecklenburg County, the Urban Libraries Council, and the ALA/ARL. She is a contributing author to the book *Outreach Services for Teens: A Starter Guide* (2020) by Jess Snow.

ANDREA McNEIL is a children and teen librarian with more than twenty-five years' experience developing library programming and leading community events to engage children and families with library services.

FREDERICK PAIGE is a cofounder of the hip-hop studies program "Digging in the Crates" and an assistant professor at Virginia Tech in the Civil and Environmental Engineering Department. His main scholarly goal is to share the knowledge needed to develop an informed public that lives in a sustainable built environment.

LA' PORTIA J. PERKINS is a scientist and rapper. She serves as the federal lands associate at Defenders of Wildlife and was formerly the creative director and community engagement program specialist for the hip-hop studies program "Digging in the Crates" at Virginia Tech. Perkins holds an MS degree in forestry and a BS in wildlife and fisheries biology.

DONNELL PROBST is the deputy director of the National Association for Media Literacy Education (NAMLE) and a faculty associate at Arizona State University's Walter Cronkite School of Journalism and Mass Communication where she teaches Digital Media Literacy. Probst holds a BA in media studies from Arizona State University and an MLIS from San Jose State University.

LAUREN KRATZ PRUSHKO had been a public librarian for twelve years and is currently a children's librarian at the Los Angeles Public Library. Prushko has taught both children and teens how to create and record their podcasts. She records a podcast with her monthly children's book club called Children Chatting with Authors.

NICOLE RAMBO is a youth services librarian at the Middle Country Public Library (on Long Island, New York) whose passion for zines helped spark the idea for zine programming at her library. She received an award for her work on "The Zine Project" from the Young Adult Services Division of the Suffolk County Library Association.

JAMEY RORIE is a librarian at the Allegra Westbrooks Regional Library in Charlotte, North Carolina. He has more than eight years' experience working with teens in a public library setting and is focused on bringing teens new experiences and ways for them to express their voice and their own individuality.

BRIANNE SKYWALL is an Iowa transplant with several library positions under her belt. She joined the Boston Public Library system in 2019. Christopher Jacobs and Brianne Skywall collectively form the Teen Technology Team at the Central location of the Boston Public Library. Both help to run Teen Central, a teen-exclusive community space equipped with robust technological resources.

MICHAEL A. SPIKES studies news media literacy through the Learning Sciences at Northwestern University. He has engaged in news media literacy with Stony Brook University, the DC Public Schools, and the Newseum. He has also produced content for NPR, the *PBS Newshour*, and the Kellogg School of Management.

**CHRIS SPRADLIN** is a teen services specialist at the Mint Hill branch of Charlotte Mecklenburg Library. He loves to share the world of tabletop role-playing games with the community. Spradlin is currently running two D&D 5E programs, a Call of Cthulhu Harlem Unbound program for the library's Black Lives Matter initiative, and will soon start a QueeRPGs program highlighting queer creators and narratives for inclusive audiences.

**KRISTINE TANZI** is the coordinator for teen services at the Middle Country Public Library on Long Island, New York.

**LAURA VALLEJO** is a teen services library staff member at the South Boulevard Library Branch in Charlotte, North Carolina. She enjoys cosplaying in her spare time, as well as reading comics and manga and tabletop gaming.

**LONNA VINES** is a neighborhood branch manager at the Myers Park branch of Charlotte Mecklenburg Library. She has worked in public libraries for more than ten years and has served on the leadership team for Girls Rock Charlotte since 2017.

**JASMINE WEISS** is a senior sociology major with an Africana studies minor at Virginia Tech University. She is the creative director for the hip-hop studies program "Digging in the Crates" at Virginia Tech and the vice president of the Virginia Tech chapter of the NAACP. Her interests include social justice, music, and real estate.

**SHIMIRA WILLIAMS** is a Pittsburgh-based innovation consultant who seeks to integrate technology with informal educational environments to support children, youth, and their families. Community organizations consult with her to brainstorm, prototype, and implement data-driven projects that improve their ability to collaborate with partners and the community at large.

# INDEX

## A

access
    digital divide, 90–91
    equity of access, 48–49
    for media literacy education, 38–39
    as part of information literacy/media
      literacy, 43–44
    screen time differences and, 22
    to tools/instruction in library, 46
accessibility, 56–57
Ackerman, Patricia, xiv
action
    for media literacy, 41–42, 208
    as part of information literacy/media
      literacy, 43–44
active listening, 78–80
Adams-Bass, Valerie N., 27
Adobe Premier editing software, 146
adults
    broadband access, 22
    fear of urban teens, 76–77
    Intergenerational Media Literacy
      program, 96–97
    social capital of teens and, 9
advertising, 99
affinity space
    display work, 74
    flexible furniture, 73
    overview of, 72
    staff desk, 73–74
agency
    in JLI framework, 165–166
    media literacy education builds, 26
    of students with journalistic learning,
      167

ALA
    *See* American Library Association
Alitu.com, 118
Allegra Westbrooks Regional Library,
    181–184
Allen, Liz
    information about, 216
    on the Zine Club, 137–141
Alper, Meryl, 24
"Alright" (Lamar), 80
American Corner, North Mitrovica,
    Kosovo, 91–93
American Library Association (ALA)
    information literacy, adoption of, 161
    information literacy, definition of, 43
    media literacy education, 209
    *Media Literacy in the Library: A Guide*
      *for Library Practitioners*, 174
analysis
    of media content, 39
    as part of information literacy/media
      literacy, 43–44
"Analyzing and Creating Infographics"
    curriculum map (Edwards), 177
Anchor App
    ease of use/free, 121
    for editing podcast, 123
    for podcasting program, 118
Anderson, Brittany N., 30
Anderson, Jimmeka
    on Black Girls Film Camp, 149–154
    Chance W. Lewis on, xviii
    "The Education of Blacks in Charlotte
      (1920–2020), An Online Youth
      Exhibition" project, 130–136

Anderson, Jimmeka (cont'd)
  information about, 215
  Keepin' It Reel: Black Girls Film Camp,
    149–154
  on relationship-building, 83–84
  "Remembering the Why," xxi–xxvi
  on space/relationships for media
    literacy with urban teens, 69–84
  themes of book, xiii–xiv
  "The Train Has Arrived: Understanding
    Their World," 3–17
Anderson, Monica, 168, 179
Anderson, Ross C.
  information about, 216
  on journalistic learning approach, 163
  Journalistic Learning Initiative, 162–168
Anyon, Jean, 5
appeal factors
  for readers' advisory, 127–128, 130
  teen interest in, 129
appointments, 121, 122
art
  display of teens' work in library, 74
  Girls Rock Film Camp, 144–149
  Keepin' It Reel: Black Girls Film Camp,
    149–154
  in Zine Club, 138, 139, 140
  See also film; music
Arthur, Craig
  information about, 216
  on Virginia Tech's "Digging in the
    Crates" Hip Hop Studies program,
    110–114
articles
  on critical media literacy/media
    literacy education, 213–214
  on serving teens in urban
    communities, 212–213
artists, 141
ASA@MyLibrary program series, 141
Ashley, Seth, 169
asset-based approach
  critical lens for media literacy
    education, 26–27
  to media literacy, 24–25
Associated Press, xiv
Audacity, 116
Auphonic.com, 117
authorship, 39
Auxier, Brooke, 168

**B**
Baldwin, James, 69
Ballard, Parissa J., 26
Bankert, Alexa, 26
Bansal, Anusha
  Blissful Coding Club, 195–201
  information about, 216
Barman-Adhikari, Anamika, 23
Barnard College, 138
barriers
  cultural context and, 61
  at-home stressors, 63–64
  identities of librarians as, 58–60
  leading with curiosity, 60–61
  librarians as barriers to urban teens in
    libraries, 53–54
  library outreach programming for
    addressing, 66–67
  security in libraries, 61–63
  to teens, observing/evaluating, 208–209
  See also challenges
Barrington Middle School, Rhode Island,
  174–177
Barrington Public Library, 174–177
Barron, Brigid, 27
Bates, M. J., 44
beat battle, 112
The Beauty of S.T.E.M., 191–195
beliefs
  evaluation of media content, 40
  views of teens, 62
Belle Booth, 23
Berry, R. Alan
  information about, 216
  "Power Lines: Empowering Teens Who
    Have Been Disempowered through
    Partnerships," 87–105
Beverley, Heather Love
  "ALT RA: Looking beyond Books in
    Readers' Advisory," 127–130
  information about, 216
Beyoncé, 3
bias
  of all media messages, 42
  evaluation of media content, 40
  identities of librarian and, 55
  youth interaction with media and, 126
Biden, Jill, 197
BIPOC (Black, Indigenous, and people of
  color) communities
  generational poverty among, 6

librarians as barriers to urban teens in
libraries, 53–54
media representation of, 13
BIPOC (Black, Indigenous, and people of
color) students
"The Education of Blacks in Charlotte
(1920–2020), An Online Youth
Exhibition" project, 130–136
library outreach programming for
marginalized youth, 66–67
literacy, disparities among
marginalized students, 10–11
Teen Technology Mentor program,
population served, 187
*Black Feminist Thought* (Collins), 150
"Black Girl Magic" term, 150
Black people
in inner-city urban communities, 5
*Power Lines* for Black parents, xviii
segregated communities and, 7–9
"urban" term as socially constructed
reality, 3
Black women
as guest speakers for Black Girls Film
Camp, 152–153
impact of Black Girls Film Camp, 153–154
Black youth
Keepin' It Reel: Black Girls Film Camp,
149–154
media consumption by, 13
media creation by, 25–26
Blake, Jamilia, 151
Blinn, J. R., 164–165
Blissful Coding Club
Blissful Us logo, 201
library collaboration for, 198–200
peer-to-peer learning, 195–196
program overview, 196–197
success of, 197–198
Blissful Us
founding of, 195
logo of, 201
success of, 197
website/social media links, 200
blue screen, 143
*Board of Education, Brown v.*, 7
booklists, 129
BookRiot, 129
books
on critical media literacy/media
literacy education, 213–214

on serving teens in urban
communities, 212–213
video games *vs.*, 179
books/print literature programs
"The Education of Blacks in Charlotte,
An Online Youth Exhibition," 130–136
introduction to, 125–126
readers' advisory for teens, 127–130
Zine Club, 137–141
Booth, Belle, 25
Boston Public Library, 185–191
Bousselot, Tracy, 163
Bowles, Samuel, 14
Braun, Linda W., 70
Brayton, Spencer, 83
Brennan, Christine, 157
bring your own technology (BYOT) ethos,
101
Brinkmann, Svend, 169
broadcast journalism, 156
Brooklyn Public Library, 88–89
*Brown v. Board of Education*, 7
Buckingham, David, 25
budget, 189–190
*See also* funding
"But What Is Urban Education?" (Milner),
4–5
BuzzFeed, 129
BYOT (bring your own technology) ethos,
101

**C**
California
Journalistic Learning Initiative for
students in, 164
public libraries as hub for
marginalized teens, 65
Card, Maisy
Blissful Coding Club, 195–201
information about, 216
Cardoza, Nicole, 71
career training
The Beauty of S.T.E.M. program, 191
Digital Career Path Programs, 93–95
Girls on the Beat@ Charleston County
Public Library, 154–157
Journalistic Learning Initiative, 162–168
Carnegie Library of Pittsburgh-
Homewood, 191–195
Carnegie Mellon University, 196

Carolina School of Broadcasting, 133
Casey, Natasha
on critical media literacy, 83
on relationship-building with teens, 83–84
Cayleff, Susan, 152–153
CCPL (Charleston County Public Library), 154–157
Center for News Literacy at Stony Brook University, 168, 169–174
Cervantes-Soon, Claudia, 81
chairs, 73
challenges
of analyzing news through infographics, 175–176
experienced by teens in urban communities, 5–13
of podcasting program, 122
of Teen Technology Mentor program, 188–189
of teens in community, teen reflection on, 15–16
of teens today, 70
of Zine Club, 140
challenges/opportunities of serving urban teens in libraries
cultural context of responses, 61
at-home stressors for teens and, 63–64
identities as barriers, scenarios about, 58–60
identities/privilege of librarians, 54–57
Jasmine McNeil on library outreach programming, 66–67
leading with curiosity, 60–61
librarians as barriers to teens, 53–54
Mary J. Wardell-Ghirarduzzi on library support of marginalized teens, 65–66
politics in library space, 57
security in libraries, 61–63
teen reflection on library support of success, 64–65
Chan, Chitat, 25
Chandra, Sumit, 22
character, 127, 128
characteristic, 4
Charleston County Public Library (CCPL), 154–157
Charlotte, North Carolina
CMS schools, segregation of, 7–8
"The Education of Blacks in Charlotte (1920–2020), An Online Youth Exhibition" project, 130–136

social capital/upward mobility in, 9–10
Charlotte Mecklenburg Library
Dewey and Dragons program, 181–184
"The Education of Blacks in Charlotte (1920–2020), An Online Youth Exhibition" project, 130–136
Girls Rock Film Camp: The Future of Film, 144–149
ImaginOn, mission of, 143
teen reflection on relationships built through library programs, 102–103
*Charlotte Observer* (newspaper)
article about education in, 131
on CMS graduation rates, 8
*Charlotte Talks* (public radio show), 7–8
*Charlotte-Mecklenburg Board of Education, Swann v.*, 133
Charlotte-Mecklenburg Schools (CMS), 7–8
Chetty, Raj, 10
Chiles, Nick, xiv
Choi, Changhee, 164
Chow, Garrick, 116
Chromebook, 183
civic engagement, 95–99
civic media literacy, 95–99
Civil Rights Data Collection website, 131
Claiborne, Jeneva, 102–103
Clark, Lynn Schofield, 24
clothing fashions, 191–195
CMS (Charlotte-Mecklenburg Schools), 7–8
Code with Google, 202
Codecademy, 202, 203
Code.org, 202, 203
coding clubs
Blissful Coding Club, 195–201
guidance for, 201–203
technology club, 203–204
3D printing club, 204–205
Cohen, Alison K., 26
co-learning, 83
Coleman Report (federal government), 9
collaboration
for Blissful Coding Club, 198–199
community engagement for partnerships, 100
for "The Education of Blacks in Charlotte (1920–2020), An Online Youth Exhibition" project, 132
of teens in coding clubs, 203
*See also* partnerships
college students, 196, 200

Collins, Patricia, 150, 151
*The Color of Law* (Rothstein), 8
Common Sense Media, 22, 175
communication
    for Girls Rock Film Camp, 146
    youth-produced publications, 163–164
community
    engaging for partnerships, 100
    identity of Black girls and, 151
    libraries as welcoming place for, xiii–
      xiv
    partnerships as conduits for
      community-building, 95–99
    steps for learning more about, 208–
      209
    Virginia Tech's "Digging in the Crates"
      Hip Hop Studies program, 110–114
    Zine Club and, 141
computers
    access to, 90
    from Charlotte Mecklenburg Library,
      183
    digital divide and, 12
    for podcasting program, 123
    tech equity for virtual Teen Tech
      Mentor program, 189
    for 3D printing club, 205
concentration effect, 6–7
connectors
    music as connector, 109–110
    people at the library as, 192
    urban teens as, 54
consistency, 80
content creators
    display of teens' work in library, 74
    media literate, skills of, 41
context, 39
conversation, 130
Coover, Darcy
    Girls on the Beat@ Charleston County
      Public Library, 154–157
    information about, 217
copyright, 41
*Core Principles of Media Literacy Education*
  (NAMLE)
    "Implications for Practice," 42–43
    media literacy definition, 36–37
    media literacy, skills for, 38–42
    YALSA's *Teen Services Competencies for*
      *Library Staff* and, 45–49
Cornelius, Ariah, 136
Corning, Sean, 95

Costner, Kevin, 75
counterspace
    Black Girls Film Camp as, 151
    as lens, 74
    library as, 70–71
COVID-19 pandemic
    digital divides and, 90
    gaming time increase during, 180
    Girls on the Beat program and, 157
    Girls Rock Film Camp and, 149
    podcasting programming and, 122
    screen time increase during, 144
    technological inequities during, 11–12
    teen reflection on interests stemming
      from experience, 15–16
    Teen Technology Mentor program and,
      187, 188
Craig, Shelley L.
    on media representation of youth, 27
    on online spaces as supports, 23
creation, 43–44
    *See also* media creation
credibility, 39, 40
Creighton, Peggy Milam, 177
Crenshaw, Kimberlé, 152
crime, 7
critical analysis, 47–48
critical lens, for media literacy education,
  26–28
critical media literacy
    active listening and, 79–80
    books/articles on, 213–214
    changing perceptions with, 13
    in education for marginalized
      students, 14–15
    function of, 14–15
    Jayne Cubbage on, 17
    Jeff Share on, 16–17
    relationship-building with teens and,
      83–84
critical pedagogy, 14
critical theory, 14
critical thinking
    about all media messages, 42
    improvements with journalistic
      learning, 167
Cubbage, Jayne, 17
cultural beauty standards, 79–80
cultural competency, 48
cultural context, 61
cultural inclusiveness, 48
Curry, Adam, 110

Czarnecki, Kelly
  on challenges/opportunities with
    serving urban teens in libraries,
    53–67
  Chance W. Lewis on, xviii
  collaboration with Jimmeka Anderson,
    xxiii, xxiv
  information about, 215
  Jimmeka Anderson's thanks to, xxv
  on relationship-building, 83–84
  on space/relationships for media
    literacy with urban teens, 69–84
  themes of book, xiii–xiv

**D**

D&D Beyond website, 181, 183
Dahya, Negin, 25
Dale, Jolly, 147–148
Daly, James, 36
data literacy, 176
Davis, Mark J.
  analyzing the news through
    infographics, 174–177
  information about, 217
Davis, Viola, 152
De Abreu, Belinha S., xiii–xv, 217
De los Ríos, C. V., 27
deconstruction, 169
DeJarnette, Ben, 163
DeMarrais, Kathleen, 14
Dennis, Everette E., 96
Derakhshan, Hossein, 168
desegregation, 7–8
design, 204–205
Dettmann, Molly
  information about, 217
  Podcasting the Possibilities program,
    120–123
Dewey and Dragons, 181–184
"Digging in the Crates" Hip Hop Studies
  program, Virginia Tech, 110–114
digital age, 173
Digital Career Path Programs, 93–95
digital citizenship, 41
Digital Club Support Program, 181
digital democracy, 66
digital divide
  Digital Career Path Programs, 93–95
  Digital Storytelling with Twine
    program and, 91–93

homework gap from, 12
  partnerships for skill development/
    healthy digital relationships, 90–95
digital journalism, 155–156
digital literacy, 165
"digital natives," 22
digital relationships, 90–95
Digital Storytelling with Twine program,
  91–93
digital/makerspace, 73
disciplinary systems, 62–63
discrimination, 54
disinformation
  need for media literacy education,
    161–162
  news media literacy and, 168, 169
disparities
  experienced by teens in urban
    communities, 5–6
  literacy, 10–11
  media/misrepresentation of teens, 13
  poverty/social dislocation, 6–7
  segregated communities, 7–9
  social capital/upward mobility, 9–10
  technological inequity, 11–12
display
  of narrative infographics, 176
  of teens' work in library, 74
dispositions, 29
diversity
  critical pedagogy embraces, 14
  of Girls Rock Film Camp, 145
  library representation of diverse
    communities, 45–46, 47
  teen-centered readers' advisory tips,
    130
Dixon-Payne, Deneen S.
  on Black Girls Film Camp, 149–154
  information about, 217
Doerman, Ally
  on coding clubs, 201–205
  information about, 217
double consciousness, 8–9
Dowds, Ally, 191
DragonPad Pop Filter, 117, 118
drive, 208
DTLA Mini Maker Faire event, 120
Du Bois, W. E. B.
  on double consciousness, 8–9
  "How does it feel to be a problem?,"
    xvii

Duvernay, Ava, 149
Dvorak, Jack, 164

**E**

Ecamm recording software, 117
economics, 39
Edifier H650 Headphones, 117
Edmonds, Rachel, 135
education
    critical media literacy for teens, 16–17
    critical theory and, 14
    of teens in urban communities, xvii–xviii
    Theresa Redmond on media literacy skills in instruction, 50
    *See also* media literacy education
"The Education of Blacks in Charlotte (1920–2020), An Online Youth Exhibition" project, 130–136
educational rhetoric, xviii
educators
    *Core Principles of Media Literacy Education*'s "Implications for Practice," 42–43
    media literacy education in learning environments, 46
    teen media use, understanding of, 30
    *See also* voices from the field
Edwards, Julie Biando, 95
Edwards, Nicole, 177
effectiveness, 40
"Empire State of Mind," 1
empowerment
    of Blissful Coding Club members, 198
    as form of media literacy action, 42
    learning environment of hope, 101
    podcasting programs for empowering teens, 115
    of students with journalistic learning, 167
empowerment, through partnerships
    conclusion about, 102
    conduits for community-building/civic engagement, 95–99
    conduits for skill development/healthy digital relationships, 90–95
    Elis Estrada on library partnerships, 104–105
    for The LAMP programs on media literacy, 87–89

lessons learned for media literacy partnerships, 99–101
    Nygel D. White on library partnerships, 103–104
    teen reflection on relationships built through library programs, 102–103
environment
    *See* space
Epstein, Rebecca, 151
equipment
    for podcasting program, 120–121, 122, 123
    of Teen Central, Boston Public Library, 185
    *See also* technology
equity
    intellectual freedom for media literacy skills, 48–49
    tech equity for virtual Teen Tech Mentor program, 189
Estrada, Elis, 104–105
ethics, 41
evaluation
    of media content in media literacy education, 40
    as part of information literacy/media literacy, 43–44
Evans, Jabari, 27

**F**

Facebook, 24, 173–174
fair use, 41
fake news, 49–50
fashion, 191–195
The Fashion Apprentice program, xxiii
fashion show, 192, 193
features writing, 156
federal government
    racially segregated communities, force behind, 8
    role in maintaining poverty, 5
fiction, 171
field experts, 104–105
*Field of Dreams* (film), 75
film
    Girls on the Beat@ Charleston County Public Library, 154–158
    Girls Rock Film Camp: The Future of Film, 103, 144–149
    Keepin' It Reel: Black Girls Film Camp, 149–154
    programs for teens, 143–144

First Ward High School, 133
Fisher, Stephanie, 25
Flake, Ebony, 150
food
    at-home stressors of teens and, 64
    teen taking food at library, 60–61
format, for podcast recording, 115
Foundry VTT, 181–182, 183
Franklin, Miss, 192
Freire, Paulo
    on co-learning, 83
    on critical media literacy, 16
    critical pedagogy developed by, 14
*Full Frontal with Samantha Bee* (television
  program), 170
funding
    for The Beauty of S.T.E.M. program, 194
    for Black Girls Film Camp, 152
    for "The Education of Blacks in
      Charlotte (1920–2020), An Online
      Youth Exhibition" project, 132
    for podcasting program, 118
    for Teen Tech Mentor program, 190
furniture, 73–74
*The Future of Library Services for and with
Teens: A Call to Action* (YALSA & IMLS),
70


**G**

Game Master, 183–184
gaming
    The Beauty of S.T.E.M., 191–195
    Blissful Coding Club, 195–201
    coding clubs, 201–205
    Dewey and Dragons, 181–184
    for media literacy, 179–180
    Teen Tech Mentor program, 185–191
GarageBand, 115–117
Garcia, Antero, 27
gendered bathrooms, 57
generational poverty, 6
Genner, Sarah, 22
genre, 127, 128
gentrification, 208
Gillig, Traci, 27
Gingold, Jessica, 26
Gintis, Herbert, 14
Girls on the Beat@ Charleston County
  Public Library, 154–158
Girls Rock Camp Alliance website, 149

Girls Rock Charlotte (GRC), 144–149
Girls Rock CLT website, 149
Girls Rock Film Camp: The Future of Film,
  103, 144–149
Girls Who Code club, 199, 202
goals
    of media literacy partnerships, 102
    shared goals of partnership, clarity
      about, 100
    student goals for Zine Club, 138
Goldfarb, Brian, 25
González, Thalia, 151
*Good Hair* (film), 79
Goodreads, 129
Google Codelabs, 202
Google Forms, 188
Google search, 173–174
Google Slides, 174, 188
graduation rates, 8
graphic design skills, 93–95
Greater Cincinnati STEM Collaborative,
  204
Greenspan, Alan, 5
Gretter, Sarah, 162
Grundy, Pamela
    "The Education of Blacks in Charlotte
      (1920–2020), An Online Youth
      Exhibition" project, 131
    historical workshops by, 132
Guadiano, Nicole, 11
guest speakers
    for Black Girls Film Camp, 152–153
    for Girls on the Beat@ Charleston
      County Public Library, 155–157
    for Girls Rock Film Camp, 148
Guldin, Rachel
    information about, 218
    on journalistic learning approach, 163
    Journalistic Learning Initiative, 162–168
    on student awareness of issues, 167
guns, 61–63
Gunton, Lyndelle, 161


**H**

Haddix, Marcelle, 154
Halpin, Catherine, 191
Hamann, Cyndi
    "ALT RA: Looking beyond Books in
      Readers' Advisory," 127–130
    information about, 218

Hamer, Fannie Lou, 153
hands-on projects, 157
"hanging out," 81
Hanif, Zakariyah, 64–65
Haque, Yousuf S., 169
Harrison, A. Kwame, 111
Harvard University, 10
Headliner website/app, 118
Helms, Ann Doss, 8
Hicks, Alasia, 28–29
hip-hop, 110–114
Hispanic youth
    literacy of, 10
    in urban communities, 5
history
    capturing through media, 131–132
    of community, researching, 208
    "The Education of Blacks in Charlotte
        (1920–2020), An Online Youth
        Exhibition" project, 130–136
Hobbs, Renee, 177
Holosko, Michael J., 25
homework gap, 12
hooks, bell, xiii
hope, 101
Hornik, R., 169
Horsley, Suzanne, 23
Huddy, Leonie, 26
Hudson Guild, New York City
    Intergenerational Media Literacy
        program, 96–97
    partnership for Digital Career Path
        Programs, 93–95
Hughes-Hassell, Sandra, 125, 126
*The Hunger Games* (Collins), 171
Huntsville-Madison County Public Library
    Online LibGuide, 174

**I**

I AM not the MEdia, Inc.
    digital media workshops by, 133
    "The Education of Blacks in Charlotte
        (1920–2020), An Online Youth
        Exhibition" project, 130–136
    Jimmeka Anderson's creation of, xxiii
    We Can Imagine workshop, 134
Ibrahim Mazreku school, Malisheva,
    Kosovo, 98, 99
ICT (information communication
    technology), 11–12

ideas, 44
identities
    examination of identity
        characteristics, 54–55
    multiple identities of teens in urban
        communities, 4
    relationship-building before rule
        enforcement, 58–59
    story you are telling yourself, 59–60
Igielnik, Ruth, 22, 23
ImaginOn branch of the Charlotte
    Mecklenburg Library
    affinity space of, 72–73
    blue screen for teen space, 143
    Girls Rock Film Camp: The Future of
        Film, 147–149
    Jimmeka Anderson's work at, xxi–xxiii
    teen reflection on media-centered
        programs of, 82–83
IMLS (Institute of Museum and Library
    Services), 70
"Implications for Practice" (NAMLE), 42–43
implicit bias, 55
inappropriate language, 78
inclusion, 38
inequities, 11–12
Infogram, 177
infographics, 174–177
information
    access to, 38–39
    analysis skills, 39
    evaluating media, 40
    media literacy and, 35–36
    search process, 44
information communication technology
    (ICT), 11–12
information literacy
    definition of, 43, 161
    as essential skill, xxv
    with media literacy, 43–45
    need for, 161–162
    in post-truth era, 12
Information Neighborhoods lesson plan,
    169–174
"infotainment" media genre, 170
Instagram
    Blissful Coding Club links, 200
    presidential election information on,
        23, 24
Institute of Museum and Library Services
    (IMLS), 70

integration
  Rachel Edmonds on, 135
  We Are Equal workshop about, 133
intellectual freedom, 48–49
interest, 76–78
Intergenerational Media Literacy program, 96–97
International Institute for Restorative Practices, 63
International Society for Technology in Education, 209
internet
  media access/use among youth, 22–26
  media creation, benefits of, 24–26
internet access
  digital divide and, 12, 90
  in Kosovo, 92
  for teens, 180
  youth screen time and, 22
interpretations, 40
interviews
  with community experts in JLI, 165
  for "The Education of Blacks in Charlotte" project, 133
  for The LAMP program, 88–89
  podcast programming ideas, 120
  for Teen Tech Mentor program, 188
investigative journalism, 155
iPad, 115, 116–117

**J**
Jacobs, Christopher
  information about, 218
  on Teen Technology Mentor program, 185–191
Jacovkis, Judith, 6
Jay, Eileen, 29
Jay Z, 1
Jayne, Pamela
  on coding clubs, 201–205
  information about, 218
Jenson, Jennifer, 25
Jiang, Jingjing, 179
JLI
  See Journalistic Learning Initiative
Jocson, Korina M., 12
Johnson, G. M., 169
Johnson C. Smith University, 133
Johnston-Goodstar, Katie, 27
Jones, ScottBey, 71

Jones, Sosanya Marie, 150
Jones, Stimulator, 112–113
*Journal of Research in Science Teaching*, 70
journalism
  Girls on the Beat@ Charleston County Public Library, 154–157
  Journalistic Learning Initiative, 162–168
  lesson plan in news media literacy, 168–174
  library partnerships with journalists, 104–105
  reasons to integrate, 163–164
journalistic learning
  design of, 163
  Journalistic Learning Initiative for, 164–166
  outcomes of, 166–167
  youth-produced publications, 163–164
Journalistic Learning Initiative (JLI)
  core framework, 165–166
  description of, 164–165
  journalistic learning, 162–163
  journalistic learning successes, 166–167
  reasons to integrate journalism, 163–164
  resources for, 167–168
*Juárez Girls Rising: Transformative Education in Times of Dystopia* (Cervantes-Soon), 81

**K**
Kabongo, Jonathan
  information about, 218
  on Virginia Tech's "Digging in the Crates" Hip Hop Studies program, 110–114
Katz, Vikki S., 24, 90
Kawashima-Ginsberg, Kei, 26
Kay, Matthew, 79–80
Keepin' It Reel: Black Girls Film Camp, 149–154
Kellner, Douglas
  on critical media literacy, 15, 83
  on media literacy education, 27
  on teaching media literacy, 24
Kendi, Ibram X., 62
Kersch, Dorotea Frank, 27
Keys, Alicia, 1
Kiesa, Abby
  information about, 218

"It Never Sleeps: The Current State of Teens and Media," 21–30
on media literacy education, 26
King, Maya, 11
Kirsh, Steven J., 13
"Know Your Neighborhood" lesson plan, 169–174
Kosovo
Digital Storytelling with Twine program, 91–93
"Photography as Activism" project/"PSAs for Social Change" project, 98–99
Kosovo War, 91
Kuhlthau, Carol C., 44
Kwon, L., 27


**L**
"Lab" of Teen Central, Boston Public Library, 185, 190
The LABS@ CLP program, 194
Ladd, Helen F., 6
Ladson-Billings, Gloria, 110, 153
Lamar, Kendrick, 80
The LAMP (Learning About Multimedia Project)
Digital Career Path Programs, 93–95
Intergenerational Media Literacy program, 97
media literacy education programming, 87–89
Lapus, Merve, 29–30
*Last Week Tonight* (television program), 170
*Latinitas* (digital magazine), 27–28
Latinx youth
JLI program for, 167
media creation by, 25–26
leadership, 60–61
learning
as lifelong pursuit, 96–97
media literacy in learning experiences, 47
objectives of Information Neighborhoods, 172
learning environment
of hope, creation of, 101
media literacy education in, 46
*See also* space
LeCompte, Margaret, 14

Lee, Ah Ram, 23
Lee, Chungmei, 7, 9
leisure reading, 125, 126
Leorke, D., 180
Lesley, Mellinee, 27
lesson plans, 168–174
lesson setup, 122–123
lessons learned, 99–101
Lewis, Chance W.
information about, 218
preface, xvii–xviii
on social capital, 9
LGBTQ+, 130
LibGuides, 170, 174
librarians
critical media literacy in library programs for teens, 16–17
cultural context of responses, 61
diversity of, library as counterspace and, 70–71
at-home stressors for teens and, 63–64
identities as barriers, scenarios about, 58–60
identities/privilege of librarians, 54–57
Jasmine McNeil on library outreach programming, 66–67
leading with curiosity, 60–61
lesson plan in news media literacy for YA librarians, 168–174
librarians as barriers to teens, 53–54
library support of marginalized teens, 65–66
media literacy and, 207–210
music in programming, 110
politics in library space, 57
reading motivation of children and, 11
relationships, building, 75–81
relationships with teens, 7
security in libraries, 61–63
social capital of teens and, 10
space, creating, 69–74
teen reflection on challenges, 15–16
teen reflection on library support of success, 64–65
teens' perceptions/realities and, 9
libraries
for access to computers/internet, 12
accessibility of, 56–57
affinity space, 72–74
barriers to teens, 208–209
classification systems of, 54

libraries (*cont'd*)
    community-building by, 95
    as counterspaces, 70–71
    gaming programs in, 180
    at-home stressors of teens and, 63–64
    library outreach programming for,
      66–67
    media literacy and, 207–210
    opportunities/learning environments
      for media literacy, 49
    partnerships for empowering teens,
      87–89
    partnerships for media literacy
      programs with teens in urban
      communities, 103–104
    politics in library space, 57
    security in, 61–63
    space, creating, 69–74
    support of marginalized teens, 65–66
    as welcoming place, xiii
    YALSA's *Teen Services Competencies for
      Library Staff* and, 45–49
*The Library as Playground: How Games
  and Play Are Reshaping Public Culture*
  (Leorke & Wyatt), 180
library liaison, 146
library partnerships
    *See* partnerships
*Library Staff as Public Servants: A
  Field Guide for Preparing to Support
  Communities in Crisis* (Subramaniam et
  al.), 72
library stakeholders, 118–119
"Life Told by a Stranger" podcast, 117
Light Up Hoodies project, 193
LinkedIn, 200
LinkedIn Learning, 115, 116
Lipkin, Michelle Ciulla
    "Flashing Lights: What Is Media
      Literacy?," 35–50
    information about, 219
Lipman, Pauline, 5
listening, active, 78–80
literacy
    challenges of teens in urban
      communities, 10–11
    critical media literacy for teens, 16–17
    technology proficiency and, 12
Littenberg-Tobias, Joshua, 26
Livingston, Gretchen, 144
Lorde, Audre, 4, 150

Los Angeles Public Library, 114–120
"Lounge" of Teen Central, Boston Public
  Library, 185, 190
Lu, Marie, 179
Lucas, George, 36
Luke, Allan, 83
Lynda.com, 115


**M**

Macedo, Donaldo, 16
Mack, Mckensie, 53–54
Madison, Ed
    information about, 219
    on journalistic learning approach, 163
    Journalistic Learning Initiative, 162–168
Madison Public Library, Wisconsin, 63
magazines, 137–141
Malcolm X, 21
*Malcolm X* (film), 79
marginalized youth
    double consciousness of, 8–9
    library outreach programming for,
      66–67
    library support of, 65–66
Martin, Trayvon, 193
mass media, 13
Mattern, Shannon, 53
Maxwell, Angie, 23
Mayer, Lillian, 207
McCarter, Pamela
    "The Education of Blacks in Charlotte
      (1920–2020), An Online Youth
      Exhibition" project, 130–136
    information about, 219
McElvane, Maia
    on Girls Rock Film Camp, 103
    photo of, 149
McInroy, Lauren B.
    on media representation of youth, 27
    on online spaces as supports, 23
McNeil, Andrea
    The Beauty of S.T.E.M. program,
      191–195
    information about, 219
MCPL (Middle Country Public Library)
    media literacy programs, 64–65
    Zine Club of, 137–141
meaning, 44
media
    access/use among youth, 22–26

analysis of, 39

Brittany N. Anderson on teen media use, 30

consumers, 44

evaluation of, 40

Journalistic Learning Initiative, 162–168

lesson plan in news media literacy, 168–174

library partnerships with media, 104–105

media creation, 40–41

messages, media literacy for, 44

misrepresentation of teens in urban communities, 13

"Photography as Activism" project, 98–99

readers' advisory service and, 127

teen reflection on engagement with, 28–29

teens' use of, 29–30

young people's relationships to, 21

media creation

benefits for teens, 24–26

for media literacy, importance of, 40–41

media genres, 169–174

media information literacy (MIL), 162

media literacy

access, 38–39

action for, 41–42

analyzing media content, 39

approaches to teaching, 24–26

changing perceptions with, 13

conclusion about, 49, 207–210

Core Principles of Media Literacy Education, 36–37

Core Principles of Media Literacy Education's "Implications for Practice," 42–43

definition of, 35–36, 43

evaluating media content, 40

focus on teens in urban communities, xxv–xxvi

gaming for, 179–180

with information literacy, 43–45

Jeff Share on critical media literacy, 16–17

Jimmeka Anderson's focus on, xxiii–xxiv

media creation, 40–41

need for, 161–162

opportunities/learning environments for, 49

power lines, meanings of, xxiv

serving teens in urban communities via, xvii–xviii

teen reflection on importance of, 49–50

Theresa Redmond on, 50

YALSA's *Teen Services Competencies for Library Staff*, 45–49

media literacy education

benefits of, xiv–xv

Brittany N. Anderson on, 30

for comprehensive understanding of information landscape, 35

*Core Principles of Media Literacy Education*, 36–37

*Core Principles of Media Literacy Education's* "Implications for Practice," 42–43

critical lens for, 26–28

incorporation into learning environments, 46

The LAMP programs for, 87–89

media access/use among youth, 22–26

Merve Lapus on, 29–30

need for, 161–162

partnerships, lessons learned, 99–101

partnerships as vital to, 102

partnerships for community-building/ civic engagement, 95–99

relationships between teens/types of media, 21

representation/context/voice and, xiv

resources for, 211–214

teen reflection on, 28–29

*Media Literacy in the Library: A Guide for Library Practitioners* (ALA), 174

Media Literacy Now, xxiii

media literacy programs

ALT RA: Looking beyond Books in Readers' Advisory, 127–130

analyzing the news through infographics, 174–177

The Beauty of S.T.E.M. program, 191–195

Blissful Coding Club, 195–201

for building relationships with teens, 75–81

coding clubs, 201–205

Digital Career Path Programs, 93–95

media literacy programs (*cont'd*)
Digital Storytelling with Twine program, 91–93
"The Education of Blacks in Charlotte, An Online Youth Exhibition," 130–136
gaming, 179–180
Girls on the Beat@ Charleston County Public Library, 154–157
Girls Rock Film Camp: The Future of Film, 144–149
Journalistic Learning Initiative, 162–168
Keepin' It Reel: Black Girls Film Camp, 149–154
lesson plan in news media literacy, 168–174
music/podcasting programs, 109–123
overview of chapters on, 107
podcasting programming for your library, 114–120
Podcasting the Possibilities program, 120–123
Teen Technology Mentor program, 185–191
Virginia Tech's "Digging in the Crates" Hip Hop Studies program, 110–114
Zine Club, 137–141
media structures, 43
mentoring
in Black Girls Film Camp, 152–153
with media professionals, 105
Teen Technology Mentor program, 185–191
Meyer, Leila, 12
microaggressions
library space and, 71
security in libraries and, 75
microphone, 117, 118
Middle Country Public Library (MCPL)
media literacy programs, 64–65
Zine Club of, 137–141
Mihailidis, Paul
on media literacy education, 26
on media literacy framework, 95–96
MIL (media information literacy), 162
Military Child Educational Summit, 197
Milner, Richard, 4–5
Mind Over Media, 177
Mirra, Nicole, 12
mirrors/windows concept, 67
misinformation
media literacy and, 49–50

need for media literacy education, 161–162
news media literacy and, 168, 169
misrepresentation, 13
Mitrovica, Kosovo, 91–93
"Moon Zine" program, 141
Moore, James L., III, 9
morality, 69
Morgan, Kristin, 194
Morrell, Ernest, 14, 30
Morrison, Toni, 87
Muhammed, Gholnecsar E., 154
Murphy, Sheila, 27
music
Music Over Violent Entertainment (MOVE) program, 78–79
"The Top 10 Teen Video Countdown" program, 77–78
Virginia Tech's "Digging in the Crates" Hip Hop Studies program, 110–114
Music Over Violent Entertainment (MOVE) program, 78–79

**N**

narrative infographics, 175–176
narratives, 40
National Assessment of Educational Progress (NAEP)
on literacy gap, 10, 11
on technological inequity, 11, 12
National Association for Media Literacy Education (NAMLE)
on access, 38
on action, 41
on analysis of media content, 39
*Core Principles of Media Literacy Education*, 36–37, 45–49
*Core Principles of Media Literacy Education*'s "Implications for Practice," 42–43
on evaluation of media content, 40
Jimmeka Anderson's volunteer work with, xxiii
on media creation, 40
media literacy, definition of, 35, 43
on media literacy education vision, 25
professional development, 209
National Library, Prishtina, Kosovo, 98
*National Teen Space Guidelines* (YALSA), 72

Nation's Report Card (NAEP)
    on reading proficiency, 10
    on technological inequity, 11, 12
Nesi, Jacqueline, 22
*Neuron* (journal), 109
New Jersey Institute of Technology, 196
New Settlement Community Center,
    Bronx, NY, 93–95
New York State Education Department, 137
Newark Public Library
    Blissful Coding Club offered by, 196
    collaboration for Blissful Coding Club,
    198–199
Newman Library, Virginia Tech, 111–114
news
    analyzing through infographics, 174–177
    Journalistic Learning Initiative, 162–168
news media literacy
    The LAMP program at Brooklyn Public
    Library for, 88–89
    lesson plan in news media literacy for
    YA librarians, 168–174
    need for, 162
    overview of, 168–169
Nins, Tasha, 53
NKY Makerspace, 204
Norman, Mark, 95
Norman North High School, 120–123
Norman-Haignere, Sam, 109
North Carolina Humanities Council, 132
*Not Light, but Fire: How to Lead*
    *Meaningful Race Conversations in the*
    *Classroom* (Kay), 79
Novelist, 129
N.W.A., 107

**O**
Obama, Barack, 35, 161
O'Brien, Soledad, 157
Oldenburg, Ray, 69–70
Older Adults Technology Services, 96–97
Oluo, Ijeoma
    on implicit bias, 55
    on school-to-prison pipeline, 62
Ong, Maria, 70
online learning, 11–12
online participation, 22–23
online resources, 174
online spaces
    media access/use among youth, 22–26

media creation, benefits of, 24–26
    *See also* virtual programs
oppression
    barriers to teens, observing/
    evaluating, 208–209
    of Black females, 150
Oregon
    Journalistic Learning Initiative for
    students in, 164
    pilot JLI program in, 166
Orfield, Gary, 7, 9
#OscarsSoWhite, 13
outreach
    Jasmine McNeil on library outreach
    programming, 66–67
    library outreach to marginalized teens,
    66
    relationships, building, 80
*Oxford English Dictionary*, 4

**P**
pace, 127, 128
Paige, Frederick
    information about, 219
    on Virginia Tech's "Digging in the
    Crates" Hip Hop Studies program,
    110–114
"The Pale Codex" game, 182
Palo Alto High School, California, 163
parents
    Blissful Coding Club , responses to, 197
    library services for urban teens, xiv
    media literacy lesson and, 175
    *Power Lines* for Black parents, xviii
Parker, Kim
    on benefits of social media on teens, 23
    on smartphone ownership among
    youth, 22
partnerships
    for The Beauty of S.T.E.M. program,
    192–193
    for Blissful Coding Club, 197
    conclusion about, 102
    conduits for community-building/
    civic engagement, 95–99
    conduits for skill development/healthy
    digital relationships, 90–95
    for "The Education of Blacks in
    Charlotte (1920–2020), An Online
    Youth Exhibition" project, 136

partnerships (*cont'd*)
    Elis Estrada on library partnerships,
        104–105
    for Girls Rock Film Camp, 145, 146
    for The LAMP programs on media
        literacy, 87–89
    lessons learned for media literacy
        partnerships, 99–101
    Nygel D. White on library partnerships,
        103–104
    teen reflection on, 102–103
    for 3D printing club, 204
    for Zine Club, 141
Patton, Desmond Upton, 22
Payne, Deneen Dixon, 149–154
peer influences, 9
peer-to-peer training, 195, 196
Perkins, D. N., 29
Perkins, La' Portia J.
    information about, 219
    on Virginia Tech's "Digging in the
        Crates" Hip Hop Studies program,
        110–114
Perrin, Andrew, 22
Personal Passion Project (PPP), 186–187
Pew Research Center
    on internet access, 22
    on smartphone ownership among
        youth, 179
"Photography as Activism" project, 98–99
photojournalism, 155
Piktochart, 177
Pinos, Jaume Castan, 91
*Places Journal*, 53
podcasting, 110
podcasting programming
    buy-in from library stakeholders,
        118–119
    podcast program ideas, 119–120
    Podcasting the Possibilities program,
        120–123
    teens listening to podcasts, 114–115
    what you will need for, 115–118
Podcasting the Possibilities program,
    120–123
politics
    in library space, 57
    media literacy skills for post-truth era,
        162
pop filter, 117, 118
post-truth era, 12, 162

poverty
    generational poverty in U.S., 6
    literacy and, 10–11
    segregated communities and, 8
    social capital/upward mobility and, 9–10
    of teens in urban communities, 6–7
    urban poverty, 5
power
    identities and, 55
    librarian shifting power dynamics, 58
    media literacy education and, 27
    morality and, 69
    of music, 109–110
power lines
    conduits for community-building/
        civic engagement, 95–99
    conduits for skill development/healthy
        digital relationships, 90–95
    Elis Estrada on library partnerships,
        104–105
    lessons learned for media literacy
        partnerships, 99–101
    meanings of, xxiv
    Nygel D. White on library partnerships,
        103–104
    as opportunities for empowering
        teens, 207
    partnerships for The LAMP programs
        on media literacy, 87–89
    teen reflection on relationships built
        through library programs, 102–103
*Power Lines: Connecting with Teens in*
*Urban Communities Through Media*
*Literacy* (Anderson & Czarnecki)
    preface, xvii–xviii
    themes covered in, xiii–xiv
    title, reason for, xxiv
power structures
    critical literacy for analyzing, 14
    influence of, xxiv
PPP (Personal Passion Project), 186–187
Preparatoria Altavista high school, 81
presidential election of 2020, 23–24
pressure, 80–81
Price, Robert J., Jr., 13
Price-Dennis, Detra, 150, 151
Principles of Community, Virginia Tech,
    113
print literature programs
    *See* books/print literature programs
printed materials, 179

privilege, checking, 54–57
Prizren Library, Kosovo, 98, 99
Probst, Donnell
  "Flashing Lights: What Is Media
    Literacy?," 35–50
  information about, 220
process, 101
product, 101
professional development
  pursuing, 209
  websites, links for, 212
profiling, 59–60
programming ideas, xxii–xxiii
projector, 117
Prushko, Lauren Kratz
  on creating podcasting programming,
    114–120
  information about, 220
  podcasting program photo, 119
"PSAs for Social Change" project, 99
public service announcement (PSA), 99
publication, 165–166
purpose, 39

**Q**

questions, for reflection, 209–210

**R**

racial equity, 66
racism
  barriers to library participation, 48
  microaggressions, library space and, 71
  security in libraries and, 62–63
  segregated communities, 7–9
  teens' experience in library and, 54
Racshenberg, Kaella, 49–50
Ramasubramanian, Srividya, 28
Rambo, Nicole
  information about, 220
  on the Zine Club, 137–141
Rasi, Päivi, 96
readers' advisory, 127–130
reading
  ALT RA: Looking beyond Books in
    Readers' Advisory, 127–130
  habits of youth, changes in, 126
  leisure reading, 125
  literacy, disparities among
    marginalized students, 10–11

*Real-World Teen Services* (Velásquez), 72
Reavis, Allyson, 126
recording software, 120–121, 123
"redlining," 8
Redmond, Theresa, 50
reflection
  after reading book, 209–210
  in JLI framework, 165–166
relationships
  with media technologies/content,
    90–91
  partnerships as conduits for, 90–95
  relationship-building before rule
    enforcement, 58–59
  social capital and, 9
  with teens, for inclusion of diverse
    voices, 46
  with teens, identities of librarian and,
    56
  of teens with security guards, 63
  *See also* partnerships
relationships, building
  active listening, 78–80
  consistency, not force for, 80–81
  importance of, 75–76
  interest, taking, 76–78
  Natasha Casey on, 83–84
  teen reflection on media-centered
    programs and, 82–83
Remake Learning, 193
remote learning, 90
reporting, 154–157
  *See also* journalism
representation
  access directly impacts, 38
  of Black girls in visual media, 151
  *Core Principles of Media Literacy
    Education*'s "Implications for
    Practice," 42–43
  of diverse communities, 47
  of diverse voices in library
    programming/collections, 45–46
  library as counterspace and, 70–71
  media literacy's exploration of, 48
  negative representations of older
    adults/teens, 97
  "Photography as Activism" project,
    98–99
  teen-centered readers' advisory tips,
    130
research, 186

resources
  books/articles on critical media
    literacy/media literacy education,
    213–214
  books/articles on serving teens in
    urban communities, 212–213
  for infographic lesson, 177
  for Journalistic Learning Initiative,
    167–168
  library outreach programming for
    marginalized youth, 66–67
  for news media literacy, 168
  for news media literacy lesson plan,
    174
  professional development websites,
    212
  for Teen Tech Mentor program, 191
  websites with media literacy
    curriculums, activities, handouts,
    films, or games, 211–212
restorative justice, 63
Rice, Condoleezza, 125
Rice, Eric, 23
Rideout, Victoria, 22, 29
Robb, Michael B., 22, 29
Rock the Mic event, 82–83
Rode Procaster Broadcast Quality Two-
  Person Podcasting Kit setup, 120–121, 122
Rodge, Pradnaya, 125, 126
Roll20 platform, 181–182, 183
Rorie, Jamey
  on Dewey and Dragons program,
    181–184
  information about, 220
  "The Pale Codex" game by, 182
Rosa, Matthew, 82–83
Rothstein, Richard, 8
Rottmund, Kelly, 194
Rudolph, Wilma, 53

## S

safe space
  Black Girls Film Camp as, 153
  library as counterspace, 70–71
  library as "third place," 69–70
  microaggressions and, 71
  relationships as key to, 75–76, 81
  Zine Club as, 138
Saunders, Laura, 95
schedules, 189

Scheerder, Anique, 90
"School Library Infographics: How
  to Create Them, Why to Use Them"
  (Creighton), 177
schools
  library partnerships with, 104
  "school-to-prison pipeline," 62
  technological inequities experienced
    by teens, 11–12
Schulte, Stephanie R., 23
Scott, Rachel, 95
Scratch, 202
screen time
  conversations about youth/media, 21
  differences among youth, 22
  of teens, increase in, 144
security
  in libraries, as barrier to teens, 61–63
  in libraries, safe space and, 75
segregation
  challenges of teens in urban
    communities, 7–9
  resegregation of Charlotte schools, 134
self-definition, 151
self-reflective lens, 40
Share, Jeff
  on asset-based perspective, 24
  on critical media literacy, 15, 16–17, 83
Shared Foundation, 27
shared goals, 100
skill development, 90–95
Skype, 117
Skywall, Brianne
  information about, 220
  on Teen Technology Mentor program,
    185–191
sleeping, 64
smartphones
  for Blissful Coding Club, 200
  smartphone ownership among youth,
    22
  teen ownership of, 179–180
Snapchat, 23, 24
Snow, Jeff, 191
social capital, 9–10
social dislocation, 6–7
social justice, 193
social location, 54–55
social media
  benefits for teens from, 23
  Blissful Coding Club links, 200

conversations about youth/media, 21
global impact on news/information-
sharing, 162
information about presidential
election on, 23–24
Journalistic Learning Initiative, 162–168
in "Know Your Neighborhood" lesson
plan, 170–171
media creation, benefits of, 24–26
news media literacy, need for, 168
teen reflection on engagement with,
28–29
teen reflection on media literacy,
49–50
socioeconomic status, 11
software
downloadable, avoidance of, 202
for Teen Tech Mentor program, 190
*The Souls of Black Folk* (Du Bois), 8
Sousa, Alexandra, 28
South Boulevard Branch Library, Charlotte
Mecklenburg Library, 183–184
space
affinity space, 72–74
for Black girls, 150
of Black Girls Film Camp, 150–151
counterspace, library as, 70–71
microaggression, role in need for safer
spaces, 71
"third place," library as, 69–70
for 3D printing club, 205
speakers
*See* guest speakers
Spheros, 203
Spikes, Michael A.
information about, 220
lesson plan in news media literacy for
YA librarians, 168–174
on news media literacy, 169
sports journalism, 156
Spradlin, Chris, 181–184
staff desk, 73–74
stakeholders, 118–119
STEAM
technology for Teen Tech Mentor
program, 190
Teen Technology Mentor program for
STEAM literacies, 185–186, 188
Steinkuehler, Constance, 179
Steinmetz, Jesse, 7

STEM
The Beauty of S.T.E.M. program,
191–195
Blissful Coding Club, 195–201
Stevens, Robin, 23
STIKK Kosovo ICT Association, 92
*Stolen Sharpie Revolution* (Wrekk), 138
Stone Avenue Branch of the Brooklyn
Public Library, 88–89
stories
at-home stressors of teens and, 64
stories librarians tell themselves about
teens, 59–60
Stornaiuolo, Amy, 25
story line, 127, 128
storytelling
Digital Storytelling with Twine
program, partnership for, 91–93
with hip-hop, 113
videos for, 143, 144
writing music encourages, 110
Straight Outta Compton (N.W.A. album),
107
students
analyzing the news through
infographics, 174–177
*Core Principles of Media Literacy
Education*'s "Implications for
Practice," 42–43
"The Education of Blacks in Charlotte
(1920–2020), An Online Youth
Exhibition" project, 130–136
Journalistic Learning Initiative, 162–168
security in libraries and, 61–63
Studio City Library of the Los Angeles
Public Library, 114–120
Style, Emily, 66–67
Subramanaiam, Mega, 72
subtexts, 40
successes
of analyzing news through
infographics, 175–176
of Blissful Coding Club, 197–198
of Teen Technology Mentor program,
188–189
of Zine Club, 140
Süss, Daniel, 22
sustainability, 101
*Swann v. Charlotte-Mecklenburg Board of
Education*, 133

**T**

tables, 73
Talk Sync App, 118
Tanzi, Kristine, 137–141
Tarabini, Aina, 6
Taxonomy of Information Neighborhoods, 174
teaching, 43
  *See also* education
teams, 165
technique, 39
technology
  Blissful Coding Club, 195–201
  bring your own technology (BYOT) ethos for programs, 101
  coding clubs, 201–205
  literacy, need for, 161
  for podcasting program, 115–118, 120–121
  technological inequity, 11–12
  technology club, 203–204
  for Teen Tech Mentor program, 189, 190
Teen Central, Boston Public Library, 185–191
"Teen Leadership Development through a Teen Gaming Program" (Dowds, Halpin, & Snow), 191
teen librarians
  *See* librarians
Teen Podcasting Workshop
  at Studio City Branch, 115
  technology for, 116–117
teen reflection
  on challenges in community, 15–16
  on "The Education of Blacks in Charlotte (1920–2020), An Online Youth Exhibition" project, 135–136
  on engagement with media, 28–29
  on media literacy, importance of, 49–50
  on media-centered programs at library, 82–83
  on relationships built through library programs, 102–103
*Teen Services Competencies for Library Staff* (YALSA), 45–49
teen tech mentors (TTMs)
  successes/challenges of program, 188–189
  work of, 185–187

Teen Technology Mentor program
  overview of, 185–187
  population served by, 187–188
  replication of program, 189–191
  successes/challenges of, 188–189
teens
  The Beauty of S.T.E.M. program for, 191–195
  Blissful Coding Club for, 195–201
  books/print literature programs for, 125–141
  coding clubs for, 201–205
  critical lens for media literacy education, 26–28
  Dewey and Dragons program for, 181–184
  film/video programs for, 144–157
  Intergenerational Media Literacy program, 96–97
  Journalistic Learning Initiative, 162–168
  library affinity space for, 72–74
  library support of marginalized teens, 65–66
  media, relationships to, 21
  media access/use among, 22–26
  media literacy education for, 29–30
  music, power of, 109–110
  news media literacy of, 168
  partnerships for community-building/ civic engagement, 95–99
  partnerships for empowering, 87–89
  partnerships for skill development/ healthy digital relationships, 90–95
  podcasting programming for library, 114–120
  Podcasting the Possibilities program, 120–123
  relationships with, building, 75–81
  steps for learning more about, 208–209
  Teen Technology Mentor program, 185–191
  video skills, programs for, 143–144
  YALSA's *Teen Services Competencies for Library Staff*, 45–49
  Zine Club for, 137–141
teens in urban communities
  books/articles on serving, 212–213
  challenges/disparities experienced by, 5–13
  contextualizing "urban" as characteristic, 4–5

critical media literacy in library
programs for, 14–17
education of, xvii–xviii
Jimmeka Anderson's work with, xxi–
xxiv
learning more about, 207–209
marginalization of, 4
media literacy, conclusion about,
207–210
misrepresentation of, 13
reason for book's focus on, xxv–xxvi
relationships with, building, 75–81
space for media literacy, 69–74
"urban" term, use of, 3
*See also* urban teens, serving in
libraries
TekStart, 194
Temesgan, Bereket, 15–16
Thevenin, Benjamin, 92
"third place"
library as "third place, 69–70
role of public libraries as, 95
Thomas, Ebony Elizabeth, 25
Thompson, Cashawn, 150
3D printing club, 204–205
Thussu, Daya Kishan, 170
TikTok, 23, 24
time, 202
TinkerCAD
for 3D printing club, 204–205
for technology club, 203–204
Tishman, Shari, 29
tone
as appeal factor, 127, 128
identifying, 129
"The Top 10 Teen Video Countdown"
program, 77–78
training
professional development, 209
by teen tech mentors, 186
*See also* career training
trauma, 152
TTMs
*See* teen tech mentors
Tully, Melissa, 169
"Tween Time," 187, 188
tweens, 191–195
Twenge, Jean M., 22
Twine, 91–93
Twitter
Blissful Coding Club links, 200

information about presidential
election on, 24
in Information Neighborhoods lesson,
173–174

**U**

UC Berkeley, 10
UNC Charlotte Chancellor's Diversity
Fund, 152
UNESCO (United Nations Educational,
Scientific and Cultural Organization), 162
University of Michigan, 55
University of North Carolina at Charlotte
"The Education of Blacks in Charlotte
(1920–2020), An Online Youth
Exhibition" project, 130–136
funding for Black Girls Film Camp, 152
University of Prishtina, 98–99
upward mobility, 9–10
urban
as characteristic, 4–5
representation question, xiv
as socially constructed reality, 3
urban characteristic frame, 4
urban communities
history of, 208
libraries for media literacy education,
xiv
serving teens in, xvii–xviii
*See also* teens in urban communities
urban education
contextualizing "urban" as
characteristic, 4–5
Jimmeka Anderson's PhD in, 3
Urban Education Collaborative, 152
urban intensive frame, 4–5
urban schools, 7
urban teens, serving in libraries
cultural context of responses, 61
at-home stressors for teens and, 63–64
identities as barriers, scenarios about,
58–60
identities/privilege of librarians, 54–57
Jasmine McNeil on library outreach
programming, 66–67
leading with curiosity, 60–61
librarians as barriers to teens, 53–54
Mary J. Wardell-Ghirarduzzi on library
support of marginalized teens, 65–66
politics in library space, 57

urban teens, serving in libraries (*cont'd*)
    security in libraries, 61–63
    teen reflection on library support of
        success, 64–65
urban-emergent community, 5
use, 43–44

**V**
Vallejo, Laura, 181–184
values, 44–45
Values for a Better Future, 99
Van Dijk, Jan A. G. M., 90
Velásquez, Jennifer
    on displaying teens' work in library, 74
    *Real-World Teen Services*, 72
"video diary" assignment, 189
video games
    The Beauty of S.T.E.M., 191–195
    Blissful Coding Club, 195–201
    coding clubs, 201–205
    Dewey and Dragons, 181–184
    for media literacy, 179–180
    Teen Tech Mentor program, 185–191
videos
    for "The Education of Blacks in
        Charlotte (1920–2020), An Online
        Youth Exhibition" project, 133
    Girls on the Beat@ Charleston County
        Public Library, 154–158
    Girls Rock Film Camp: The Future of
        Film, 144–149
    Keepin' It Reel: Black Girls Film Camp,
        149–154
    in "Know Your Neighborhood" lesson
        plan, 169–170
    programs for teens, 143–144
Vimeo Girls Rock Charlotte website, 149
Vines, Lonna, 144–149
violence, 78–79
Viotty, Samantha, 26
Virginia Tech Digging in the Crates
    (VTDITC), 110–114
Virginia Tech University Libraries' Digital
    Literacy Initiative (DLI), 112
virtual programs
    of Blissful Coding Club, 197–198
    Dewey and Dragons on virtual
        platform, 181–184
    Girls on the Beat program, 157

    Teen Technology Mentor program,
        switch to virtual, 187–189
    virtual Black Girls Film Camp, 152–153
    of VTDITC, 113
    Zine Club online, 140
virtual tabletop platforms
    choice of, 184
    for Dewey and Dragons program,
        181–182, 183
Visme, 177
Vito, DC, 26
vocabulary, 172
voice
    controlling for active listening, 79
    in JLI framework, 165–166
    podcasting programs for teen voices,
        114–120
    representation of diverse voices, 45–46
voices from the field
    Brittany N. Anderson on teen media
        use, 30
    Elis Estrada on library partnerships,
        104–105
    Jasmine McNeil on library outreach
        programming, 66–67
    Jayne Cubbage on critical media
        literacy, 17
    Jeff Share on critical media literacy,
        16–17
    Mary J. Wardell-Ghirarduzzi on library
        support of marginalized teens, 65–66
    Merve Lapus on media literacy
        education for teens, 29–30
    Natasha Casey on relationship-
        building, 83–84
    Nygel D. White on library partnerships,
        103–104
    Theresa Redmond on media literacy
        skills, 50
Volpe, Vanessa V., 28
volunteers, 196, 200
VTDITC (Virginia Tech Digging in the
    Crates), 110–114
Vuk St. Karadžic City Library, Kosovo,
    91–93

**W**
walk, 208
Wardle, Claire, 168

Warschauer, Mark, 90
Waves NS1 Noise Suppressor plug-in, 117
We Are Equal workshop, 133
We Are Here workshop, 133
We Are Worthy workshop, 134
We Can Develop workshop, 134
We Can Explore workshop, 134
We Can Imagine workshop, 134
We Will Create workshop, 134
We Will Inspire workshop, 134
We Will Lead the "Exhibit Launch"
  workshop, 135
website
  of Blissful Coding Club, 200
  for coding clubs, 201–202
  for "The Education of Blacks in
  Charlotte (1920–2020), An Online
  Youth Exhibition" project, 133, 134,
  135
  professional development websites,
  212
  websites with media literacy
  curriculums, activities, handouts,
  films, or games, 211–212
Weiss, Elaine, xiv
Weiss, Jasmine, 110–114
welcoming space
  library as, xiii
  library as counterspace, 70–71
  library as "third place," 69–70
West Charlotte High School, 133
Whatcha Mean What's a Zine? (Todd), 138
white lens, 54
white librarians
  as barriers to urban teens in libraries,
  53–54
  identities of librarians as barriers,
  58–60
  at ImaginOn library, relationship to
  teens, xxii
  privilege, checking, 54–57
white people, 8–9
white students, 10
whiteboard, 123
Williams, Shimira, 191–195
Wilson, Carolyn, 162
Wilson, William J., 6
Wittig, Corey, 194
Wix web development platform, 133
Wizards of the Coast, 181

women
  Black women as guest speakers for
  Black Girls Film Camp, 152–153
  Girls on the Beat@ Charleston County
  Public Library, 154–157
  Girls Rock Film Camp: The Future of
  Film, 144–149
Women + Girls Research Alliance and
  Civitas Education Management, LLC, 152
Women and Hollywood website, 149
workforce training, 93–95
writing
  Girls on the Beat@ Charleston County
  Public Library, 154–158
  Journalistic Learning Initiative, 162–168
  for literacy, 41
  music, 110
  writing cafe of MCPL, 64–65
  Zine Project, 138–141
Wyatt, D., 180

**Y**
YA librarians, 168–174
Yadav, Aman, 162
Young Adult Library Services Association
  (YALSA)
  award from, xxiii
  on dedicated spaces for teens, 72
  The Future of Library Services for and
  with Teens: A Call to Action, 70
  media literacy education, 209
  Summer Learning Resources Grant,
  137
  Teen Services Competencies for Library
  Staff, 45–49
  Teens' Top Ten list, 121
  YALS issue on trauma-informed
  responses, 63
Yousafzai, Malala, 109
youth
  critical lens for media literacy
  education, 26–28
  library outreach programming for
  marginalized youth, 66–67
  library support of, 65–66
  media access/use among, 22–26
  See also teens; teens in urban
  communities
youth-serving organizations, 104

YouTube
    presidential election information on,
      24
    videos in "Know Your Neighborhood"
      lesson plan, 169–170
YPulse, 180

**Z**
Zine Club
    description of, 138–140
    of MCPL, 64–65
    population served by, 137
    replication of program, 140–141
    successes/challenges of, 140

Zine Project, 137, 138
Zine Showcase, 138
zine swap, 139
Zittoun, Tania, 169
Zoom, 117, 188
Zurkowski, Paul, 161
Zvobgo, Kelebogile, 84